What Angel Magick Can Do for You

What if you could contact your personal guardian angel for help with your toughest problem? Or if you could invoke an angel to infuse your magickal rituals with divine energy? What if you could tap into angelic power to improve your health, prosperity, and every other aspect of your life? Whatever your goals, this book will show you how angels can help you achieve them.

Popular author Silver RavenWolf wrote this book to share her personal experiences on working magick with angels. She provides imaginative, down-to-earth directions for working angel magick of your own. Her magickal system has the ability to meld itself around nearly every religious structure, making angel magick open to people of all beliefs—including you!

Whether you write an "angel want ad" or choose another mode of communication, now is the time to contact your first angel. Angels work their magick in such subtle ways, you may be tempted to call all those good things that start happening a "coincidence." But after you read this book, you'll discover that when angels are around, there's no such thing as coincidence. There's only a new world of personal empowerment … a world that you can begin to experience today.

About the Author

Silver RavenWolf is a true Virgo who adores making lists and arranging things in order. The mother of four children, she is currently working toward her clinical hypnotherapy certification. Silver has attained Wiccan priesthood and is the Tradition head of the Black Forest Clan, which covers six states, and is an Elder of the Family of Serphant Stone. As Director of the International Wiccan/Pagan Press Alliance, she is actively involved in the magickal community. She also runs a healing circle for people of all religions. When she has the time, Silver teaches several magickal sciences on a one-to-one basis.

"The best way for a magickal person to be accepted is to let people get to know you," explains Silver. "Once they understand your personal values and principles, their attitudes about your alternative religious interests tend to be more positive. Let them know you and the work that you do."

To Write to the Author

If you wish to contact the author, write to:

Silver RavenWolf
P.O. Box 1392
Mechanicsburg, PA 17055-1392, U.S.A.

Please enclose a legal-sized self-addressed, stamped envelope for reply, or $1.00 to cover costs. The author will not reply unless this guideline is met. Both the author and publisher enjoy hearing from you and learning of your enjoyment of this book and how it has helped you. If you wish more information about this book or other Llewellyn titles, please write to:

Llewellyn Worldwide
P.O. Box 64383, Dept. K724–2
St. Paul, MN 55164-0383, U.S.A.

Free Catalog from Llewellyn

For more than ninety years Llewellyn has brought its readers knowledge in the fields of metaphysics and human potential. Learn about the newest books in spiritual guidance, natural healing, astrology, occult philosophy, and more. Enjoy book reviews, new age articles, a calendar of events, plus current advertised products and services. To get your free copy of *Llewellyn's New Worlds of Mind and Spirit,* send your name and address to:

Llewellyn's New Worlds of Mind and Spirit
P.O. Box 64383, Dept. K724–2, St. Paul, MN 55164-0383, U.S.A.

Angels

COMPANIONS IN MAGICK

Silver RavenWolf

1997
Llewellyn Publications
St. Paul, Minnesota 55164-0383, U.S.A.

FIRST EDITION
Second Printing, 1997

Cover design: Lynne Menturweck
Cover art: Stephanie Henderson
Chapter illustrations: Robin Larsen
Book design, layout, and editing: Jessica Thoreson

Library of Congress Cataloging-in-Publication Data
RavenWolf, Silver, 1956–
    Angels: companions in magick / Silver RavenWolf. -- 1st ed.
      p.   cm.
    Includes bibliographical references and index.
    ISBN 1-56718-724-2 (pbk.)
    1. Angels--Miscellanea. 2. Occultism. I. Title.
BF1623.A53R38   1996
    291.2'15--dc20   96-27953
                                            CIP

Llewellyn Publications
A Division of Llewellyn Worldwide, Ltd.
P.O. Box 64383, Dept. K724–2, St. Paul, MN 55164-0383

Other Books by the Author

To Ride a Silver Broomstick
HexCraft
Beneath a Mountain Moon (fiction)
To Stir a Magick Cauldron
The Rune Mysteries (with Nigel Jackson)

Of Sparks, Flames, and Moonbeams

(The Presence of Angels)

Sparks from the Soul,
Flames from the Sun,
The glimmer of moonbeams,
As Angels they come!

Sometimes wings enfolding
Sometimes brilliant light
They rise like the dawning,
They illumine the night

We look for their power
In Miracles grand
Some watch, never seeing,
Their wondrous plan

But I sense them most
In the warmth of my home
And their touch on my shoulder
When I am alone.

—David O. Norris

Table of Contents

Introduction

I work with angels all the time now, but it wasn't always that way. When I was growing up I believed in angels, but thought they were simply mythical creatures belonging to a particular religion. It would be nice if they were real, but hey—I always wished the character Samantha from the old television show *Bewitched* was real, too.

I guess for some of us it takes a good punch in the gray matter to wake up and see the angels. I was one of those people. Angels have immensely affected my adult life, and I cannot believe I shut my brain up for so long to their existence.

I believe certain truths travel along universal lines, but I shy away from religions that try to decide how everyone should respond to divinity. Instead, I try to find aspects of these religions that will fit into my practices, while not giving up the mystery or the focus of the work. This isn't always easy.

In my studies of magick and religion, I've discovered that magick functions universally. No one religion can lay claim to it, though some religions incorporate magick more than others. We can take the best of the religions we love, use their fulfilling properties, and still reach our goals.

I also learned not to listen to other people about my choice of spirituality. I know that sounds rather harsh. However, I don't apologize. I believe that there is only one expert in the world on your relationship and belief in divinity—you. When it comes time for you to explore the world beyond, no one else is is going to be with you. You'll be doing it alone. Whatever you have believed as far as religion and spirituality goes is going to ride with you. Let's hope you've managed to pick up some semblance of universal truth along the way.

I frequent the information highways (computer bulletin boards and on-line services) now and then. I like to see how others think, what they feel is important in religious practice, and how they coordinate their lives with their spiritual aspirations. This interests me, of course, because I am a Wiccan, but I am also a writer, searching for ideas to help make my life, as well as the lives of my readers, better.

I have found that angels appear to transcend all cultures, races, and systems. They are a part of human history and civilization, sometimes at the forefront, other times in the shadows, but they are always there. They don't belong to any one particular religion, although many modern people try to associate them with Christianity, Judaism, and Islam. No one religion holds total responsibility for the belief in angels. In truth, these religions only support the existence of angels, they didn't create them (though some sects have taken great pains to name them).

During my research on angels I have discovered the following:

Angels aren't anybody's property.

Angels don't belong to any particular religious system.

Angels don't discriminate based on religious faith.

Angels create bridges between various religions.

To call on an angel is to rise above religious dogma and touch the universal spirit.

I also found something very exciting. Angels *love* to work magick with humans. That is the whole purpose of this book—to tell you how to work magick successfully with the angels. I know I'm a better person for inviting the angels into my life. It is my deepest desire that you reap the same benefits, and more.

SILVER RAVENWOLF
aka Jenine E. Trayer
April 1995

One

Seek and Go Find the Angels

There is no substantial and concrete evidence save for what the witness saw and felt. The rest is the stuff of myth, legend, and speculation.

—Malcolm Godwin,
author of *Angels:*
An Endangered Species

By picking up this book, you've already listened to the words of an angel. Your guardian angel could be whispering in your ear. Celestial angels may have urged you to peek inside this book because they are interested in working with someone like you. Perhaps a friend's guardian angel hopes you will pass along what you learn to his or her special charge, helping your friend in a time of need. Whatever the case, angelic forces are at work in your life.

The angels have been with you since the day you entered the earth plane. They won't abandon you. They know you are spirit first, and that the human body is the clothing you wear while you live on Earth and fulfill your destiny. The angels are spiritual guides and helpers, assisting you in the tasks you have set out to do. They are as real as you are. Angels are an integral part of the universal plan, as important as you are, and just as busy. Our spirits can easily attune to the angels; we only need to try.

Did you ever get the haunting feeling that you don't belong here? In a sense, that feeling is correct. Earth is not our natural habitat, and our spiritual selves remember that there are other things "out there" that we have already experienced and will experience again. When you come to Earth, you take an oath that you will try to do your best for the amount of time given to you. The oath is all-important, but often we forget it. As we spiritually progress, we receive a clearer picture of our mission.

The angels do not forget the oath we have taken, or what we have promised to do while we are here on Earth. They help us remember and aid us in our personal mission. We have to learn to listen, for if we block the angels out, they become only the fairy beings of dreams and pleasant stories. If you don't remember anything else you read in this book, then remember this message: *you are not alone.*

A Smattering of Religious Thought

There is no one right way to believe in an angel or to practice religion. Many angel legends stem from tribal beliefs, genetic memory, and spiritual recall. Choose whatever ideas seem best for you.

Most of the written information about angels does not come from the orthodox scriptures of the four Western religions that believe in the existence of these heavenly beings (Christianity, Judaism, Zoroastrianism, and Islam). Over the centuries, ideas about the angelic hosts have changed, depending on who wrote about them. Many scholars believe that angels are the result of cross-breeding among belief systems and include Egyptian, Sumerian, Babylonian, and Persian archetypes. Through further research we find that belief in angelic hosts and spirits is far older than any of the structured religions practiced today, which supports the idea that they aren't tied to what humans want them to be. Angels simply are.

During human history, angels have risen and fallen in popularity many times over.[1] Sometimes angels appeared fashionable, other times they've been swept to the

---

1. In A.D. 745, Pope Zachary denounced a series of angels. In the Middle Ages they rose to prominence again, heralded by Milton and Dante. Scientific materialism came into fashion shortly after, and by the late 1800s, angels no longer held sway in the lives of the people (*Know Your Angels* by John E. Ronner, page 135).

bottom of the Bible cabinet at the whims of religious leaders. One thing we know for sure: stories of angels have been intertwined in human myth and legend long before Christianity. Where there is legend and myth, there is an underlying grain of truth. Angels have touched each culture in the manner in which that culture can most understand and use their energies. For example, the Romans knew the angels as Lares, protective household guardians. The Viking version of angels are the Valkyries, those beautiful, robust females who descended from the heavens to retrieve the souls of slain warriors and take them to Valhalla.

The "golden age of angels" occurred in the late Middle Ages in Europe, but ended during the fourteenth century as the Black Death strode across the land, spitting its venom at humans and angels alike. The inquisition followed.

Unlike most fads, angels have managed to keep themselves in the picture—foreground or background, it doesn't seem to matter to them—throughout the turbulent history of humankind. They've also kept up with current clothing fads, accepted styles of the fine arts, and made their presence known in church communities as well as scholarly circles. Their pictures have adorned the walls of castles, churches, temples, brothels, family homes, and halls of higher learning. Clothed in anything from white goat skins to celestial silks, angels have moved with us. Regardless of their popularity, their work continues—steady, ongoing. One thing angels are not, is fickle.

Followers of Eastern religions (Hindus, Jains, and Buddhists) have a less structured belief in angels. They depend on messages from departed loved ones, meditation, valuable information received through the higher self, reincarnated sages, and other assorted spirits. They have incorporated the forces of the angelic hosts into their own belief systems, often dispensing with the "being" part of angels. However, they still believe in helpful spirits, which is what counts in the long run. How we deal with the thought isn't important—how we use the belief is the main concern.

To the Western mind, the intangible must be made concrete in order for us to understand it. Western religions cannot agree on who or what angels are, nor how much they interact in our lives. They can't even decide how to include the angels in their structures.

Religious structures seem to thrive on debate and argument. For example, conservative Catholics argue for a fallen angel (devil), but other Catholics feel each individual is responsible for his or her own actions. Blaming a mythical beast is not the answer to all our problems. Martin Luther, foremost in the Protestant march, denounced the angelic hosts, but held on to Satan. Looks like Luther, and his followers, got the dark end of the bargain.

With some digging, we find that angels are actually archetypes of universal energies. They are thoughts that pre-date all the religions mentioned previously, stemming back into our tribal cultures, our genetic memories, and our spiritual recall. Angels do not exist to serve a particular structure. They do exist to help humans and other inhabitants of this planet.

The structured religions borrow heavily from each other when it comes to legends and lore on the angels. Angels, you will discover, can be reached through meditation, will assist you in connecting with your higher self, bring important messages and advice to you, and yes, even help you work through reincarnation memories. Above all, you will discover that angels do not depend on our religious structures to exist; rather, they are a mystery that religious structures have tried to unravel.

The material in this book is designed for individuals of all faiths—you can be Wiccan, Druidic, Faery, Alternative Christian, Judaic, Christian, Islamic—it doesn't matter. It is better if you can move beyond the constructs of your faith, then mix and match the information given here, and assimilate it with your faith along the way. As long as you believe in a higher, positive power in our universe and are willing to work magick with the angels, this book is for you.

How the Angels May Contact You

Angels will tailor their contact with you to your needs. Some individuals will hear voices in their heads—not bad words, but thoughts of wisdom, peace, and enlightenment. Joan of Arc (1412–1431) heard the voices of angels, starting when she was about thirteen years old. Some legends indicate it was St. Michael who spoke to her. In other historical references, she heard the angel Gabriel. We all know the history of Joan and how she inspired the soldiers of France. We also know that she was accused of Witchcraft and burned at the stake for her beliefs.

Although Joan met an unfortunate end (a result of the patriarchal times), many others have claimed to find guidance from the angels. Thomas Aquinas (1225–1274), student of Albertus Magnus, has been called by some historians the "Angelic Doctor." The Roman Catholic Church regards him as their greatest theologian and philosopher. He spent most of his life in service to his order and wrote *Summa Theologica*, which gives a detailed description of angel existence. It appears his angels worked with him through more of a channeling method, in which he wrote down the divine thoughts and shared them with others. (I like Thomas Aquinas because he felt that many of the Apostle Paul's writings were wrong.)

Other people receive messages in dreams. *The Book of Mormon* was first published in Palmyra, New York, in 1830. Mormons accept the book as a divinely inspired work revealed to Joseph Smith in a dream. (Rumor has it that Joseph Smith was actually a ceremonial magician.)

The legend surrounding the Mormon religion begins in 600 B.C., before the destruction of Jerusalem. A Hebrew family fled the city and traveled to North America by boat. Their descendants became two nations—one the lineage of our Native American Indians. The other nation was supposedly destroyed by the first. Records of the elders of the surviving nation tell of the appearance of a prophet, whom they believed to be Jesus Christ after his execution. This information was recorded on gold plates by another prophet named Mormon. His son, Moroni, buried the plates. They remained buried for 1,400 years until Moroni appeared to Joseph Smith as an angel, showing him where to find the plates and how to translate them. The translations became known as *The Book of Mormon.* After Joseph translated the plates, they were returned to the angel and never seen again.

Finally, there are those who receive help from angels in the form of visions. Two of the above could also be considered visionaries (Joan of Arc and Joseph Smith), since both legends also speak of the participant actually "seeing" an angel. There is debate on whether they saw the angels in the waking state or whether they had entered an alpha or theta state (common during meditation).

While doing research on this book, I spent several hours on the computer service America Online.® Just through common chatter on the "boards" I found that many individuals claim to either have seen angels for themselves, or have felt the effects of them in their lives.

Of course there are many other examples I could give you, but that's not the idea of this book. Here, you are going to have angelic experiences of your own.

The Timeless Quality of the Angels

Authors have devoted many books to the idea of angels, and many scholars have dedicated their lives to learning about them. The bibliography of this text provides several sources from historical to modern popular reading. As this is a how-to book, I'm not going to delve into the complete lineage of the angels, except with respect to their magickal applications. If you are interested in this aspect, by all means consider the bibliography, then browse through your local library, or if you wish, check out both regular and metaphysical bookstores. Several chapters later in this book will present specific angels and give a brief historical overview of them and their purpose. To further delve into the subject will require research on your part. I do this on purpose. One cannot learn from any single text, conversation, or work of art. You need to gather as much information as possible to fashion your own beliefs. This process stabilizes your position on any matter and helps you keep an open mind.

Who and What Are Angels to You?

I believe the simplest answer to the above question is this: Angels are what you personally perceive them to be. Before you begin working with them, you are going to have to decide what constitutes an angel to you and what doesn't, and go on from there. It's best that you leave your mind open, simply because no single expert on angels (except the angels themselves) exists to tell you what they are like. When it comes right down to it, the historical writers on angels were no better than you, nor were they more gifted in sight, thought, or deed. They were human, as you are, with the same feelings, drives, intuitions, hopes, and dreams. Those religious scholars told the world what they thought about angels. However, these are only their ideas. Their perceptions do not have to be your perceptions, nor does the fact that they are now dead make their legends and lore any more valid than when they first set pen to paper.

I urge you to think for yourself. You are not a monk in a dusty cell, whose only occupation is to record his visions and design truths that will satisfy the hierarchy of his church. You are not a scholar seated at a round table, reinventing Pagan lore to suit the needs of a religious structure. You are free to believe as you choose. Your thoughts on angels today may require you to get rid of some of the old ideas stuffed into your head as a child, so get that mental trash can ready. It's okay to change your mind. It's perfectly acceptable to meet the angels on your own terms in a process of spiritual education. As you work through this book, your vision and thoughts on angels will change. You will re-evaluate the patterns in your life. You will mold your beliefs to bring harmony into your personal space. You will be working toward spiritual attunement to make the most of your destiny.

A trip to your local bookstore will show you that there are more books on encounters with angels (commonly called testimonials) than any other type of angel text currently sold. As of this writing, one particular publishing company has at least ten angel books out, only two of which belong in categories other than first- and second-person accounts of angelic experiences. Historical information runs a weak second, and how-to books are a distant third. Some of these books keep strictly to the Christian or Hebrew religious structures, where others are more open-minded and represent a larger cross-section of believers, trying their best not to focus on any system. Each author has a distinctive view on angels. None of them is incorrect, because each is following his or her intuition. Each author sees angels in the manner he or she best understands. Readers who share their ideas will also understand these author's books; therefore, each text contributes to the fabric of human learning.

Rather than tell you what is right and wrong about angelic structure, let's cover some frequently asked questions (at least the ones that are relevant to this work). You might like to get out a notebook and jot down your insights as you read these questions. You may be surprised to find out that angel diaries are not something new, but have been food for creative thought for many people throughout history. Angels are not adverse to technology, so if you want to slap a disk in that computer and create a file for your angel ramblings, be my guest. If you can't stand writing, then perhaps you may opt for a tape recording.

I'll give you the questions first, then I'll tell you what I think. You don't have to agree, but I thought you might like to have some background to help understand my reasoning in handling the material later on in the book. Remember, angels are as you perceive them to be. You need to feel comfortable with your thoughts. If you have doubts about a question or can't answer it at the moment, don't worry about it. You'll come back to it later when you are ready. Remember, the purpose of these questions is to make you think, not to give you (or me) a passing or failing grade.

Do you believe all angels look like humans?

I believe angels are energy forms that can change at will, appearing in the state of being that is necessary to get the job done. When working with human beings, they may appear as humans to keep from scaring us half to death. This means that angels may appear as any race of being on our planet, male or female. You will see and visualize angels as you most need to see them, when you need to see them. For those people who work with archetypes, they may appear half-animal and half-human. Be assured that there is no politically correct way to envision or "see" an angel.

Do you think angels will appear before you in this dimension, talk to you in your head, or just send you ideas and impressions?

I have experienced all these types of angelic visitations. Most common for me, however, are messages through ideas and impressions.

Do you think guardian angels and celestial angels are the same, or different?

I believe they can be the same, and be different. It is thought that celestial angels help your guardian angel on occasion, becoming your guardians for a time. Other people believe that the guardian angel stays by the assigned human's side. Finally, some feel that humans who are trying to make great strides in the development of others may have a celestial being as their guardian angel. This would be an angel who normally does not function as a guardian, but because the person has come to Earth for a special mission, this angel is assigned. Quite a lot to contemplate, isn't it?

Do you think ghosts and angels are the same, or different?

I believe they are not the same thing, though I believe loved ones who have passed away certainly have the opportunity to assist you, should they so desire. Some individuals believe that helpful ghosts and guardian angels are the same thing. For example, let's say a parent died when a child was one year of age. That child may grow up to believe that the parent serves as his or her guardian angel. This is a common belief in our society where children have lost parents or grandparents at a young age. You will have to decide where you want to draw the line between ghostly help and angelic assistance.

Do you believe spirit guides and angels are the same, or different?

If you don't need to distinguish between ghosts, spirit guides, and angels, then don't. If you are the type of person who has to have everything ironed out, then this is a question you will need to contemplate. I believe that spirit guides and angels are a part of the same divine energy, but not necessarily the same entity.

Do angels have to have a name?

I don't think so, though some individuals do find names for the spirits/angels they depend on regularly. Other individuals like to stick with what an angel might represent, such as healing, laughter, success, compassion, etc., and leave the naming process alone. There are also people who choose to find angels who already have historical names. We'll cover all these subjects later in the book.

Do all angelic names have to end in -el or -irion?

I don't believe these suffixes are necessary. This is generally considered a Hebrew practice. There is nothing wrong with using these suffixes; however, it is not a necessity. The *-el* suffix is an ancient word with quite a history of its own:

Sumerian *el:* "brightness" or "shining"
Akkadian *ilu:* "radiant one"
Babylonian *ellu:* "the shining one"
Old Welsh *ellu:* "a shining being"
Old Irish *aillil:* "shining"
English *elf:* "shining being"
Anglo-Saxon *aelf:* "radiant being"

Do you feel that because an angel received its name through a religion that is different from yours, you can't work with it?

If you are strong enough to cross religious boundaries and biases, then it really doesn't matter what the historical name might be. If you answer yes to this question, meaning that other religious beliefs than your own bother you, then don't call the angel by name, but by the purpose of the work. However, remember that names hold power, and to call something or someone by its name puts you closer to the energy you are contacting, not necessarily to the structure that gave the name. Don't forget that angels transcend religious bias—discrimination is a purely human burden.

What do angels look like?

This is up to you. Wings and halos didn't show up in the Christian images of angels until the time of the Roman Emperor Constantine (A.D. 312), though the Greek pantheon includes the winged gods such as Hermes and Eros. Pre-Christian depictions of angels include beings in white goat skins, or show them to be very young in build and features. I have seen angels with dark skin, powerful limbs, and heavy wings; angels who are tall and swathed in white robes (standing beside a police officer, if I remember correctly); and angels with the body of a human and the head of a lion.

Can humans be angels or are angels a species unto themselves?

Some people believe that certain humans are "angels in training," while others subscribe to the idea that angels were created at the dawn of time as a species unto themselves. Still others believe that many of the Pagan gods or archetypes were/are angelic beings, and are neither human nor lower spirit, but represent a portion of the God/dess.

I'm sure you have other thoughts on angels that I've not covered. That's okay. The idea in asking these questions is to get you thinking about angels, not to test you on what the right or wrong answer may be. You may think you will never see an angel, then—guess what—you have a visitation. You may feel you can't possibly call an angel by name because you don't follow a particular religion, then your child gets sick and while working magick, you call the name anyway. In shock you find that calling the angel by name worked for you, even though you don't practice the religion from which it derived its name.

Historical scholars and angel authors cannot agree on the answers to many of these questions. While reviewing several works on the subject, I found a few authors to be condescending of their peers and their viewpoints—not very angelic of them, is it? The animalistic and spiritual sides of humans are always at war. It is up to you to help the two sides meet in the middle and bring harmony into your life, as well as the lives of others. If you think angels are dressed in silks and satins and your friend sees angels in Hawaiian shirts, so be it.

Why Use Angel Magick?

I thought you'd never ask! First, I'm sure there are lots of things in your life you'd like to change, and I'll bet you think some of those things are out of your league. Ask the angels for help.

Second, how about planetary harmony? Perhaps you are working magick for yourself and things are going along just fine. Why not ask the angels to help you work toward honing your abilities? No request is too small or too large for angelic intervention. All of us come up between that proverbial rock and a hard place—time for angels here.

Does your family have difficulty understanding your alternative religion? Do they give you a rough time about your beliefs? Enter the angels. Everybody likes angels. Imagine their shock when they discover you like them, too. Even better, you work with them! Having difficulty relating divinity to your children? Say hello to the angels. Children and angels get along wonderfully. Friends and family having difficulty with self-esteem? Angels will provide the lift.

Is there is a custody battle going on in your life and one of the rocks or arrows shot at you has the name of your religion on it? Are visits between parents a nightmare because either one side or both is trying to shove a particular religion down the kid's throat? It's angel time. Almost everyone believes in angels.

Do you work with people in the fields of hypnotherapy, psychology, tarology, I-Ching, scrying, psychometry, or runic knowledge? What better way to understand you are non-threatening and grasp the information you are giving them than by using angels to bridge the gap.

Has disaster struck? Bring on the angels. They don't want to see you wallowing in a puddle of poo, either.

Again, these are just a few examples of how angels can be incorporated into your life. Angel magick has enabled me to bridge the gap between all types of people in all walks of life. Angels break the barrier between the many universes we experience. Most of all, however, working with the angels has brought me true enlightenment. Not a day passes that I don't feel their presence in my life. If you don't believe me, it's time for you to try it.

Welcome, My Angel Friend

It's time to find your first angel. Don't get excited; finding an angel is not too hard. There is only one requirement—you can't be kidding around when you call an angel. First, I'd like you to sit back and think seriously about why you want to contact the angelic realms. Be honest with yourself. Is there something you want to improve within yourself or your lifestyle, or is there a rough spot in your life that you would like to smooth out? Are you merely curious?

Take your time. I'm not going anywhere.

Got it? Good. Now, get a piece of paper or an index card and write a want ad for your angel. I kid you not. Sit down and compose an ad as if you were looking for a teacher, a friend, someone who has a service you would like to contact, etc. Here's a sample angel want ad:

WANTED: Angel from the celestial realms. Seeking an angel who can help me improve my self-image. Need one who can get through my stubborn streak.

Or:

SEEKING: Angel who is willing to help me with my money problems. Seeking loving assistance to help me create peace and prosperity in my life.

When you've finished the ad, hold it in your hand, close your eyes, and concentrate on bringing a being of light toward yourself. Read your ad out loud if you think it will help. Don't worry about not doing it right—there is no wrong way to ask an angel to help as long as you use good manners. If you would like to utter a little prayer, be my guest. Here's a good one:

Angelic hosts please hear my call
Bright blessings I extend to all.

East and south, west and north
I circle 'round and call thee forth.
Invisible friend, messenger of love
Send me aid from the realms above.

When you are finished, tuck the card in a pocket or pin it someplace on your clothing where no one can see it. Don't announce to everyone you know that you've just placed a want ad for an angel. We don't want anyone's negative thoughts interfering with your project. After help has arrived and you feel the need to share the information with someone who can use it, then by all means do so. If you have friends or family who you know will scoff at you, don't bother. An old magickal adage is: "Teach not the mysteries to fools." Others will find their way in their own time without using you as a stepping stone.

Don't expect your angel to appear to you with trumpets of glory and lights of gold and silver. Angels are often subtle in their work. You may receive a job offer from an unexpected source. A friend may call to pull you out of your doldrums. You may pick up a book and find the answer you were looking for there. When angels are around, there is no such thing as coincidence. It is your job to heighten your sensitivity. If you open your mental eyes, you will see angels everywhere.

Angels Seeking Magickal People

The angels are looking for magickal people. They want to work with Witches, Ceremonalists, Druids, Faeries, and other Pagans. They want to work with divinely inspired Christians and Jews. Magickal, spirit-filled people usually have their act together and are already working for the betterment of humankind. If you can summon the elementals, stir the ancestral dead, and call on deity and archetypes, there is no reason why you cannot work with angels. Angels are eager to work with people who are well-grounded and strong in their beliefs. Remember, angels don't discriminate. They are looking for tarologists, Kabbalists, hypnotherapists, astrologists, herbal experts, and holistic healers. You've got the chance to be part of something big. Don't let preconceived ideas rooted in misinformation get in your way.

Don't think angels aren't interested in your everyday problems or are too busy in the celestial realms to listen to you. That nonsense belongs to stuffy theologians, not to angels. The angels are guides, helpers, and friends, and they are waiting for you to call on them. Ask them for help, or offer your help to them. The universe is multi-tiered and multi-faceted—there is a place for all of us.

Angelic Brainstorming

Angels are great at helping you brainstorm any problem, choice, or situation. This next exercise is designed to get you involved with angels right away. You will need a pen or pencil, a few sheets of paper, a watch, and a tape recorder, if you wish. If you are into computers, create an angel file and get ready to send those fingers flying.

Turn on your tape recorder and record the steps. Remember to leave two-minute breaks where indicated, and short pauses after the breathing instructions. Play the tape when you are ready to do the exercise.

Close your eyes. Take a deep breath and relax. Another. One more. Let all the cares of the day leave your system. Feel them flow away from you.

Now open your eyes and write the word "Angel" at the top of your paper. For two minutes (and two minutes only), write down every word or phrase you can think of that is associated with angels. It doesn't matter how odd the associations are. Just let yourself go. No one will see this exercise, so don't worry about what you write. At the end of two minutes, put your pencil down. Take a deep breath and relax.

Close your eyes. Take another deep breath. Envision the angels circling around you. You don't have to make this visualization elaborate. Feelings are fine. Open your eyes and write the word "Universe" at the top of the next sheet of paper. For two minutes (and two minutes only), write associations to the universe down on your paper. Write down everything that pops into your head. When the two minutes are up, put your pencil down and take a deep breath. Relax and let yourself go.

Close your eyes one more time and take another deep breath. Envision one angel touching your shoulder. This is your guardian angel. Open your eyes and write the word "Message" at the top of the last piece of paper. For two minutes (and two minutes only) write down everything (and I mean everything) that comes into your mind. When the two minutes are up, put your pencil down and take a deep breath. Close your eyes and say "thank you," because you have just communicated with the angelic hosts. It's that easy.

Read over your papers. Don't dissect the meanings of what you wrote right now. If something jumps out at you, you may wish to contemplate the thought, but don't bend your brain over it.

Twenty-four hours later, read over your associations. Did you find something new? I always do.

You can use this exercise for any project. The hardest thing about any task is getting started. The angels love to help people get their motors running, whether it is to create something or to solve a problem. The more you practice this exercise, the better at angelic brainstorming you will become.

Here is what I wrote when I did this angelic skill-builder. (You see, I believe in sharing what I do, and trying everything out before I give the idea to someone else. You will never find any exercises in any of my books that I haven't tried first.)

Angel: Soft, kind, light, helpful, full of fun, difficult to find, research, stars, legends, assertive, archetypes, willing to assist in all situations, testimonials, garbage truck, soothsayer, healing, treasure, to be an angel, delight, happiness, to go beyond, laughter, encompassing, Goddess helpers, wisdom, teachers, non-judgmental.

Universe: Whole, one, intuitive, connected, all, omnipresent, balanced, love, no bargaining, caring, worthy, circular, never-ending, talent, time, respect, individual, soul, travel, astral, ignorance, prayer, unity, levels of being, space, warmth, excitement, levels of existence, animals, decisions, music, dance.

Message: Leap of faith, mystery, prophets, togetherness, interest, unencumbered, bright future, opportunities, guidance, love, teachers, service, to be or not to be, get off your duff, get rid of negative people that clutter your life, be an individual, walk and others will follow, be an angel, don't live by others' judgments, be strong and wise, wisdom is in your heart.

If you've written one word over and over, don't worry about it. That means there is something on your mind and your angels are trying to help you come to terms with it. Reread your message and think about what it means to you.

Planning an Angel Day

One of my favorite things to do is plan an "angel day." It doesn't cost any money, and I'm never disappointed in what I find or the experiences I have. You can choose to spend a day with nature (pack a picnic lunch), visit friends, or go to a busy shopping mall. It doesn't matter. There is only one requirement: before you start out, say to yourself, "I'm going to have an angel day today. That means I'm open to whatever the universe has to show me about angels, and how I can help others." Then off you go.

Keep in mind that every occurrence and everyone you meet is orchestrated by the angels to educate or entertain you. You are on an adventure, a treasure hunt. Be nice to every person you meet. Look people straight in the eyes if they speak to you. I'm not saying that you are supposed to go to the worst part of town and waltz around like you own the place. Use your common sense.

If you are a "shopper," tell yourself that you will only look for angel things today. You will find that you spend less money and ferret out items you've really been looking for, not the junk you usually collect through impulse buying. Ask the angels to help guide you to the right store, or library, if you are looking for a particular book or reference material.

When you return home, jot down the significant events of your day. Spend time meditating and clearing out your body. During meditation, envision your angel as a tour guide to help you work out any unanswered questions about your experiences.

In essence, there are many ways you can have an "angel day." You can begin every day as an "angel day." You will be surprised by how much more in tune with the universe you will be, and it is a great feeling to have with you every single day.

Onward...

Together, you and I are going to journey into celestial realms. We will seek and go find the angels, and we will work magick with them. That's right; we won't throw the burden of the work on the shoulders of the angels. You are going to try to remember precisely why you are here on this planet, and what your mission might be.

This book is only one tool you can use to work with the angels. Check the books listed in the bibliography for more information about the angels you meet here. The angels are happy to work with you in any way you choose.

Two

The Angelic Altar

Angels love magick. They like the energy and adore the connection with divinity. Angels and magick are—excuse the pun—a match made in Heaven … Summerland … sacred space … pick one. Why shouldn't they want to work with magickal people?

Angels are not adverse to cast circles. They will stay out if you ask them, or they will come in if you call them. They work well at quarters. Sometimes they will simply ring the circle with their presence, adding extra energy to your working.

In this chapter we will cover information on creating an angelic altar. You'll also find material on the primary angels of Western culture. To some of you, this will be old news, but I hope you read it anyway. You may find something different, or something you might like to try. If this is new to you, don't worry if you can't get it all straight right away. You'll get the hang of it.

Creating an Angelic Altar

Some of you may already have altars you use in your daily workings. An important function of an altar is to centralize power. Each item placed upon the altar should have a specific purpose. Frivolous decorations or favorite pieces should not be on your working altar. A wall display above your altar would be a good place for these things.

Your altar also serves as a work surface. Make sure there is plenty of space for creating talismans, making conjuring bags, etc. The altar also enables you to honor the universe and your beliefs, even when you are not physically present.

Altars can be as large or small as you choose, depending on your personality and space requirements. Some individuals have a "high" altar and a "low" altar. The high altar is mainly for decoration, and only used on holy days. The low altar is a general, all-purpose one, designed for everyday magick. Both my high and low altars consist of large stones. My high altar remains in the north. My low altar is a large, flat stone that I can move around. Every item on your altar (as well as the altar itself) should be cleansed, consecrated, and charged before it is used. (More on this later in the chapter.)

Some people like to use altar cloths, either buying them from magickal shops or using exotic scarves found at a thrift store. Others like to make the altar cloths themselves, stitching magickal designs to match their belief system. For an angelic altar you may like to embroider angelic script (see Chapter 15) on a piece of cloth bordered by angels. Rather than an altar cloth, you may like to make an angel banner to hang above your altar. You don't even need to sew it—you could find a design you like, cut it out of felt, and glue it with a glue gun to a plain, felt banner.

You may wish to put an oil lamp or candles on your altar for illumination purposes. Oil lamps are very magickal. The treasured temple oil lamps of the priests and priestesses of old represented the light of the divine in an otherwise dark world. I've found that I prefer working by oil lamp, and save candles for actual magickal work. When using candles, please be sure your candle holders are sturdy and non-flammable. If you are going to let a candle burn all night, put a large metal dish underneath the candle holder to ensure the safety of yourself and your home, should the holder tip over or catch fire. I received a letter from a girl who used a wooden candle holder (as she had always done) and let her candle burn all night. The holder caught fire and destroyed her altar. Luckily, she awoke before it caught the rest of her apartment on

The Angelic Altar

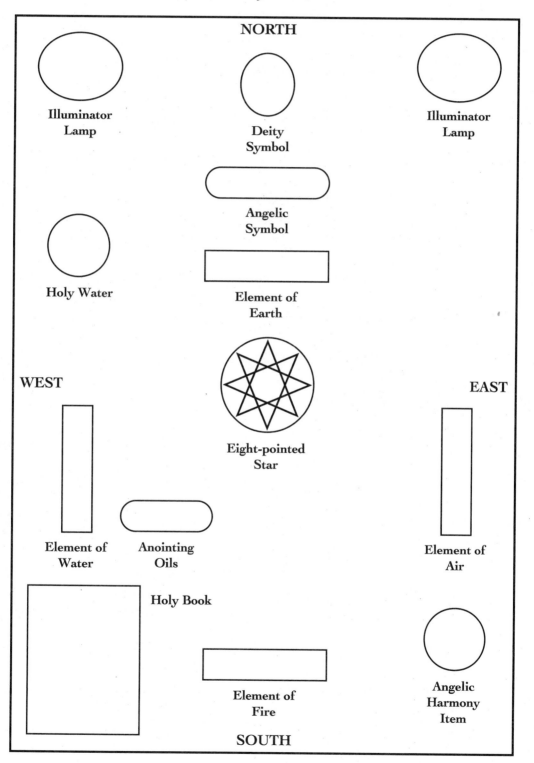

NORTH

Illuminator Lamp

Deity Symbol

Illuminator Lamp

Angelic Symbol

Holy Water

Element of Earth

Eight-pointed Star

WEST

EAST

Element of Water

Anointing Oils

Element of Air

Holy Book

Element of Fire

Angelic Harmony Item

SOUTH

fire. Another young man lost his apartment by leaving a wooden incense burner unattended. Wooden candle holders are just for looks and not designed for a long magickal working. I always choose fire holders/containers that are non-flammable.

Many magickal people like to place a representation of deity on their altar. This is your choice. Sometimes I have a statue on my altar representing the Goddess; other times I put a rack of deer antlers on the altar to represent the God. When I work Pennsylvania Dutch German magick (Pow-Wow), I use a plaque painted with a six-petaled flower, called a Hexefus (which represents the power of the Witch under the direction of the Veiled Goddess and the Hooded God). If you are of another religion, you may wish to put a statue, or perhaps a picture, of your deity on the altar. For example, magickal Catholics may choose the statue of a saint or the Virgin Mary. Someone of the Protestant faiths may choose a picture of Jesus. If you believe God energy to be faceless, then you may not wish to put any representation on the altar at all.

To me, the angelic hosts are a part of divinity, guided by the grand plan of universal light. In my mind, the Goddess commands those angels dealing with the process of birth, nurturing, learning, wisdom, and growth. The God commands those beings who keep order, give strength to those in need, relegate justice, etc. Therefore, I often call upon both the angels and my belief in the divine when involved in a serious working. This is a matter of personal choice.

When working with angels, I like to put a representation of an angel on my altar. I am not worshipping the angels, but keying myself into their energies. A representation helps me connect with that energy. Another powerful connector to the angelic realms is the eight-pointed star. You can either purchase one, or make one on a disc of wood or metal. I often place this disc in the center of my altar (at least through the opening devotion before the actual magickal working) when working with angels.

Your representation of an angel does not have to be an expensive item of china or something beyond your budget. One evening my eight-year-old son sat down with a piece of plain paper and a pair of scissors. After a while, he strolled over to my desk and handed me an angel he had created. I liked it so much, I framed it and hung it above my altar.

Angels get along well with the elements and element magick. Most magickal people put representations of these elements on their altar. The elements are earth, air, fire, and water. Later on in the text we will discuss angels that have an affinity for the elements, but for now, you may want to choose something from each of these categories to put on your altar. Here are some examples:

Earth: A bowl of dirt from your area, sand, salt, crystals, or, in some magickal traditions, ice. The earth item goes on your altar at compass point north. North stands for mystery, growth, fertility, material abundance, the combined forces of nature, birth, healing, business, industry, and possessions.

Air: Incense, a feather, a fan. The air item goes on your altar at compass point east. East represents intellect, communication, knowledge, concentration, telepathy, memory, wisdom, the ability to know and understand the mysteries, to unlock secrets, and to contact the angels.

Fire: A special small candle, lamp, small burning cauldron. Place the fire item at compass point south on your altar. It stands for energy, purification, courage, the will to dare, creativity, the higher self, success, refinement, the arts, and transformation. If you are not able to have fire where you practice magick, use a bowl of grain, corn meal, or rice.

Water: A bowl of water, a flute of water, a small cauldron of water. Place the water element at compass point west on your altar. West stands for intuition, emotions, the inner self, flowing movement, the power to dare, cleansing, sympathy, love, reflection, tides, and also represents the gates of death.

We've almost finished with the things you may wish to put on your altar. There are three items left that you might want to consider:

Holy oil/anointing oil: To anoint oneself during prayer or before a working.

Holy book: The book that is most important to your religion. The Witch would use his or her Book of Shadows, a Christian would use the Bible, etc.

Calling piece: During your workings with angels you may pick up something special that allows you to get yourself in tune with angelic energy quickly. It could be a gemstone, a plaque, a piece of jewelry, or a small talisman. Perhaps it is an item you discovered on a meditational walk. It doesn't matter what it is in the physical. What is important is that it assists you in creating harmony with the angelic forces.

First, let's look at the basic angelic forces you will be using. Their names are Raphael, Michael, Uriel, and Gabriel.

A Simple Angelic Altar

So what if you don't want to put everything shown previously on your altar? Will that hurt anything? No. On the next page is a simple angelic altar you may like to try.

The purpose of showing you more than one altar set-up is to stress that what you find comfortable in your spirituality is right for you. If you want your altar to hold only an angel statue that has a cup for tea-candles in it, then that is how it will be. There is no one right way to worship divinity or call the angels into your life. You always have a choice.

A Simple Angelic Altar

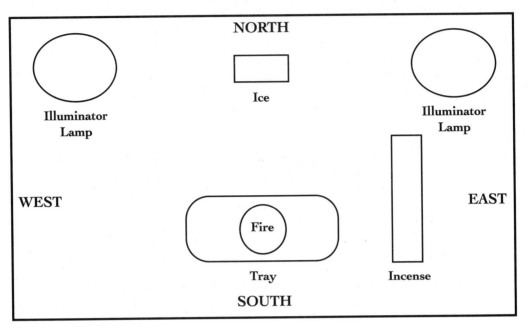

NORTH

Ice

Illuminator Lamp

Illuminator Lamp

WEST

EAST

Fire

Tray

Incense

SOUTH

The Basic Angelic Forces

The Jewish sect of the Essenes, which flourished at the time of Jesus, imposed an oath on those entering the order never to reveal the names of the angels. For in the knowledge of the names, they believed, was power that could be abused, and that would distract the spiritual aspirant from his principal reason for being a member of the community.[1]

Names have power. To name something is to meld with its energy, for good or ill. Personally, I think that if you abuse angelic power, you will suffer for it. As with all decisions we make in life, to work for good or ill is a matter of choice. As with all choices, you will reap the consequences, positive or negative.

Modern thought on the subject of angels links them more with the positive aspects of the universe, such as healing, success, security, and safety. We have left (hopefully) the medieval times of tickling our brows with a feather quill, and salivating over how many names we can create for legions of fallen angels. Some humans have transferred the failings of humanity to other entities, creating unpleasant thoughtforms—hence the ranks of the fallen angels.

In this text we will deal primarily with angelic energies that have a history of positive attributes and dealings with humans. The first of these are the Archangels, who are common to most religions—Raphael, Michael, Gabriel, and Uriel.

---

1. *In Search of Angels* by David Connolly, page 87.

The description of each Archangel includes an invocation for working with them. An invocation is the drawing forth of the powers of any divine being. With the invocations given, you will be drawing the energies of the Archangels into a magick circle (which we will cover in Chapter 6). Sometimes the drawing forth of the angelic brings a change in personality for the magickal person. You may find yourself surrounded by shining light and, as a result, became a shining being yourself, cloaked in the energies of the angel you have called.

Employ invocations for a specific situation to manifest those energies that can best help you in a situation. For example, if I wanted to manifest healing powers, I would call on Raphael. If I wanted transformation in my life, then Gabriel would be the angelic force to manifest my desire. Use the energies of Michael if you find yourself in a situation where defense is needed. If I wanted to improve my prophetic abilities or learn a divination tool, such as the Tarot, I would call on Uriel. These are just a few examples. Each angel has many talents they are willing to share with you.

Raphael, Angel of the East

I am the Angel of the Sun
Whose flaming wheels began to run
When God's almighty breath
Said to the darkness and the Night,
Let there be light! and there was light
I bring the gift of faith.
—Longfellow, "The Nativity"

Colors: Yellow or gold and blue

Season: Spring

Time of day: Dawn

Element: Air

Astrological signs: Gemini, Libra, and Aquarius

The original Chaldean version of Raphael was named Labbiel. The Hebrew word *rapha* means healer, doctor, or surgeon. Raphael, strictly speaking, would mean "shining healer." Information about Raphael stems back to the Near East before the time of Christ. Ugarit, a city-state that blossomed on the Mediterranean seacoast, had a pantheon that included the high god El and his consort Atirat (whose child was Raphael), the storm god Baal and his sister Anat, other divinities, and (of course) angels. Therefore, Raphael was originally an archetype, not an angel.

Raphael's task is to heal the Earth, and through him the Earth protects and nourishes humankind. This includes energies of love, joy, light, prayer, compassion, and honor. Raphael's main function is to take care of sickness, disease, and imbalance in all Gaia's children. Known as the angel of the Sun, he rules science and knowledge.

21

He is the ruling prince of the second heaven, overseer of evening winds, guardian of the Tree of Life (Biliomagas), governor of the south, and sometimes seen as the guardian of the west, though in most of our work he will remain in the east. Raphael is an angel of love and laughter. He is also a guide into the Underworld, as well as the patron angel of doctors, nurses, midwives, alternative healers, travelers, and those who have lost their sight. Raphael gave King Solomon the gift of the pentacle. Remember the points of the upright pentacle stand for earth, air, fire, water, and the spirit of humanity, surrounded by universal harmony. Raphael is the angel of magickal tools and the mysteries that surround them.

Raphael has an affinity with young people and creativity. Some say he is the "supervisor" of all guardian angels. This angel has a sense of humor, and likes jokes and playful times. He looks out for those who are starting new spiritual paths, or those who are striving to excel on their chosen journey of enlightenment. He likes to visit unsuspecting mortals and chat with them. He is the "incognito angel."

Visualize Raphael as a figure dressed in yellow robes with some purplish highlights, carrying a caduceus (a wand entwined by serpents; this symbol, representing the life force, is used by doctors), and riding upon a breeze. However, other sources feel he wears green robes tinted with blue (as seen in Botticini's painting titled *Tobias and the Angels*).

Invocation of Raphael

From azure coast and Ugarit ocean
Chaldean lineage, shining god of healing devotion,
Cresting on dawn's golden, enchanted breezes
Rising to purge humanity of insidious diseases.
I beckon thee, great angel of the Sun
To enter here with sparkling laughter and creative fun.

Whisper the secrets of the pentagram, fair Raphael
The Son of El and consort of Atriat is Labbiel.
Your wand entwined by mystical serpents
Science and knowledge are thy devoted servants,
Now command the legions when magick requires it
And bring forth the power of healing mist.

Angel guardian of spiritual leaders
Brush peacock wings on swirls of scented cedar
Floating among humanity in disguise
Spiraling from the east as bluegold prayers rise
Bringing into form Gaia's balance again
And let us ne'er cry over what might have been.

Michael, Angel of the South

Holy Michael Archangel, defend us in the day of battle; be our safeguard against the wickedness and snares of negativity and do thou, prince of the heavenly host, by the power of God thrust down all evil and wicked spirits ....

—Pope Leo XIII

Color: Red or scarlet

Season: Summer

Time of day: Noon

Element: Fire

Astrological signs: Aries, Leo, and Sagittarius

Michael means "who is God," and therefore can be seen as the Pagan godform. In many religions, Michael ranks as the top angelic being. Like Raphael, he was worshipped as a god of the Chaldeans. Therefore, before his involvement with Christianity, Islam, or Judaism, he was (drum roll, please) Pagan. Yes, just like the good old Christmas tree and the Easter Bunny, guess who had him first? Not the current structured religions. They borrowed him, like many of the other angels, and made him over to fit within their belief structures.

So we see that Michael actually comes from a Pagan archetype. He is chief in the order of Virtues; chief of the Archangels; angel of repentance, righteousness, and mercy; and the ruler of the fourth heaven. (We'll get to the explanations of all this unusual terminology later on in the text.) His mystery name is Sabbathiel, so if you would like to call him that, be my guest. In Islam he goes by the name of Mika'il.

Michael's popularity with the patriarchal religions is easily understood. He is an avenging angel who has put down quite a few bad guys in legend and lore, meaning he appeals to those with a testosterone overload—smash it and trash it. In medieval times, he wore armor. Today you would find him decked out in the best military equipment our world has designed. He is an undisputed hero, the terminator of the angelic realms. Let's not be too hard on Michael, as his lore is a product of male wishful thinking combined with the true need for justice, strength, protection, and balance in our world. In legend, he is the only angel who defends the heavenly hosts through thick and thin. His loyalty is unquestionable.

Michael's history includes more than just Christian lore. For example, he assumed the task of "weighing the souls" once performed by Anubis in the Egyptian pantheon. In Persian mythology, Michael carried the name Beshter, meaning one who provides sustenance for humanity. In an earlier Akkadian version, the people named him Kasista, meaning prince or leader. Pagan peoples from Roman Gaul found themselves bribed into Christianity by more tampering with his essence. The Church gave many of the qualities of Mercury to Michael. Thus the "Michael's Mounts," found throughout Europe and associated with the old custom of mounds of the dead, are based on mystical Pagan beliefs. These mounts link to ley line energy. The Church allowed Michael to assume many of the Pagan archetypal powers in an effort to lure the people away from their mother religions. In lore, it is the angel Michael who appeared to Mary (Jesus' mother) to tell her that her time to leave this plane had come. Michael manifests as an angelic being not beyond mercy, patience, and compassion.

In Islamic tradition he is the angel of food and knowledge; in Egypt, he is a patron of the Nile. His festival and feast occur each year at the rise of the Nile.

Michael's wings unfurl to a blazing emerald green, sometimes depicted with peacock feathers (a remnant of the Egyptian Goddess Maat?). At times, Michael carries a glowing sword; however, in the modern era, his weapon of truth lies in the written word and not, thankfully, the rockets of our military. In some traditions he holds a scepter in place of the sword.

Michael is the chief guardian of police officers, security guards, hunters, and armed service personnel. He stands firm as the guardian of the Goddess on the astral planes, wherein he protects Her energy from the onslaughts of the patriarchy. Michael has a special talent for cleansing anything, from people to places. He is also the conglomeration of ancient spirits who watched over the holy creeks, streams, fountains, lakes, etc., before the Christian era, and the guardian of the shrines erected in honor of the healing energies of divinity.

Michaelmas, the Feast of Saint Michael, celebrated by the Church of England and the American Episcopal Church, draws crowds of the faithful on September 29 of each year. Much pomp and ceremony leads up to the Michaelmas festival. In the Isles, Michael is spoken of as brian Micheil (god Michael):

> *Thou wert the warrior of courage*
> *Going on the journey of prophecy*
> *Thou wouldst not travel on a cripple,*
> *Thou didst take the steed of the God Michael,*
> *He was without bit in his mouth*
> *Thou didst ride him on the wing,*
> *Thou didst leap over the knowledge of Nature.*[2]

When erecting sacred space within your home or on your property, turn to the angel Michael for guidance on both the structure and placement. Visualize Michael as a figure dressed in scarlet with green or gold highlights who holds a flaming sword.

> *Michael the victorious*
> *Thou Michael the victorious,*
> *I make my circle under thy shield,*
> *Thou Michael of the white steed,*
> *And of the bright brilliant blades,*
> *Conqueror of evil*

---

2. *Carmina Gadelica Hymns and Incantations* by Alexander Carmichael, page 588.

Be thou at my back,
Thou ranger of the heavens
Thou warrior and king of the angels
O Michael the victorious,
My pride and my guide,
O Michael the victorious,
The glory of mine eye.

I make my circle
In the fellowship of my guardian angel
On the field, on the meadow
On the cold heathery hill;
Though I should travel ocean
And the hard globe of the world
No harm can ever befall me
Neath the shelter of thy shield;
O Michael the victorious
Jewel of my heart,
O Michael the victorious,
Goddess' shepherd thou art.[3]

Invocation to Michael

Chaldean prince and Pagan god
Avenging lance of sword and rod
Warrior angel of noon fire's grace
Who guards herein this sacred space,
Into form burst forth my Michael
The scarlet flame, Sabbathiel.

Loyal fighter and astral guardian
The crimson leader, man's perfect specimen.
Mercy, patience, and warm compassion
Whose divinity's hand took care to fashion
Hail unto thee, O patron of the Nile
I call thee forth, strong Michael.

Courage and trust bring into form
Time-favored angel of legends worn
Center thy energies wise and just
The Goddess' champion in whom She trusts.

---

3. *Carmina Gadelica Hymns and Incantations* by Alexander Carmichael, page 87.

This terminator angel, heavenly hunter
My battle angel of blazing summer.

Gabriel, Angel of the West

Most beautiful of maidens
Like the moon amongst the stars
Dear Gabriel clothed in light
Bringing peace into my heart.
                    —Unknown

Color: Blue or aquamarine

Season: Fall

Time of day: Dusk

Element: Water

Astrological signs: Cancer, Scorpio, and Pisces

Gabriel is second only to Michael in both Christian and Jewish lore. The root word for her name is Sumerian in origin. Her name means "governor of light" (*gabri* means "governor" and the suffix *-el* means "shining"). She is the angel of resurrection, mercy, vengeance, death, birth, transformation, and mystery revealed, as well as a peacemaker. She bears before her an olive branch, the symbol of peace. Gabriel, considered the ruling princess of the first heaven, sits on the left side of divinity. Mohammed claimed that Gabriel had 140 pairs of wings; unfortunately, he said she was male. She is known as Jibril to the Moslems. They believe that it is the angel Gabriel (the male version) who dictated the Koran to the prophet Mohammed.

Gabriel is the chief of the angelic guards who watch over Paradise (Heaven, Summerland, etc.). She is also seen as the angel of the Moon. Her gifts include hope and messages from the divine realms through the written word. Great golden wings unfurl around her slender body. Gabriel is another "terminator" angel, meaning many of her duties included stomping out the bad guys. Gabriel is the guardian of Goddess energy on Earth, protecting those who are in service to Her. She enjoys flowers, and legend states her face is stupendously beautiful and her build could win any beauty contest. Beside her snort wild and flamboyant white horses. Horses, especially winged ones, are the animal associated with this angel.

Gabriel is thought to be the protector of childbirth and pregnancy, and she is the angel, by testimony of Joan of Arc, who persuaded Joan to help the Dauphin. Gabriel heralds the birth of those who are holy or favored by the universal forces of light, and Sumerian lore indicates she once held human form (archetypal energy again) and rose to the state of a Goddess. Gabriel's symbol is the lily, the *fleur-de-lis*, which represents the triple aspect of the Goddess. In legend, Gabriel foretold the births of Samson, the Virgin Mary, John the Baptist, and Jesus.

Gabriel is also connected in legend and lore with Lilith, Adam's first wife, who scorned him and fell from the grace of both humans and heavenly hosts. In one account, Lilith was not human at all, but a being from the stars who refused to mate with the animalistic Adam (who was a cross-breed of low humanoid and stellar genes). Gabriel and Lilith are not the same being; Gabriel is the geneticist who oversaw the project.

Although Michael is in charge of the heavenly armies, Gabriel works on strategy and orchestrates the movements of the troops. In Moslem lore, Gabriel delivered the Black Stone of the Kaba to Abraham in Mecca. The stone exists today and many followers make an annual pilgrimage *(haj)* to the city of Mecca to kiss the stone.

In modern times, Gabriel finds herself chosen as the patron of messengers and postal employees. In 1951, Pope Pius XII declared Gabriel to be the patron angel of all aspects of telecommunications. Visualize Gabriel as a figure dressed in blue with some orange highlights, holding a cup surrounded by waterfalls.

Invocation to Gabriel

Sumerian Priestess of the Light
I seek thy presence here this night,
As aquamarine fog enchants the dusk
And autumn blooms its sacred musk.
Arise sweet Gabriel of the Moon
With gold-tinged wings and crying loon.

Goddess energy here on earth
Bring transformation and rebirth
The lily opens, fed by the chalice
This angel removes and avenges malice.
Governess of mystical light divine
Resurrection and mercy her design.

Come now, unite my Warrior Queen
Who tells of birth and things unseen
From wisdom's fountain I seek to drink
And open mystery I've yet to think.
While fairies paint the starry skies
And Jibril guards this paradise.

Ariel, Angel of the North

The angel who watches over thunder and terror …
—Malcolm Godwin

Colors: Green and brown

Season: Winter

Time of day: Midnight

Element: Earth

Astrological signs: Taurus, Virgo, and Capricorn

Ariel means "Earth's great lord" or "shining Earth." This angel is the guardian of visions, dreams, and prophecy. He is often depicted carrying a scroll. Ariel is known as the angel of mystery, and assists Raphael in healing the children of the Goddess. Ariel is another angel who first appears to be a god in legend and lore, so he too has risen (or fallen, as you perceive it). According to John Dee, astrologer-royal in Queen Elizabeth's day, Ariel is a conglomerate of Anael and Uriel. Modern writers on angels often confuse Ariel and Uriel, probably because they stand for much the same thing. Uriel gave the interpretations of the mysteries of magick to humans, and is especially kind to those born in the month of September. He is the protector of psychics and all who seek to foretell the future for the good of humankind, as well as journalists, teachers, and writers. He is in charge of natural phenomena such as tornadoes, thunderstorms, hurricanes, volcanoes, and earthquakes. Uriel's archetype is the god of the Sun. However, beware—Uriel is another "terminator" angel and more aggressive in his handling of offenders. Not a fluff-and-bubble angel, he enjoys ripping out tongues and roasting the evil ones. One recent writer on angels says Uriel's energy applies itself to the earth plane "as unswerving in the pursuit of duty as a forty-ton truck traveling ninety miles an hour" with no brakes.

Ariel is also responsible for overseeing the work of all nature spirits. He holds the keys to the fairy kingdoms.

Visualize Ariel/Uriel as a figure dressed in greens and browns on a fertile landscape holding sheaves of wheat, corn, or barley. His totem animal is the lion.

Invocation to Ariel

> *Forest green and sienna brown*
> *The winter rolls out, to touch the ground*
> *Where frosty midnight brings mystery*
> *Of visions, dreams, and prophecy*
> *Nature spirits dance the spell*
> *To call the thunderous Uriel.*

Volcanoes of information now burst forth
On crystal snowflakes from the north
With lions roar and Sekhmet force
I call this angel of secret source
Shining earth and truth to tell
I seek the knowledge of Ariel.

Of rocks and stones and forest trees
A hawk-eyed being who endless sees
The truth cut cold of human lies
And brings the gift of angel eyes
Spread thy wings of hurricane scroll
Enlighten my poor mortal soul.

You might notice that I have called three of the four Archangels "he." However, angels are neither male nor female, and can be either, should they have the inclination. Have you ever noticed that the names Michael, Gabriel, Raphael, and Uriel lead to names for both boy and girl children? If you feel more comfortable dealing with the angels in a feminine sense, do so. You may also keep their masculine attributes, and then call in Goddess energy to make a more balanced, harmonious atmosphere—the choice is yours.

These are four of the "Clan of the Seven" in the angelic realms, sometimes known as the Eighth Choir or the Archangels. Christian and Jewish faiths agree there are seven, but don't agree on the other three angelic members. Islam recognizes these four (and no others), but the Koran only mentions two—Gabriel and Michael. You will meet the six disputed angels later on in this book. They are Metatron, Remiel, Sariel, Anael, Raguel, and Raziel.

Throughout the remainder of the book you will be meeting all sorts of angels. If you do not wish to use the historical name of the angel, you can call the force/energy instead. Be specific and do it with feeling, and you will get the results you seek.

The Banishing (Earth) Pentagram

The pentagram (the five-pointed star) and the pentacle (the five-pointed star with a circle around it) is/was a gift from the angel Raphael to humankind. The key to using the banishing pentagram lies in your visualization techniques.

If you have not done this before or are having trouble, follow these steps. First, draw a pentagram on an index card. Stare at the pentagram, then close your eyes. See it outlined behind your eyelids. Imagine now that it is a bright blue or white light. Now, open your eyes and follow the diagram on the next page that shows you how the banishing pentagram is drawn. Practice this until you have it down.

Banishing pentagram

Cleansing, Consecrating, and Charging

Cleansing, consecrating, and charging remove any negative residue that has attached itself to an item or place, create harmony so you may work in tandem with divinity and universal forces, and instill positive, harmonic energy into the object or place, ensuring the success of your work.

Therefore, cleansing removes any negative vibrations. Consecrating dedicates the item or place to the divine. Charging instills that divine energy into the item or place. Before you set up your angelic altar (or use any tool for the first time, such as Tarot cards, jewelry, or any item on the altar) you should cleanse, consecrate, and charge it.

The first step in our altar cleansing, consecrating, and charging is the Lesser Banishing Ritual, often called the LBR. You should learn this ritual and perform it every night and every morning. In ceremonial magick one often uses a dagger; in the Wiccan realms we may use a wand or athame. In angelic magick neither is necessary; the fingers of your dominant hand will do nicely. The LBR cleanses both your body and the area you are in, and provides you with a path of harmony during the day.

The Lesser Banishing Ritual

1. Take a deep breath, then another, then one more. Relax. Close your eyes if you like. Visualize yourself filled with divine light, growing larger, yet rooted to Mother Earth. Allow your center (around your navel area) to enter a state of complete calm, a floating sensation of peace and tranquility. Imagine that your feet, like the roots of a tree, dig deeply, securing your body in the earth. This procedure is called grounding and centering.

2. Bring the index finger of your dominant hand down your body until you are pointing to the ground. As you do this, visualize the white light of divinity

entering the top of your head and circulating down through your body. Say *Mahl-KOOT.*

3. Bring your index finger to your right shoulder. Visualize the white light running down the center of your body, forming a beam from the heart area out to your right, past the finger at your right shoulder. Say *Vih-g'boo-RAH.*

4. Move your finger horizontally to your left shoulder. Visualize the white light extending through infinite space to your left. Say *Vih-g'doo-LAH.*

5. Cross your arms in the God position (fists up touching your chest, with wrists crossed). Visualize within your chest, at the point covered by your crossed wrists, a brilliant golden glow. Say *Lih-oh-LAHM, Ah-MEN.*

6. Turn to the east. In one fluid motion, step out with your left foot, point your finger to the east, and draw the banishing pentagram in the air. Many people visualize this pentagram as blue flames or blazing white light. Some spiral the energy/visualization out from their fingers and explode the visualization of the banishing pentagram. The choice is yours. Say *Yud-heh-vahv-heh.*

7. Bring your hand back down to your side and turn to the south. Repeat the pentagram as above and say *Ah-doh-NYE.*

8. Bring your hand back down to your side and turn to the west. Repeat the pentagram as before and say *Eh-heh-YEH.*

9. Bring your hand back down to your side and turn to the north. Repeat the pentagram and say *AH-glah.*

10. Turn to the east, raise your hand, and begin to connect the pentagrams with glowing white light, moving from the east, to the south, to the west, to the north, and back to the east.

11. Visualize this circle expanding to form a sphere around yourself and the room you are in.

12. Spread your arms straight out from your body, so that you form a cross. This equal-armed cross represents the four elements and the four archetypal angels. In the east, say *Before me, Rah-fay-EL. Behind me, Gahb-ray-EL. On my right hand, Mee-chai-EL. And on my left hand, Ohr-ree-EL.*

13. With your arms still up, spread your feet apart (this is the Goddess position) and say *For about me flames the pentagram....*

14. Visualize a golden six-pointed star descending on the top of your head and moving down into your body; say *And above me, now within me, shines the six-rayed star. Service* [touch your head], *devotion* [touch your heart], *honor* [touch your thigh], *Shekinah, descend upon me now!*

15. Repeat steps 2 through 5.

Holy Water

There are a variety of ways to make holy water. The basic ingredients are salt and water. Magickal traditions vary on how holy water is made, and sometimes extra ingredients are added for a specific purpose. For angel magick, however, we need only salt and water. Sea salt or kosher salt is best, but if you can't get your hands on anything else, table salt will do. One way to make holy water is given here.

Hold the bowl of water in your hands and say the following:

> *In the name of the angel Michael* [he guards holy wells and springs] *and the angel Raphael* [he cleanses the baptismal waters and instills them with healing], *I banish all negativity from this water, through time and in the phantasm. I cleanse and consecrate it in the name of the holy ones. So mote it be.*

You can name the "holy ones" if you like. For example, if you are Wiccan you may say "In the name of the Lord and the Lady," or "In the name of the Veiled Goddess and the Hooded God." If Protestant, "In the name of Jesus." If Catholic, "In the name of Mary." The choice is yours. Draw a banishing pentagram with your finger over the water, then visualize the water being blessed and filling with divine light.

Hold the salt out before you and say:

> *In the name of Gabriel* [the guardian of Earth and its inhabitants], *I banish all negativity in this salt, through time and in the world of phantasm. I cleanse and consecrate it in the name of the Holy Ones. So mote it be.*

Draw a banishing pentagram with your finger over the salt and visualize the water being blessed and filling with divine light.

Add three pinches of salt to the water bowl. Stir the water clockwise three times with the index finger of your dominant hand.

Here is where the procedure changes depending on your religious preference. If you are Wiccan, lower your athame into the water and say:

> *As the rod is to the God, so the chalice is to the Goddess.*
> *Together they are one.*

If you are Protestant, recite the Lord's Prayer.

If you are Catholic, say:

> *As mother Mary is representation of divine union,*
> *So together they are one.*

If you are a Ceremonialist, say:

> *Behold, this is the divine union of water and earth!*

All recitations carry the same visualization procedure, in which the container is visualized transmuting into divine and holy light. If you are not using an athame, put your index fingers and thumbs together to form a triangle. Look through this triangle to the water in the bowl, and imagine the brilliant light of the holy ones beaming through the triangle and changing the water. Ceremonialists call this the Triangle of Manifestation.

Hold the container with the holy water and say:

> *In the names of Michael, Gabriel, Raphael, and Uriel, I call upon the positive powers of the universe to transmute this water into divine essence in the name of* [your deity], *and enable me to work positive magick for the betterment of humankind.*

Cleansing, Consecrating, and Charging Your Angelic Altar

The sanctification and purification of the altar is a part of most religions, whether they are structured, alternative, or tribal. To cleanse, consecrate, and charge your angelic altar, you will need your holy water and something that represents the four elements, as well as your anointing oil. Inexpensive oils can be purchased at metaphysical shops, herbal stores, or ordered through the mail.

Do the Lesser Banishing Ritual (see page 30).

Pick up the lit incense and make a banishing pentagram with the incense over the altar, then circle the incense clockwise over the altar three, seven, or nine times. Say the following:

> *Angel of the east, guardian of eternal healing and wisdom, element of air, I call upon the angel Raphael to cleanse and consecrate this altar stone in the name of* [chosen deity].

Light the candle and say:

> *Element of fire*
> *Work thy will by my desire.*

Make a banishing pentagram with the candle over the altar, then pass it three, seven, or nine times over the altar and say:

> *Angel of the south, guardian of eternal strength and Goddess energy, element of fire, I call upon the angel Michael to cleanse and consecrate this altar stone in the name of* [chosen deity].

Pick up the bowl of water and sprinkle the water over the altar in the shape of a banishing pentagram, then circle the bowl over the altar in a clockwise motion three, seven, or nine times, saying:

Angel of the west, guardian of earth and its inhabitants, element of water, I call upon the angel Gabriel to cleanse and consecrate this altar stone in the name of [chosen deity].

Pick up the bowl of salt (or whatever you chose to represent earth) and sprinkle the substance over the altar in the shape of a banishing pentagram, then circle the bowl over the altar in a clockwise motion three, seven, or nine times, saying:

Angel of the north, guardian of the mysteries, element of earth, I call upon the angel Uriel to cleanse and consecrate this altar stone in the name of [chosen deity].

Pick up the anointing oil. Anoint your forehead. On the altar, draw a pentacle in oil at each of the four corners.

Hold your dominant hand over the altar and circle in a clockwise direction four times (once for each element). You are now mixing the elemental energies together to form one substance. Tap your hand on the altar three times to seal this energy.

Hold your hands over the center of the altar and say:

In the names of Michael, Gabriel, Raphael, and Uriel, I cleanse and consecrate this altar in the name of [chosen deity]. *I do bid the unseen positive angelic hosts to gather close about me, for I do call them forth into this time and this place to make holy this altar in the name of* [chosen deity]. *Round and about course the positive energies of the universe, and through my hands and the hands of the angels doth a permanent current of power pulse.*

Wait several heartbeats until you feel the power pulsing through the altar, then allow that power to grow until you feel you are finished. Say:

By the beat of angel wings, the drums of the universe now sound the call of perfection. It is done.

Remove your hands from the altar, and make the sign of the equal-armed cross over the altar to seal it permanently. Now, you may complete your altar with whatever you see fit. When you are finished, you may wish to say:

Mystic angels, bold and pure
Thank you much for being here.
Angel of earth, who carries Her mysteries
Angel of water, who guards Her children
Angel of fire, who protects Her countenance
Angel of air, who channels Her wisdom and heals Her body
Go safely to thy heavenly realms
Peace and divine energy be your guiding light.
Hail and farewell.

Stamp your foot on the ground or clap your hands and say:

This circle is open, but never broken.

Now your angelic altar is all set and ready to go! You will use your altar while performing daily devotionals, working minor and major magicks, creating and working with healing energy, performing angelic ritual, and praying.

You will notice I often recommend doing your work by or on your altar. This is to keep you attuned to the energies there; however, sometimes we can't get to the altar. For example, maybe my daughter is studying on the dining room table (my altar is in the dining room) and I don't want to disturb her. I may do the preliminary work at my desk, perhaps listening to my portable tape player using the earphones. Later in the evening, after the family has cleared out of the dining room, I will go to my altar and finish my work. This is where I will connect with deity and the angels.

There are times, though, when you are away from your altar. This doesn't mean you can't contact the angels simply because you don't have a physical representation, or you are unable to light a candle. Angels will hear you when you call for them no matter where you are. The idea of using your altar is to encourage you to find harmony in your work by localizing your energies and focusing your ideas and aspirations.

General Invocation to the Angels

In the eyes of the universal spirit,
In the love of the Divine Ones,
In the power of the angels.
Bless me with
Love toward the universe,
The affection of the angels,
The wisdom of the Queen,
The grace of the God,
The strength of the human spirit,
And the will and power to perform magick for the service of humankind.
May I perform
In shade and light
Each day and night
In perfect love and perfect trust
Descend upon me thy loving spirit.
So mote it be.

Three

Angel Hierarchy and the Queen of Angels

*W*hile researching this book, I discovered several systems presenting levels of hierarchy in the angelic realms. All these recorded systems and structures, which can seem overpowering at first, have their roots in the human mind. Often, they appear stuffy and so tied to a particular religious structure that their original purpose is lost. Yet, if we choose to ignore these works, are we being absolutely fair? Obviously someone spent a great deal of time creating them. What the originator's passions and driving force at the time could have been, we do not know. But is it right for us to ignore their work, re-create the same thing, and call it something else for the sake of modern philosophy?

I grappled with this question and finally decided to stick with what is already in place, but expand that knowledge into the magickal realms. I did have a few setbacks in my studies. For example, I can't believe that divinity created a huge bunch of angels whose only function is to "praise the heavenly hosts." Nothing like making your own cheerleading squad. That suggests that ultimate divinity has an ego, and not a small one at that. In my mind, only the human is shackled with that ego thing. Instead of "praising the heavenly hosts," perhaps their job is to raise a reservoir of positive energy from which all planes of existence can draw.

I also had a problem with the passages indicating the angels (assumed to be male, in this case) were so smitten by the beauty of the daughters of men that they flung aside their holy obligations and sought the women for their sexual favors, condemning themselves to eternal damnation, thus creating some of the fallen angels.

This is a wonderful plot for a novel, but not particularly practical for the smooth action of the universe, in which the element of chaos is humanity, not angels. Just because some human men can't learn to control their lust doesn't mean that the male of every other species in the universe has the same problem.

This doesn't get us into the hierarchy of the angels, does it? Perhaps it does. By understanding our own failings, we realize that the systems in place may have a few problems here and there. That's fine. We can work around these and get on to the more important stuff. How to use the hierarchy of the angels in our lives without feeling like we are not good enough to work with them is the first step.

Remember in Chapter 1 when I told you that angels came with us and are here to help us fulfill our destinies? With every chapter in this book I'll urge you onward and upward into the hierarchy of the angelic realms, and try to show you that by interacting with the angels, you can make your life better, more fulfilled, and gather a sense of harmony about you.

The system most commonly followed by Westerners comes from a book written by Dionysius the Areopagite during the sixth century. Through the ages these choirs of angels have performed specific duties and carried energies inherent only to them. Some structured religions believe that many humans are working through earthly incarnations to become a member of one of the Nine Choirs. The Nine Choirs are divided into three groups, or spheres, as follows:

Angels of the First Sphere

Seraphim   Cherubim   Thrones

Angels of the Second Sphere

Dominions   Powers   Virtues

Angels of the Third Sphere

    Principalities   Archangels   Angels

Angels of the First Sphere

The first sphere of angels is collectively concerned with the universe and the manifestations of divinity within it, operating at the highest level of the astral. Some see these as the angels of pure contemplation, but to me, contemplation means sitting on your duff and thinking about things. Perhaps, then, this means that they manifest energy through pure thought. I like that idea a lot better. These angels possess the deepest knowledge of divinity, and its inner workings and manifestations. The angels of the first sphere are the Seraphim, the Cherubim, and the Thrones.

Seraphim

The Seraphim, those closest to divinity, concentrate on vibrational manifestations to keep divinity constant and intact, and are considered the angels of pure love, light, and fire. They make sure nothing rocks the boat, no negative energy gets through to divinity, and help create and carry positive energy through all the choirs of angels and into the physical realms. They don't encircle God and sing pretty songs to keep everybody happy. They encircle divinity to ensure its continued existence, and funnel that energy toward us so we can keep going. Supposedly, there are four chiefs of these angels, corresponding to the four winds of the Earth, who beat the air with six wings each. The ruler of the Seraphim is either Jehoel, Metatron, or Michael. Other angels named in this order are Seraphiel, Uriel, Kemuel, and Nathanael. As you study and work with the Nine Choirs, you will find that several angels are mentioned in more than one category, moving up and down the celestial ladder as the universe has need of them. This movement is especially true of the four Archangels (Michael, Gabriel, Raphael, and Uriel).

The Seraphim (beings of pure light) shine so brilliantly that a human would die of fright should he or she see a Seraphim in all his/her/its glory. Only the Lord and Lady, and Michael, are capable of complete interaction with these beings. Some say their faces are like lightning and their clothing as blinding as arctic snow. They never stop moving and doing—they are ceaseless in their work.

Magickal people can access the Seraphim because we are excellent at praying and raising power. However, as a friend once said to me, "Would you want to come up against those little old ladies who sit in the back of the cathedral, mumbling over their rosaries? There's more magick with them than in many bragging adepts." I don't doubt it.

The word Seraphim means "ardor." In other words, these angels work with consuming divine love and compassion. One cannot just walk up to the Seraphim and say, "How ya doing?" on the astral plane. Humans encounter them by invitation only. This is not to say that the Seraphim don't interact with humans at all, or don't listen to what you have to say. You can talk to them and request their aid in working magick, but you may never see them (obviously; if they are scary, you may not want to). If your guardian angel belongs to the order of Seraphim, you may find yourself involved in some sort of world change or human consciousness change, where you need their inspiration, divine love, and power to complete your mission.

In other mythology, the Phoenixes were angels of a high order, classed with the Seraphim and Cherubim. They become the elements of the Sun and were associated with specific planets. They were twelve-winged and associated with birds; their plumage is purple.

Magickally, work with the Seraphim when you wish to raise energy for humanitarian or planetary causes. They listen to group ritual. To reach the Seraphim, burn a white candle for divinity, and a purple candle for the Seraphim.

Cherubim

The Cherubim function as the guardians of light and stars. They also create and channel positive energy from divinity, and appear exquisite in form. They supposedly outshine all the other angels. They are Assyrian or Akkadian in origin, and their name means "those who intercede"—mighty spirits of knowledge and boundless love. I find it interesting that they often rise in the human consciousness as half-human, half-beast, usually with the faces of lions. Ancient architecture placed statues of them with human faces and the bodies of bulls or lions at temple entrances to protect holy ground. Originally, the Cherubim were not angels at all, but made their way into the heavenly hierarchy over time. Could they have been a lost race that now functions on the astral rather than on the physical plane? Humans see them as a sort of Beauty and the Beast combined into one creature. Is it any wonder that Vincent on the popular television show *Beauty and the Beast* generated such admiration among its viewers? The Cherubim watch over all galaxies, collecting and dispensing energy where needed, as well as guard any religious temple, from the architecturally glorious to an adobe shack.

The Cherubim can also function as personal guards, wielding flaming swords, should this be necessary. A more horrid glimpse of Cherubim paints them with four faces and four wings, which could be a mythical representation associating them with the four winds. They appear as both holy beasts and the charioteers of divinity. By name we have Ophaniel, Rikbiel, Cherubiel, Raphael, Gabriel, Uriel, and Zophiel. Why the art world has shrunk these strong and attractive angels to little midget beings that look more like babies, I'll never know. I prefer to stick with the lion face and human body. Of course, you may see them differently.

In magick, when you are seeking divine protection, wisdom, and knowledge, look to the Cherubim. Many of the Egyptian deities, especially Sekhmet, Bast, and

Anubis, could be considered Cherubim. Some archeologists now believe that the famed Sphinx (the giant structure of a human's face and lion's body) may pre-date the Egyptian culture, hinting of a civilization yet to be uncovered. To reach the Cherubim, burn a white candle for divinity and a blue candle for the Cherubim.

Thrones

The Thrones are assigned to planets, therefore most of the planetary angels you'll find mentioned in this book belong in the Throne category. They create, channel, and collect incoming and outgoing positive energies. The Thrones carry the name "many-eyed ones," sort of private investigators for divinity, as well as instructors of humility. Their name—Thrones—comes from the idea that all the power of divinity rests on their stable shoulders. Justice and its dispensation are important to them. They will shine their light on injustices, and send healing energy to any victim. Again, who rules whom is in question. The prince of the Thrones could be Oriphiel, Zabkiel, or Zaphkiel. Other names given are Raziel and Jophiel. Thrones take great interest in what humans are doing, though they may channel energies through your guardian angel rather than deal with you themselves.

In magick, call on the Thrones for assistance in smoothing relations with groups of people or between any two individuals. If you seek stability, look to the Thrones. For any issue involving the planets or planetary energies, call the Thrones. To reach the Thrones, burn a white candle for divinity and a green candle for the Thrones.

Angels of the Second Sphere

The second sphere angels (the Dominions, Powers, and Virtues) concern themselves with the governing of a specific planet, as well as those angels assigned tasks below them. These angels flow in an intensity of power. They also carry out the orders they get from the angels of the first sphere. Second sphere angels deal with the cosmos and its interconnectedness. Some angelic scholars argue that second sphere angels don't give a diddly about humans and are far too concerned with "cosmos" matters; however, I can't believe their mail system is so lousy that prayers and the raising of energy by humans get lost. I also don't believe they carry the human attribute of being stuck-up.

Dominions

The Dominions (Dominations) fill the role of divine leaders whose efforts involve integrating the material and spiritual, without losing control. They carry emblems of authority, such as scepters and orbs. The prince of this order is either Hashmal or Zadkiel. Interestingly, Dominion is also the name of the oldest angel. Other angels mentioned as princes of the Dominions are Muriel and Zacharael.

Magickally, all issues of leadership fall under the control of the Dominions. They are the epitome of the law of cause and effect, and are very precise in their working. Dominion angels bestow "natural leadership," and work to ensure that humans are happy and healthy under that leadership. They don't approve of corrupt governments, politicians, or church or civic leaders who do not have the best interests of the people at heart. If you wish to access divine wisdom, ask the Dominions. They are perfect mediators and arbitrators. If you are beginning an important project or have come across a glitch in a continuing one, call the Dominions. To reach the Dominions, burn a white candle for divinity and a pink candle for the Dominions.

Powers

The Powers keep track of human history. The angels of birth and death belong to this lineage. They organize the world's religions and send divine energy to keep the positive aspects of them going. They function as regulators of chaos. Some theologians think the Powers were created before the other choirs. They are seen as divine warriors, who work not through fear and hatred, but through encompassing love. Although they dispense justice, there is no hatred behind the act. The Powers are the angels of warning and will send you messages when someone is out to harm you. These messages may come in many ways: feelings, dreams, or snippets of conversation. This means you must learn to calm the inner chatter and listen to what these angels are telling you. They work through the human sixth sense, accessing it to get us to listen to them. Again, there is debate on who heads this order. According to hermetics, the chief is Ertosi. Sammael and Camael are also mentioned as leaders. Other angels in this category are Gabriel and Verchiel.

Magickally they are warrior angels, and you should call them when you are in trouble. The Powers are excellent at ferreting out hidden agendas that are designed to serve only one ego and harm others. They will assist you whenever you think the proverbial wool covers your eyes. These angels will defend your home, property, children, or any group of people who call on them for protection and defense. To reach the Powers, burn a white candle for divinity and a yellow candle for the Powers.

Virtues

The Virtues' primary job is to move massive quantities of spiritual energy to the earth plane and the collective human consciousness. Known as "the miracle angels," they bestow grace and valor. In the planetary scheme of the Egyptians and in hermetics, the chief of Virtues was Pi-Rhe. Among the ruling princes of the order are Michael, Raphael, Barbiel, Haniel, Hamaliel, Tarshish, Peliel, Sabriel, Uzziel, and Peliel.

Virtues are especially fond of those who try to go beyond their capabilities to achieve more than everyone else says they can. They love go-getters and positive people who try to enlighten and lead others toward harmony.

The Virtues are the spirits of movement, working and guiding the elemental energies that affect our planet. Earth, air, fire, water, spirit, weather patterns, and planetary upheavals associated with the elements fall under the auspices of the Virtues. These are the angels of nature. When working elemental magick, it is the Virtues who will listen to you and assist you. When you are in trouble or working a healing, turn to the Virtues. When you are sick or scared, call on the Virtues. To reach the Virtues, burn a white candle for divinity and an orange candle for the Virtues.

Angels of the Third Sphere

The third sphere angels find themselves intricately involved in human affairs and are considered the angels of the Earth. They constantly weave in and out of our lives, listening closely to human affairs. The third sphere angels include the Principalities, the Archangels, and those simply called the Angels.

Principalities

The Principalities are the guardians of large groups, such as continents, countries, cities, and other human creations on a grand scale (such as NATO). They work toward global reform. You'll find them in boardrooms and swimming holes, wherever groups of people congregate for learning, decision-making, or just for fun. They too create and funnel positive energies from the physical to the divine, and from the divine to the physical. Protectors of religion and politics, they watch human leaders to help them make just decisions in human affairs. The chief ruling angels of this order include Requel, Anael, Cerviel, and Nisroc. In Egyptian lore, the ruler is Suroth.

These angels are often called Princes because of their association with towns, states, provinces, islands, countries, continents, etc. When the United Nations meet, you can imagine the host of angels that circle around and above these heads of state.

Magickally one can call on these angels in times of discrimination, extinction of animals or people (Goddess forbid), inadequate rulership of anything from a town to a company, or strength to make wise decisions for these places and inhabitants. Human rights and economic reform are top priorities for the Principalities. To reach the Principalities, burn a white candle for divinity and a red one for the Principalities.

Archangels

The Archangels are an odd bunch. They often belong to one of the other spheres, or choirs, yet enjoy dealing with humans when they can. They are the special forces of the angelic realms, used to dealing with the top brass down to the newborn babe. They also create and funnel energies both ways. Chapter 2 and other sections of this book discuss the magickal applications of the Archangels.

To reach the Archangels, check the color correspondences listed in Chapter 4.

Angels

The Angels are those beings assigned to a particular person. They are often known as guardian angels. These angels link themselves to matters of the human and physical manifestation. They too funnel energies from us to the divine, and from the divine down to us. Our guardian angels are assigned to us through all incarnations on Earth. They are our best friends and our closest companions. They are with us at our birth and help us through the transition of death. They defend us when we are in trouble, help us assimilate into the world, assist us in carrying out our divine plan, and call in the other forces of the Nine Choirs when we need them. However, they can't do a lot of these things if we don't ask for their help. Human free will is not only our gift, but sometimes our downfall. We must learn to open our tight little mouths and talk about our needs and concerns. (We'll talk more about guardian angels in Chapter 7, which is dedicated just to them.)

Our guardian angels are constantly in touch with any and all of the angels in the Nine Choirs. They pass messages along in the blink of an eye, and if we ask our guardian angels for assistance, they will ask both divinity and other angels for help. Again I must tell you that you are never, ever alone. Although all angels can act in a heartbeat, when your problems involve other humans, things may go slower than you expect or may not turn out the way you had precisely planned. When asking the angels for assistance, be sure to keep your heart and mind pure and ask that the best solution for everyone manifest, or ask that you be treated in a fair and thoughtful manner. Don't think that just because you call the angels, you aren't going to have to tie up the loose ends of a problem or not do your share. However, they will open unblocked avenues and bring you opportunities you may not have been able to cultivate yourself.

Guardian angels can come from any of the Nine Choirs. Each angel has his/her (or its, as your belief system indicates) function. None is better or more important than the others. To reach your guardian angel, burn your favorite color candle. Add a white one beside it for divinity.

The ebb and flow of energy to the human, and from the human to the divine, is the central focus of all the angels. Should this flow stop, we would all, angels included, cease to exist. All laws, both cosmic and human, are governed by the angels. They can change anyone's fate at any time. However, an angel will never be a co-conspirator in anything evil. If justice needs to be administered, they will do it with strength and love, not in vicious retribution. Those stories are to scare the stupid.

We can work magick with any of the angels in the Nine Choirs. For example, if you want to heal the planet, then you would target the specific choir that is responsible for it. All angels attune to, and follow the dictates of, the Blessed Mother and the Blessed Father. Those people who have opened their hearts to the female divinity will make major changes in our society. The Lady is most definitely the Queen of Angels, and should you need Her, all you need to do is call.

When working with the angels, our only Achilles' heel is doubt and fear. If we doubt the power of the angels to help us, we break our link with them. If we don't believe or are afraid, it's like putting a door between ourselves and the angels.

Invocation of the Nine Choirs

Brilliant Seraphim I call to thee
Circle 'round, bring love to me.
Mighty Cherubim guard my gate
Remove from me sorrow and hate.
Thrones stand firm, stable be
Keep me steady on land or sea.
I call Dominions, leadership true
May I be fair in all I do.
Circles of protection Powers form
Help me weather any storm.
Miraculous Virtues hover near
Elemental energies I summon here.
Principalities bring global reform
Bless the world and each babe born.
Glorious Archangels show me the way
To bring peace and harmony every day.
Guardian angel, Goddess might
Bless me with your guiding light.

Petition of the Nine Choir Alignment

The fact that you have picked up this book and are thinking of working magick with the angels makes you a special person. You are probably one in a thousand. Few people have the guts to work angel magick because it means they have to live honorably, which isn't necessarily an easy thing to do. Others think that angels won't fit into their religious beliefs. I've come to the conclusion that angels fit anywhere, any time, and any place. They're not as picky as we are.

One delightful winter morning, I had to run a few errands that took me to a local mall and a grocery store. As I made my transactions I suddenly started looking at people—I mean really looking at them. I realized that every person around me was not alone—that their angels (few or many) were with them. In amazement I realized that the earth plane must be a busy place indeed. At that moment the psychic senses I'd been training for so long took a leap forward. As I looked at each person, I "felt" the things that bothered them most. Some people wandered around like they were alone in the world, and I ached to tell them they were not. Others were busy going about their business, thinking of family, friends, etc. I knew on sight those who were dishonest or mean at heart, or those who felt their lives were empty, despite their fine clothing or expertly applied make-up—I thought I'd stepped into the twilight zone.

As I walked, I felt my angels beside me. They were very big and I felt them pulsate. I don't know why I knew this; I just did. People looked at me and smiled, and I smiled back. This is unusual because most strangers in my neck of the woods are not extremely friendly, especially to someone in passing. I felt that those who smiled broadly could sense the angels, but had no idea what they were sensing. I felt big. I felt good. I felt loved. I touched harmony.

As I wandered out to the parking lot, the idea came to me for the Petition of the Nine Choirs. It is your introduction to all types of angels, and lets them know that you are truly ready to invite them into your lives and work magick with them.

You will need one white candle to represent the Lady, and one white candle to represent the Lord. You will also need a candle to represent each of the levels of the Nine Choirs, so that makes eleven candles in all. If you like, use the candle colors I gave you earlier.

Make sure that you will not be disturbed during this ritual. You need time to talk to the angels alone, and not be bothered by the telephone, television, visitors, or family members.

Go to your angelic altar and light your illuminator candles or lamps. Take a deep breath and hold both white candles tightly in your hands. Whatever your religious preference, utter a prayer or invocation, stating precisely what you wish to do. I'm not going to give you one because it has to come from your own heart. Light both white candles, saying:

> *I light this candle for the Lord.*
> *I light this candle for the Lady.*

If magick is familiar to you, this is the time to cast your magick circle. Choose whatever circle casting you like best. If you do not know how to cast a magick circle, check Chapter 6 in this book; if the idea of a circle makes you uncomfortable, simply envision yourself surrounded by white light.

Line up the candles and begin with your guardian angel candle. Say the following:

> *I light this guardian angel candle and invite my guardian angel into my life. I pledge to work magick with the angels and to help my fellow humans and the planet to the best of my ability. So mote it be.*

Relax and meditate on what you have just said. Feel your guardian angel around you, and acknowledge that you will listen to the messages given to you.

Light the Archangel candle and say the following:

I light this Archangel candle and invite the Archangels into my life. I pledge to work magick with the Archangels, and to help my fellow humans and the planet to the best of my ability. So mote it be.

As before, relax and think about the Archangels and what they mean to you.

Go through the rest of the choirs, one at a time, lighting the candle, calling the angels, then speaking the oath. Meditate on each choir.

When you are done, take a deep breath and close your eyes. Open yourself to universal harmony.

When you finish, make one petition to the angels you have called. It can be a large one or a small one—it doesn't matter. Speak the petition out loudly and firmly.

Take another deep breath and relax. Thank all the angels for attending and helping you. If you have cast a magick circle, it is time to take it up.

You can align yourself with the Nine Choirs anytime, whether you are in a good mood or experiencing some sort of dysfunction in your life. The angels are always there to help you.

The Queen of the Angels
(The Story of Saint Catherine Laboure)

I am not Catholic now and never have been, but when I first read this story my heart leaped and the hairs on my arms raised. I think there is no better account than this to exhibit the power and existence of the Queen of Angels, the entity we Wiccans know as the Lady.

On July 18, 1830, Catherine Laboure, a woman of the Sisters of Charity, awakened at 140 Rue du Bac in Paris, France, to the sight of a brilliant angel, who bade her to go to the chapel quickly. When Catherine got there she beheld the Queen of the Angels, who imparted a special message to her. In this first message She told Catherine that She was the blessed mother of all children. She called herself the Queen of Angels.

After this first visitation, Catherine devoted herself to deep solitude and prayer for many months. Every morning Catherine returned to the chapel, hoping to see the Queen of the Angels again. One morning She appeared, standing upon a globe bathed in brilliant light, and clothed by the Sun. She wore rings on each finger. When She opened the palms of Her hands, blazing rays of fire leaped forth to ignite the globe. The angels radiated an immense, pulsing light as the Queen spoke the following words:

The sphere you see represents the planet Earth. These rays that shine from my hands symbolize the graces entrusted to me to give to those of our children who ask me for them.

The gems from which the rays do not shine are the graces of which my children forget to ask. The light of the angels symbolizes their power and presence on earth. Allow me to help you, my children. Seek the light of the angels.

Catherine's visitation intensified. The rays from the Queen's hands burst forth fire upon all parts of the sphere. A golden door, the door to the Summerland, undulated in an oval shape around the vision. The Queen of Angels now said:

It is divine will that a medal be made bearing the image of this heavenly vision granted you. The medal will always be a sign of my protection and the presence of the angels to carry you along the paths of divinity's unconditional love for you. All who wear this medal with confidence will have great graces, blessings, and strength.

This medal was produced and distributed to Catholics all over the world. Legend indicates that those who wore the medal with confidence and faith reaped thousands of miracles and divine favors. The medal became known as "The Miraculous Medal." Individuals all over the world continue to wear this medal of angel power, a gift from the Queen Herself—Our Lady.

After studying this story, I decided to take a jaunt to the local Catholic inspirational shop. I felt odd wandering among religious items that were strange to me, but at the same time, I felt good that I was secure enough in my own faith to look someone else's full in the face, and honor their belief system without feeling condescending about theirs or stupid about mine. I found the Miraculous Medal and a laminated card that goes with it.

At home I set them on my angel altar (see Chapter 2), and cleansed, consecrated, and empowered them both. Although there is a prayer on the back of the card, I made up my own invocation to meet my personal spiritual needs:

Sweet Goddess, I unite myself to you under the title of my Lady, She who is the Queen of the angels, who brought forth this Miraculous Medal. May this medal be for me a sure sign of your motherly affection and a constant reminder of the oath I have taken to my religion. May I be blessed by your loving protection and preserved in the grace of your Consort. Most powerful Maiden, Mother, and Crone, keep me close to you every moment of my life so that like you, I may live and act according to the oath I have taken. With this medal I will call forth the powers of the angelic realm to assist my fellow humans and empower my own life. So mote it be.

If you don't like using the Miraculous Medal, don't worry about it. It took me a while to find a Miraculous Medal without a cross on the back of it. I won't use any jewelry that has a cross, as that sigil denotes attack, and has negative connotations for me. If you like, choose some other piece of jewelry that is comfortable for you. If you are Jewish, you may wish to use the Star of David. If you are Wiccan, you may desire to use the pentacle. The symbol should be important to you, and you must believe it will work for the purpose you stated in the consecration and blessing given above.

Catholics have a prayer that they use in all sorts of difficulties. I'm going to give it to you here, and then we are going to rewrite it a bit to fit alternative religious faiths. As all gods are one god and all goddesses are one goddess, I don't think Our Lady will mind. Legend has it that this prayer was first recited by the angel Gabriel.

Hail Mary, full of grace, the Lord is with you. Blessed are you among women and blessed is the fruit of your womb, Jesus. Holy Mary, Mother of God, pray for us sinners, now and at the hour of our death. Amen.

If you are of an alternative faith, you may wish to try the following:

Hail Lady, full of grace, the God is with you. Blessed are you among women and blessed is the fruit of your womb, the Consort and Son. Holy Goddess, Mother of Earth, work the mystery for your children, now and at the hour of our need. So mote it be.

The Queen of Angels and the Magick Circle

The Queen of Angels sends the Seraphim to gather human prayers and funnel them to the divine. All angels are deeply reverent of Her and She has her own entourage of angels. Therefore when you cast a magick circle and invoke either the Lord or Lady, you are also invoking the angelic hosts that travel with them, regardless of your belief system or whether or not you are even thinking of them, or even believe in them. If you acknowledge the presence of angelic beings when you cast your circle, you will see the difference. If you don't believe me, try it and find out.

It is true that many of us feel the presence of angels in our lives most acutely when things are not going well. Look at me. I'd been plodding along on this angel book, sometimes frustrated, but thinking my life was as it should be, when a professional disagreement that really had nothing to do with me landed me in the middle of a difficult time. Acutely unhappy, thinking my entire life was soon to be in the toilet, I went to my angelic altar and lit two white candles. I called on my guardian angel and asked that this transition in my life be as painless as possible, and that I see the truth for what it was, not blinded by human emotions and ego.

I remembered reading that humans are conduits of spiritual energy into the material world, and that angels are conduits of material energy into the spiritual realm. That makes both species a sort of bridge linking the material realm and the spirit realm together. I also understood that before I could continue any work, I needed to release my negative feelings of doubt, anger, inadequacy, rejection, and self-criticism. A nasty cauldron full of mental grime indeed.

First, I took a shower and visualized the water cleansing both my physical body and spiritual body. Then I empowered a glass of cold water (any drink will do) and imagined that as I took each sip, I was filling my body with angelic and universal energies. After that, I breathed in, envisioning healing energy coming into my body. I breathed out, expelling any doubts, fears, or unhappy thoughts.

I invoked the Lady through a poem by Edgar Allen Poe:

At morn, at noon, at twilight dim,
Lady, thou has heard my hymn:
In joy and woe, in good and ill,
Goddess Mother, be with me still.
When the hours flew brightly by
And not a cloud obscured the sky,
My soul, lest it should truant be,
Thy grace did guide to thine and thee.
Now, when storms of fate o'ercast
Darken my present and my past,
Let my future radiant shine
With sweet hopes of thee and thine.

Then, I recited Gabriel's prayer several times, melding it into a mantra, raising power:

Hail, Lady, full of grace, the God is with you. Blessed are you among women and blessed is the fruit of your womb, the Consort and Son. Holy Goddess, Mother of Earth, work the mystery for your children, now and at the hour of our need. So mote it be.

Within twenty-four hours, the problem vanished.

Other Hierarchies

I've mentioned before that several hierarchies exist when you begin mixing angels with religion. Although I picked the Nine Choirs to work with in this book, I certainly don't want to discount Jewish mysticism. In the Kabalah there are ten sephiroth (singular, sephirah). Each represents a world of its own that involves a great deal of study through visionary journeys, personal meetings with divinity, and other requirements. Each sephirah contains an angelic presence. The names of the sephiroth include Foundation, Splendor, Eternity, Beauty, Power, Grace, Knowledge, Wisdom, Understanding, and Perfection (Crown). The diagram showing these powers appear in the form of a tree. At the roots of this tree stands the guardian angel Sandalphon, who extends through the tree and out into the universe. Other angels on the tree are Saphkiel, the angel of contemplation; Raphael, the divine physician; Gabriel, who commands spiritual wisdom; and Michael, the commander of god's heavenly armies. At the top is Metatron. We will be discussing all these angels throughout the text of the book.

Four

Angels and Magickal Correspondences

The word *angel* comes from a Greek version of the Hebrew word *mal'akh*, which means "shadow side of deity." Angels do work in the shadows, meaning that we normally cannot see them, but we feel the effects of their presence and their workings. Magick is an art of shadows, of causing change in the universe through will.

This chapter gives plenty of material for working magick with the angels. If people tell you angels aren't magickal or you can't work magick with them, they don't know what they are talking about. I do it all the time. This section contains correspondences (things that are harmonious and work well together), as well as exercises to work through with each set of correspondences. We'll cover days of the week, seasons, months, colors, planetary hours, and of course, we'll learn more about the historical and modern functions of angels.

Your Angelic Journal

If you are going to work angel magick, you will need a journal to keep track of the things you learn, as well as the work you do. The journal doesn't have to be a dramatic tome of flowery prose, or a scientific plan of action with every step listed (although the more specific you are, the happier you'll be when you want to refer back to it). Some people like to decorate their journals with pictures of angels, artwork, ribbons, calligraphy, etc. To be honest, it will become a beautiful collector's item that a student or family member can use in their own studies.

The Angelic Days of the Week

Certain days of the week are better for planned ventures than others. When planning magick, be sure to check what day would be most harmonious for the working.

Monday

Monday centers on the energies of the Moon. Things like psychism, dreams, feminine energy, health, success in spiritual pursuits, domestic matters, and things of family origin are especially important today. Monday's colors are silver and white.

Angels of Monday are Gabriel (see page 26), Arcan, Missabu, and Abuzaha. Arcan is known as the king of the angels of air and the "ruler" of Monday. Abuzaha (Abuzohar) serves Monday, and is very responsive to invocations and ritual magick. Missabu is a ministering angel of Arcan.

Tuesday

Tuesday revolves around the energies of Mars. Tuesdays are good for business, mechanical things, buying and selling animals, hunting, beginning studies, gardening, sexual activities, and confrontation. Tuesday's colors are red, rose, or scarlet.

Angels of Tuesday are Camael, Samael, Satael, Amabiel, Friagne, and Hyniel. When invoked, Camael takes the form of a leopard. In Druid mythology he is a god of war, which is why we see him associated with Mars (again, notice the influence of the Pagan belief system). Camael is said to be a member of the "Magnificent Seven" in some circles. Camael is another "terminator" angel. However, some claim he tried to keep Moses from receiving the Torah and met his permanent demise, though Cabbalists often claim he survived the destruction.

Samael walks both worlds as a magician and sorcerer. Some see him as the angel of death, others as "the bright and poisonous one." Many consider him more of a demon, and accuse him of being Satan. However, there is reference to the satans (plural) as enforcers of the law, a sort of angelic police, if you will. Supposedly, when Samael is around, dogs howl in the night. On one hand, he is the ruler of the fifth heaven and in charge of two million angels; on the other, he is the one who changed into a serpent and convinced Eve to partake of the forbidden fruit of knowledge.

Satael is an angel of air invoked in magic rites and is the presiding spirit of the planet Mars. Amabiel is another spirit of the planet Mars; however, he spends his energy on issues of human sexuality. Friagne, also an angel of this day, is invoked from the east. He is a member of the fifth heaven. Hyniel also belongs to this day and is subject to the east wind.

Wednesday

Under the guidance of Mercury, Wednesday is a day of swift activity, communication, correspondence, and phone calls. This is a good day for journalists, writers, poets, bargaining, hiring employees, and visiting friends. Wednesday's colors are orange, light blue, and gray.

Wednesday's angels are Raphael (see page 21), Miel, and Seraphiel. All three of these angels function as the guardians of the planet of Mercury. Not much information can be found about Miel, but Seraphiel is a chief in the order of Seraphim. He seems to rank as the highest of the princes. Invoke him from the north.

Thursday

Thursday is a Jupiter day. This is a great day for money issues, as Jupiter is the ruling planet of all sorts of financial concerns. Self-improvement, research, and study are also good on this day, as well as travel and social gatherings. Thursday's colors are purple and royal blue.

Thursday's angel is Sachiel. Sachiel sort of surfs the days of the week, and in various texts can be found in the Monday, Thursday, or Friday categories. He presides over the planet Jupiter. Invoke him from the south.

Friday

Matters of love, human interaction, the fluidity of communication, sewing and the creation of artistic garments, household improvement, shopping, and party planning all fall under the aspects of Friday and its ruling planet, Venus. Friday's colors are emerald green or pink.

Friday's angels are Ariel/Uriel (see page 28), Rachiel, and Sachiel. Rachiel also concerns himself with human sexuality and is a presiding spirit of the planet Venus. (For information on Sachiel, see Thursday.)

Saturday

The planetary correspondence for Saturday is Saturn. Matters dealing with the public, farming, family ties, legal matters (such as wills and estates), taking care of debts, dealing with lawyers, financing, joint money matters, real estate, older people, banishing or binding negativity, and getting rid of bad habits all fall under the charge of Saturn. Saturday's color is black.

Saturday's angels are Cassiel, Machatan, Uriel, and Orifiel. Cassiel is the angel of solitudes and tears. He is one of the rulers of the planet Saturn and occasionally appears as the angel of patience. Cassiel links himself to dragon energy. (He adores dragons.) Regarding Machatan, the only information we get is that he works well with Cassiel and is also a power of Saturn. For Uriel, see page 28. Orifiel is an angel of the wilderness, a ruler of the second hour of the day, and also associated with Saturn.

Sunday

Sunday is influenced by the Sun. Community work, volunteer services, exercise, outdoor sports, buying, selling, speculating, meeting people, anything involving groups, running fairs and raffles, growing crops, and taking care of all health matters fall under the influence of the Sun. Sunday's colors are gold or yellow.

Michael is the primary angel of Sunday, but each hour of this day also has its secondary angel. These angels are Michael (first hour), Anael (second hour), Raphael (third hour), Gabriel (fourth hour), Cassiel (fifth hour), Sachiel (sixth hour), Samael (seventh hour), Michael (eighth hour), Anael (ninth hour), Raphael (tenth hour), Gabriel (eleventh hour), and Cassiel (twelfth hour). Notice some of the angels do double duty this day.

Seven-Day Magick to Bring Harmony into Your Life

Go through the information on the days of the week (given previously) and choose one thing you would like to improve for each of those seven days. You can have one item that spans the seven-day cycle, or choose a different request for each day. Be realistic in your choice. Write each day of the week on one index card. When finished you will have a card for Monday, one for Tuesday, etc., for a total of seven cards.

Write down your request on one side of each card, below the day, then sign your name. On the other side of the card put the angel's name that best represents that request. (I realize that for some of the days you don't have many choices.) If you don't want to call an angel by a specific name, then remember to use a phrase that indicates the type of energy you want (angel of healing or angel of business deals, etc.).

Hold the stack of cards in your hands, angel names up, and empower the cards with your overall desire to work magick with the angels.

Place the cards in a stack in the center of your altar in the appropriate order, with the day you wish to begin on top.

Choose a time when you want to work your angel magick every day. Is it when you get up, or perhaps before you go to sleep? It doesn't matter, as long as you choose the same time each day to work your magick with the angels.

When you are ready to work the magick, light your oil lamp (or candle) and burn some incense. Do the Lesser Banishing Ritual to begin (see page 30), then ground and center again. Hold the day's card in your hands and close your eyes, focusing on the positive energies of the angels helping you. Don't tell the angel how to do it or go over possible scenarios — let the angelic energy handle that.

When you are finished, burn the card and scatter the ashes in the wind.

If you wish to leave the candle or lamp burning for a period of time, be sure it is in a safe place. Be sure to thank the angel you called in your mind before you leave your altar.

Record your work in your journal, then go back later and note how this exercise helped you.

Angels of the Seasons

Seasonal magick, to me, is one of the purest forms of the art. As humans, we move in tandem with the cycles of the Earth, mingling with the various cloaks of energy and transmutation the Earth wears. With seasonal magick, the focus is on bringing prosperity and harmony into form. Invoke the angels attributed to each season on the first day of the season (or close to when it begins) for your general welfare, then throughout that season for specific matters.

Spring

The Spring Equinox occurs around March 21. Spring brings rebirth, rejuvenation, the planting of ideas, friendships, sexual union, fun, creativity, and communication. Magicks performed would be for healing, purification, psychism, bill-paying, planting out of doors, fertility, and all manner of things associated with air. Spring's colors are pastels of any shade.

Milkiel is the ruling angel of spring and all the necessary energies that create the season. Spugliguel is the head of spring. To begin the season, seek the assistance of both Milkiel and Spugliguel. Four other angels (Amatiel, Caracasa, Core, and Commissoros) associate themselves with this season as guardians.

Summer

The Summer Solstice occurs around June 21. Summer is a time of rapid growth, projects in full bloom, deep sexual union, strength, and the desire to share the wealth of the universe. Magicks done at this time are for bringing love toward yourself, beauty, protection, physical and magickal energy, courage, marriage, and all magicks involving the element of fire. Summer's colors are vibrant shades of green, blue, pink, and yellow.

The head angel of summer is Tubiel, who is also invoked for the return of small birds to their owners. The angels below him include Gaviel, Tariel, and Gargatel, who function as guardians of the season. Oranir is the chief of the Summer Solstice and is considered effective against the evil eye.

Autumn

The Autumn Equinox occurs around September 21. Autumn is the time of harvest and fruition, of laying plans for the winter months and tying up any loose ends in life. Magicks done at this time are for employment, large possessions (homes, cars, refrigerators, stoves, furnaces, additions to one's home, furniture, etc.), healing, all types of study, and all magick involving the element of water. The colors of autumn include orange, gold, tan, brown, and deep yellow.

Torquaret is considered the head of the season, with the angels Tarquam and Guabarel as guardians.

Winter

The Winter Solstice occurs around December 21. This is the time to rest, take stock of your accomplishments, and create long-term plans for the coming growing season. Relaxation through quiet creativity often occurs in the cold months; extra sleep and nourishment of the body and mind are now required. Magicks done at this time are for the banishment of any disease (whether mental or physical), meditation, breaking habits (including addictions and negative patterns), planning magicks, and any magicks involving the element of earth. Winter's colors are white, green, red, and gray.

Attaris is the head of this season's angels, with Amabael and Cetarari acting as guardians. Michael is also the angel of snow.

Knot Magick for the Seasons

Choose the season you wish to work with, and find a thirteen-inch-long string in the color of the season.

Write down specifically what you want to work for, and which type of angelic assistance you will be requesting. (Remember, if you do not want to call the angels by the names given previously, then call them by the energies you wish to manifest.)

Go to your angelic altar and light your illuminator candles or lamps. Place the string on the center of the altar. Light your incense. Perform the Lesser Banishing Ritual.

Recite the following poem, tying the knots as shown below:

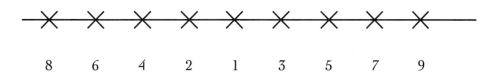

8   6   4   2   1   3   5   7   9

By knot of one this angelic magick has begun
By knot of two [angel's name] powers come true
By knot of three the desire will come to be
By knot of four my will is now secure
By knot of five this magick is alive
By knot of six this magick is fixed
By knot of seven may angelic power be given
By knot of eight the magick is now fate
By knot of nine the desire is mine!

Carry the string with you until the spell has manifested.

When the magick has proven fruitful, untie the knots and remove the energy from the string, then dispose of the string. Do not forget to thank your chosen angel for helping you.

Angels of the Months

Like the days and the seasons, each month also has its guardian angel. You can work with the angels of the months in a variety of ways.

January: Gabriel (see page 26). Color: White.

February: Barchiel, angel of hailstorms. Color: Pale blue.

March: Malahidael. Exercises his dominion for ninety-one days, from spring to summer; assists in contacting lovers. Color: Pale yellow.

April: Raphael (see page 21). Color: Pale green.

May: Ambriel. He is also helpful in warding off evil, and is a spirit cited for conjuring purposes under the planet Mars. Color: Rose.

June: Muriel. His name means "myrrh." Invoke him from the south. Legend states he can procure a magic carpet for you. Color: Emerald green.

July: Verchiel, who is well versed in the powers of the Sun. Colors: Blue and purple.

August: Michael (see page 23). Colors: Gold and yellow.

September: Uriel (see page 28). Colors: Orange and red.

October: Barbiel, who allows contact with the ancestral dead. Colors: Black and orange.

November: Advachiel. Color: Brown.

December: Hanael. His name means "glory." He carries missives to the divine ones. Invoke him as a defender against evil. There is also an association drawn with Ishtar, the Chaldean goddess. Colors: Red and green.

Angelic Magick for Monthly Goal Planning

Beginning with any month, your goal is to plan your accomplishments for the coming year. This working may take a while, so you will need to set aside some quiet time. Put on some soft music if you like.

You will need a marker, twelve envelopes, a calendar, and several slips of paper. If you wish, you can match the marker color (or colored pencils) to both the name of the angel and the names of the months. Put all the supplies on your angel altar, then place your hands over them. Ask the angelic powers to assist you in your work, then draw a banishing pentagram over all your supplies. Light your illuminator candles or lamps and fire up some incense.

Do the Lesser Banishing Ritual.

Write the name of one month on each envelope, then put the envelopes in order from the month you wish to start. Look at your calendar for this first month. Relax and hold it in your hands. What would you like to accomplish this month?

Write each goal on a piece of paper, then sign your name. When you have finished for the month at hand, put all the papers in the envelope. Do not seal it. Write the name of the angel you wish assistance from on the back of the envelope. Set the envelope aside.

Follow the same procedures for the succeeding months. Remember, if you do not want to call the angels by name you can simply call them angelic guardians of the month.

When you are finished, put the envelopes in a safe place.

At the beginning of the first month, take out the corresponding envelope and place it on your altar. You may wish to do the Lesser Banishing Ritual, then call on the guardian of that month to help you with your goals. Hold the envelope in your hands and envision angelic assistance flowing through your body and into the envelope. Seal the envelope and make the sign of the equal-armed cross over it. Keep the envelope on your altar all month long.

On the last day of the month, open the envelope. Burn those slips of paper where the goals have manifested, and thank the angels for their assistance. Look at the goals you haven't met. Were they too high for this month? Did something stand in the way? Reconsider if the goal is valid for your life path. If you feel it is not, discard the goal. If you think you would like to try again, choose another month to put it in. It doesn't have to be the very next month. Consider carefully where this goal should fall in your life, then place it in the appropriate envelope.

Follow the procedures listed above at the first day and last day of each month. Keep a record of how you are doing and your thoughts on this type of angel magick. At the end of the twelve-month cycle, write a summary of all the work you have accomplished, and how using this type of magick has changed your life.

If there are any goals left over, you can move them to the next year or discard them as you see fit.

Angels and Color

Angels appreciate color. Like music, color is a universal language. Some magickal people feel that only certain colors can represent a particular feeling or intent, but I have found that each person harmonizes with color in his or her own way. Until now, I have given color references for the angels, but as you might notice, I did not go into great detail about them. I feel that it is necessary for people to find the color that works best for them in any given situation.

It is true that colors affect the human psyche in general ways. Blue will often create a feeling of repose and tranquillity. Red will excite the temperament, and sometimes inflame arguments or passion. Standard color applications in magick consider these universal reactions; however, that doesn't mean you have to follow what others use to the letter. You need to experiment to find the color combinations or single colors that work best for you in any given situation.

I suggest you begin by using the color associations given here, but learn to mix and match those colors to heighten the benefits for yourself. For example, let's say you use the color green for money, but your work is not successful. First, you need to consider the reason for your failure. It could be something small (you simply weren't focused) or something large (the time is not right for you to bring this into your life). After you've considered these things, you try again.

No luck? No problem. Time to try something else. Let's say you mix the color green with another color, or perhaps don't use colors at all, but a symbol instead. This time it works. Then later on you try to use the color green again for a different working, and you find that once again you have a failure. You may have programmed your mind against the color. Now what do you do?

Change colors for a start, even if it is only by a shade. Consider what the problem color represents. Green, for example, is healing, money, or luck. Do you feel you don't deserve money? Perhaps you subconsciously think that you should be sick instead of well. There could be a lot of reasons, and the answers depend on you.

Color Correspondences

White: Purity, truth, angelic energies, sincerity, hope, spiritual strength, protection, power of divinity. Angels of light, Cancer, the Moon. All-purpose correspondence.

Purple: Clarity of thought, richness, worldly ambitions, power, religion, healing severe diseases and mental conditions, overcoming business difficulties. Angels of Sagittarius, Jupiter, the Moon (lavender), Mercury (violet), chaos (dark).

Blue: Tranquility, patience, understanding, health, psychism, intuition, wisdom, mental and emotional control, protection, happiness, transformation. Angels of water, Jupiter, Venus (light), lakes, seas, Pisces (dark), Venus (pale), Taurus, Cancer (dark), Libra (blue-green), Sagittarius (deep), the Moon, Aquarius (iridescent).

Green: Health, luck, fortune, fertility, nurturing, growth, money, prosperity, fruition of a project or plan. Angels of Venus (pale), forests, mountains, earth, Taurus, Pisces (sea-green).

Yellow: Attraction, charm, confidence, hypnosis, drawing, fascination, joy, intellect, communication, travel, captivation. Angels of air, Leo, the Sun, Mercury (pale).

Orange: Career, encouragement, stimulation, adaptability, studiousness, courage, active finances. Angels of Mercury, Leo, Virgo (sienna), Aquarius (dark).

Red: Passion, strength, virility, maintaining health, physical longevity, protection, defensive needs, impulsiveness, attack, health, energy, victory. Angels of fire, Mars, Aries, Leo (scarlet), Scorpio (deep).

Rose: Love, passion, communication with loved ones, relaxation, healing of spirit, success, clean living, compassion, honor, conquering evil. Angels of Venus, Taurus, Libra.

Gold: Male virility, success, happiness, confidence, courage. Angels of the Sun, Leo.

Silver: Female energies, psychism, strength and compassion, patience, higher wisdom. Angels of the Moon, Cancer, Virgo, chaos (pewter).

Brown: Friendship, earth energies, assertiveness, health and safety of animals, financial success. Angels of earth, mountains, forests, Virgo, Aquarius.

Black: Binding, turning back negativity, banishing, absorbing unhealthy attitudes and addictions, protection. Angels of Saturn, earth, chaos, Scorpio.

Turquoise or gray: Neutralizing; stopping gossip, balancing karma. Angels of Venus, Saturn, Libra.

Angel Color Wheel

For the angel color wheel[1] you will need a set of colored pencils or markers, a plain piece of paper, a list of what you would like to improve in your life, and the names of the angels you would like to ask for help. For now, you can stick to the angels we've mentioned so far; however, should none seem quite right, by all means leaf through the text and find one that does. If no angel name strikes you as the right one, then call the energy or essence of the angel instead.

Using a compass, draw a circle in the center of your paper. Draw another circle about half an inch larger than the first, using the same center point.

Use your ruler to divide the circle into sections (pie slices), with one slice for each request. Your wheel should not look like an intricate Celtic design. Keep the number of requests down—like four or six to start.

Match your requests to a color. For example, if you want healing energy for your favorite pet, choose green. If you want to excel in that job interview, choose orange.

Write each request in a pie slice in black marker. On the outer rim write the name of the angelic energy you need, then color in the pie slice with the appropriate colored pencil. Finally, write your own name across the middle of the wheel.

Take the wheel to your angelic altar and place it in the center. Light your illuminator candles or lamps and perform the Lesser Banishing Ritual (see page 30).

1. The idea for this project was taken from *Practical Color Magick* by Raymond Buckland.

Hold the color wheel in your hands and call on each angel, one at a time. Tell each angel what you have written on the paper. When you are finished, close your eyes and envision the angelic beings around you, each taking their slice of the pie. Thank them for helping you.

Tape your angel wheel somewhere in your home, like on your bedroom mirror, the refrigerator, etc., or leave it on your angelic altar. If you think someone in your family will see it and make fun of it, put it in a place where only you will see it. Angels don't like the negativity of others any more than you do.

When all the requests on your color wheel have come to form, it is time to "de-magick" the wheel. Take it to your altar and thank the angels for their assistance. Then imagine the magick forming into a golden ball over the paper. Let the magick either sink into your altar or the ground. Burn the wheel and scatter the ashes to the winds.

What if you didn't get everything on the wheel? That depends on what you asked for and how long you waited. Generally, two weeks to thirty days for small things, thirty to ninety days for bigger things. I caution you against predicting timing because no exact formula exists. One needs to learn patience when working magick. Again, this may not be the right time to bring it into your life, or perhaps it will take longer to bring to form than you originally thought. Remember, magick (like electricity) travels through the path of least resistance. If you have wanted something for a long time, there could be a lot of self-imposed blockages along the way,

The Wheel

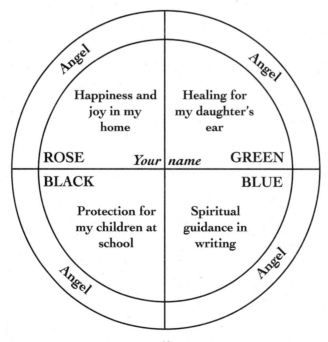

including worry, frustration, doubt, etc. If you can suspend your negativity, you have a better chance of achieving your desires.

If you feel you have waited long enough and nothing has happened, de-magick the first wheel, then do a new wheel designed for your single request.

Hourly Angels

If you are familiar with planetary hours, this section will be a snap for you. Each hour of the day has an assigned angel that can assist you in your workings. When a project begins, its hour of origin will carry the energies of that hour throughout the working. You can also judge a matter from the hour in which you were first notified about it.

Each hour of the day is ruled both by a planet and an angel. We will work with planetary hours in Chapter 13. Here, I will introduce the angels that are attributed to each hour. The only thing you need to know to use the angelic hours is the time of your local sunrise and sunset of the day (or evening) you plan to work, and the chart I have provided for you on page 65.

Once you have determined the time of the sunrise or sunset, you need to divide the daylight hours, then the nighttime hours, into twelve equal parts. The increments will not always be sixty minutes in length due to the seasonal changes. In the summer you will have longer hours of daylight than of night. During the winter months, the opposite will be true. When you have calculated this, you are ready to look at the chart.

Let's use an example of how I can use the angelic hours to foretell the outcome of a situation, or at least get a grip on the energies that surround it. While writing this manuscript, I received a telephone call at 10:28 P.M. Eastern Standard Time on Wednesday, February 15. Sunrise on this day was 7:00 A.M., and sunset occurred at 5:42 P.M. That means there were 10 hours and 42 minutes of daylight, or a total of 642 minutes of daylight. Had the call come in during the daylight hours, I would have divided 642 by 12 to discover the length of the daylight planetary hours.

However, it came during the evening hours. Sunset was 5:42 P.M. and sunrise of the following day (February 16) was 6:59 A.M. We experienced a night of 13 hours and 17 minutes of darkness, or a total of 797 minutes. Divide this by 12 and we find that each planetary hour would be approximately 66.5 minutes long. Round this figure to 67 minutes. We can recalculate later if we find that this decimal increment (0.5) would change the planetary hour.

Remember that my phone call came in at 10:38 P.M. Planetary hour number one began at 5:42 and lasted 67 minutes. Planetary hour number two began at 6:49 P.M. Planetary hour number three began at 7:56 P.M. Planetary hour number four began at 9:03 P.M. Planetary hour number five began at 10:10 P.M. Planetary hour number six began at 11:17 P.M. Because my call came in at 10:38 P.M., it falls within planetary hour number five, so that is the one we will study. We don't need to worry about that

0.5 difference, as the few minutes it totals would not change the planetary hour on this day.

By looking at the angel hour chart, I find that the fifth hour after sunset on a Wednesday is ruled by the angel Cassiel. What do we know about this angel? Cassiel is the angel of solitude and tears. He is one of the rulers of the planet Saturn, and occasionally appears as the angel of patience. Cassiel loves dragons and their energy. Even though we have not covered planetary influences yet in their conjunction with the angels (we will get to this later), have you figured out what my phone call was about?

In case you think I made this example up, I didn't. The call was from a friend of mine who, at that moment, had a very distraught woman at her house. The woman had been beaten by her drunken boyfriend. The call was for my help in this situation. The Cassiel energies—those of loneliness, tears, wise council, and patience—all fit into this situation. As we will discover later, the planetary hour of Saturn is also important. Saturn is the planet of challenges and tests. This woman will need to make a conscious effort to improve her situation and come out of denial (the beatings had been going on for two years). She must realize that the beater is not going to change and that she will have to "do it by the numbers," meaning she will need to seek legal assistance such as a restraining order to finish out the situation. Given the planetary/angelic hour, it is obvious she will need support and assistance from her friends and the authorities as she goes through this transition in her life.

Going back over the other correspondences in this chapter, we discover that the day I received the call was Wednesday, ruled by Mercury (phone calls, letters, communication of all types) and the angel of this day is Raphael (the energies of healing). The lady was reaching out toward healing the situation; however, the influence of Saturn made her journey far more difficult.

To make this more interesting, let's consider that these ladies made an appointment to see me on the following Friday at 7:00 P.M. Sunset on that day was 5:46 P.M. Sunrise of the following day was 6:55 A.M. The total time of darkness would be 13 hours and 11 minutes, or 791 minutes. Divided by 12, each planetary hour for the evening would be 65.9 minutes long—rounded to 66 minutes. Hour one begins at 5:46 P.M. Hour two begins at 6:52. Hour three begins at 7:58. They were scheduled to arrive at 7:00 P.M., which puts us in hour two, and they will probably stay during hour three.

The prominent angelic energies during these two hours were Michael and Uriel. Check Chapter 2 for details about these two angels and consider what types of energies were present.

Why would I like to know this information before they arrive? First, it tells me how combative the victim will be, meaning whether she is ready (or not) to hear some cold hard facts, or if I should temper the discussion. It also tells me what angelic energies to align with before she steps through the door. The corresponding planetary hours are the Sun and Venus. She will be open to me and my magick, but the Venus

Angelic Hours Chart

Day

Hour	Sunday	Monday	Tuesday	Wednesday	Thursday	Friday	Saturday
1	Michael	Gabriel	Camael	Raphael	Sachiel	Uriel	Cassiel
2	Uriel	Cassiel	Michael	Gabriel	Camael	Raphael	Sachiel
3	Raphael	Sachiel	Uriel	Cassiel	Michael	Gabriel	Camael
4	Gabriel	Camael	Raphael	Sachiel	Uriel	Cassiel	Michael
5	Cassiel	Michael	Gabriel	Camael	Raphael	Sachiel	Uriel
6	Sachiel	Uriel	Cassiel	Michael	Gabriel	Camael	Raphael
7	Camael	Raphael	Sachiel	Uriel	Cassiel	Michael	Gabriel
8	Michael	Gabriel	Camael	Raphael	Sachiel	Uriel	Cassiel
9	Uriel	Cassiel	Michael	Gabriel	Camael	Raphael	Sachiel
10	Raphael	Sachiel	Uriel	Cassiel	Michael	Gabriel	Camael
11	Gabriel	Camael	Raphael	Sachiel	Uriel	Cassiel	Michael
12	Cassiel	Michael	Gabriel	Camael	Raphael	Sachiel	Uriel

Night

Hour	Sunday	Monday	Tuesday	Wednesday	Thursday	Friday	Saturday
1	Sachiel	Uriel	Cassiel	Michael	Gabriel	Camael	Raphael
2	Camael	Raphael	Sachiel	Uriel	Cassiel	Michael	Gabriel
3	Michael	Gabriel	Camael	Raphael	Sachiel	Uriel	Cassiel
4	Uriel	Cassiel	Michael	Gabriel	Camael	Rahphael	Sachiel
5	Raphael	Sachiel	Uriel	Cassiel	Michael	Gabriel	Camael
6	Gabriel	Camael	Raphael	Sachiel	Uriel	Cassiel	Michael
7	Cassiel	Michael	Gabriel	Camael	Raphael	Sachiel	Uriel
8	Sachiel	Uriel	Cassiel	Michael	Gabriel	Camael	Raphael
9	Camael	Raphael	Sachiel	Uriel	Cassiel	Michael	Gabriel
10	Michael	Gabriel	Camael	Raphael	Sachiel	Uriel	Cassiel
11	Uriel	Cassiel	Michael	Gabriel	Camael	Raphael	Sachiel
12	Raphael	Sachiel	Uriel	Cassiel	Michael	Gabriel	Camael

influence make make her willing to "give him another chance." If I can hit her first with facts (through the Sun energy) and then go into the field of self-love and the need for growth and change because she is loved by her friends, the universe, and herself, we may do very well, turning the mindset of the "victim" into the "victor."

Going back over the chapter, we see that the angel of Friday is Ariel/Uriel, and her visit was during his hour—a good sign. She will also be open to talk of angels, or magick in general, to help bring her into balance. Friday is a Venus day, so above all, the atmosphere needs to be one of love and caring. The colors of the room should be pastel shades, music should be light, etc. In final observation, the fact that the woman has decided it's time to make her move falls in the seasonal cycle of pre-planting and preparation (February), explaining that the situation may come to balance in either May or June (the time of the next seasonal cycle). Of course, this was only a guess on my part. To examine the situation more carefully, I would ask for her birth date, time, and place and run a natal as well as a progressive astrological chart. To assist her in her recovery and self-esteem, I would recommend self-hypnosis and offer to work with her through a few sessions to assist in repairing the damage and help her deal with the trash she needed to expel to lead a happier lifestyle.

After our meeting, the woman left the abuser for one month. She was open to magickal aid, but not to counseling sessions. She did not meet the challenge or go forward in her life and went back to him. Two months later, he put her head through a wall. He is now serving jail time for a parole violation and she is attempting to put her life back together again. As the first planetary hour indicated, this situation brought on many tears.

Ethics and Magick

Many magickal people do not want to work with angelic energy because they feel that angels are perfect, and perhaps the magick they want to work might appear "less than perfect." If this were true, magicians over the centuries would not have been working with angels.

Angels understand us better than we understand ourselves. They are well aware of our temperaments and wells of emotion, yet they strive to work with us and for us in every possible aspect of our lives.

No matter what type of magick you are working, you should always keep ethics at the forefront of any venture. Repeatedly ask yourself questions like "Is this the right thing to do?" "Am I working for the betterment of all in this situation?" Even ask the questions "Will I feel better after I have done this?" or "Have I been fair in my assessment of the situation?"

The angels will help you when trying to answer some of these questions. Always remember to keep an open mind and work "to harm none."

Five

Angels and Meditation

_M_editation begins with relaxation of the body and mind. It is that simple. Meditation calms the nerves, eliminates stress, and lifts the spirit. It does take practice. I don't consider it "hard work," though it demands something precious—your time.

Once you get yourself into a pattern of meditation, whether you schedule it before you go to sleep or when you get up in the morning, it will be as natural to you as breathing. Even if you aren't good at daily patterns and couldn't stick to a schedule if your life depended on it, meditation can still be an option. If you really want to do it, you will find the time and place.

Basic Angelic Meditation

Find a relaxing room in your house, or if the weather is nice, go outside and sit by a tree or on your patio. Pick a time when all is quiet around you. You don't want to deal with disturbances while you are meditating. Learn to switch times to make it convenient for yourself. For example, on school days, I work on my meditation in the morning. On the children's days off or during the summer, I meditate at night, after they go to bed.

Take three deep breaths, relaxing your body with each breath. Find your center (near your navel) and continue to relax. Imagine your body connecting firmly to the earth—you are one with the universe.

Take another deep breath and envision an angel in front of you. This angel will touch the top of your head, sending healing, relaxing energy flowing down through you. Feel the energy moving through your body, pushing out any negativity that's stuck and refuses to move. I often have my hypnotherapy clients envision this as "black, yucky stuff" pouring from the bottom of their feet and soaking into the ground, where it is transmuted into positive energy.

Many people now tell various parts of their body to relax. For example, "Down through the top of my head, relaxing the muscles around my eyes, my nose, and my mouth. Down through my neck, my shoulders, upper arms, and lower arms. Down through my chest, down my back, into my stomach muscles, through my hips," etc.

Now envision a second angel before you. This one brings purity and alignment to your body. Follow the same procedure as before, watching and feeling the energy move from the top of your head down through your body, and out the bottom of your feet. This angel pulls in universal love. Many people experience a tingling or floating sensation at this point. This is normal.

The third angel is responsible for helping you align your chakra centers (the seven energy vortexes in your body). Chakra means "wheel" in Sanskrit; many individuals see the chakras as spinning disks, or spirals of energy. We will also be opening a new chakra, often linked to angelic matters and the cosmic consciousness, called the thymus chakra.[1] Lest you think I would be brave enough to make up a new chakra, forget it. I'm not that bold. I have found this new chakra very helpful when working with cancer patients.

---

1. The thymus chakra generates peace and love. It is connected to the thymus gland, an important part of the immune system. Awakening this chakra will boost your immune system and assist in dealing with cancer, AIDS, stroke, and other disorders (*Ask Your Angels* by Daniel, Wyllie, and Ramer, page 115).

As the angel touches you, each vortex will unfurl, like a pair of wings, and vibrate its appropriate color. First, open the crown chakra (located at the top of your head) and envision a pair of white wings unfurling and opening, then open each chakra with colored wings as listed below:

Second chakra: Middle of forehead—purple
Third chakra: Throat—blue
Fourth chakra: Thymus (between throat and heart)—pink or aquamarine
Fifth chakra: Heart—green
Sixth chakra: Navel area—yellow
Seventh chakra: Stomach—orange
Eighth chakra: Groin—red

Envision a final angel coming toward you. As this angel touches you, a bubble of pure white light will surround your body. Relax and let yourself drift into the sensation of feeling safe and secure.

Close the chakra centers, beginning at the groin and working your way up to the crown. Take three deep breaths, and ground and center again. Then open your eyes.

It is common for you to feel as if you have been asleep, as you will drift first into the alpha state of brainwave activity, and with more practice into the theta state. Spiritual enlightenment most often happens in the theta state, where the brainwaves are very slow. Theta is close to the sleep state of delta.

Keep track of your meditation progress in your angel journal. After a while, you may begin to hear voices in your head during this initial meditation process. If the voices are soft and positive in nature, you may be experiencing your first messages from the angels.

Meditation Hints

I receive hundreds of letters from people who have questions about the process of meditation. Here are some helpful hints.

In meditation, practice makes perfect. The more you practice, the better you get. Ideally, everyone should meditate every day, whether they practice magick or not. Meditation is healthy for your spirit, mind, and body, for both adults and children. Train your children from an early age, and their lives will be more harmonious and peaceful. By teaching them to meditate, you are giving them a precious gift—a tool to combat the stresses of life.

If your mind wanders, are you screwing up the meditation? No. Just let yourself go. Eventually you will be able to focus for longer periods of time. Keep practicing, and don't worry if you can't visualize objects or scenes for any length of time. Don't panic if you fall asleep. Remember, your mind follows the routines you set for it.

When you shut your eyes and lie still, your body thinks it is time for sleep. It takes a while for you to establish a new pattern. Eventually, you will stop falling asleep. If you fall asleep while into the pattern of meditation, that means you needed the rest.

If you are having problems learning to meditate, simply sit for fifteen to thirty minutes in a dimly lit room. Don't turn the lights all the way off, because this is a signal for sleep. Breathe deeply, but not with force. Try listening to soft music that you enjoy. Surround yourself with the colors green or blue. If these bother you, try neutral colors such as beige, gray, or white. Think pleasant, gentle thoughts. Imagine yourself floating with the music. After a few days or weeks of practicing this pattern, you will be ready to do more thorough meditation sequences.

Practice staring at a candle flame or a small object, like a piece of lead crystal, suspended from the ceiling. Don't try to stare at it with great concentration. Look at it calmly until you feel your eyelids naturally getting heavy. Don't fight the desire to shut your eyes. Let your eyelids close slowly and restfully.

Practice using positive affirmations daily. "I am happy and healthy." "I am filled with love and peace." Be sure to word your statements posively. Do not use words like "not," "can't," "won't," "shouldn't," "couldn't," etc.

Try using prerecorded hypnosis tapes. My entire family has had great success with tapes from Valley of the Sun Publishing and Hewitt's tapes from Llewellyn. Both varieties are very good. Choose tapes that appeal to your intellectual level.

What Are Those Voices in My Head?

No, you are not going crazy. Many people hear, or feel, that "voice of wisdom" when they begin working with angelic energy. At first, it may be an idea about what you need to do, or a few words, or a sense of knowing. The more you work with angels, the more open you become. You will find yourself attuned to their advice and wisdom.

When I began writing this book, I said, "Who is the angel who is to help me with this project?" I relaxed, thinking I would probably hear something in my head, but nope. Instead, I looked on my desk. Someone had left a dollar bill beside my computer. In big block letters, written directly on the bill, was the name Murphy. I'd looked at that dollar several times, meaning to put it in my pocket, but had never seen the word written across it before.

At first, I thought, "some stupid person wrote on that dollar bill." Logically, that's the correct answer. I also thought that Murphy was a dumb name. Not fancy enough, I guess, for an angel. However, I also know that angels like to have fun and games. It certainly would be fitting for me to be paired up with an angel who calls himself Murphy. In the world of a magickal person, there is no such thing as coincidence; Murphy it would be.

At first, I only called on Murphy when I got stuck. Later, I would light a candle each morning and ask Murphy to assist me while I wrote. Sometimes I would get

uring research, Murphy always helped me
ia I needed. He never let me down. I don't
r for another book or whether I'll find a
I'm thankful for the assistance and energy

n and guidance of the angels. Write down
al if you can.

ngels in Meditation

hangels—Michael, Gabriel, Raphael, and
ld like to meet first. I picked Raphael, the
t a candle in the corresponding color of
blue, rose, etc. Listening to some soft music
ic angel meditation given previously, but
d coming out, remain in your altered state
Raphael. You may get to talk to the angel,
rm and comfortable all over. You may meet
a fountain, or anywhere else. Just let the
hed, close the chakra centers and finish as
r. Be sure to write your experiences in your
hangels listed in Chapter 2 in meditation
long the way. Once you have encountered
ome new energies.

Seven Archangels

f the gang. Here is where the Western reli-
r three angels in the Clan of the Seven?
belongs in the Clan of the Seven (sometimes
abylonians regarded the seven planets as
e prototype for the Clan of the Seven. How-
us the four basic energies of the universe,
el, Raphael, and Uriel/Ariel. Each person is
which they want to work.

Christian Gnostics
1. Michael
2. Gabriel
3. Raphael
4. Uriel
5. Barachiel
6. Sealtiel
7. Jehudiel

Talismanic Magic
1. Zaphkiel
2. Zadkiel
3. Camael
4. Raphael
5. Haniel
6. Michael
7. Gabriel

The Ruling Princes of the Archangels of the Celestial Orders
1. Metatron
2. Raphael
3. Michael
4. Gabriel
5. Barbiel
6. Jehudiel
7. Barachiel
8. Satan (before his fall)

Testament of Solomon
1. Mikael
2. Gabriel
3. Uriel
4. Sabrael
5. Arael
6. Iaoth
7. Adonael

Muslim Lore
1. Gabriel
2. Michael
3. Azrael
4. Israfel

Book of Tolbit
1. Uriel
2. Raphael
3. Raguel
4. Michael
5. Sariel (Seraqel)
6. Gabriel
7. Remiel (Jeremiel)

Persian Mythology
1. Justice or Truth
2. Right Order
3. Obedience
4. Prosperity
5. Piety or Wisdom
6. Health
7. Immortality

Jewish Kabbalah
1. Methratton (Metatron)
2. Ratziel
3. Tzadqiel
4. Khamael
5. Mikhale
6. Haniel
7. Raphael
8. Gabriel
9. Methrattin

Enoch 1 (Ethiopic Enoch)
1. Uriel
2. Raphael
3. Raguel (Ruhiel, Ruahel)
4. Michael
5. Zerachiel (Araqael)
6. Gabriel
7. Remiel

The Kabbalah Unveiled: The Ten Sephiroth
1. Metatron: Kether (Crown)
2. Ratziel: Chokmah (Wisdom)
3. Tzaphqiel: Binah (Understanding)
4. Tzadqiel: Chesed (Mercy)
5. Khamael: Geburah (Strength)
6. Mikhael: Tiphereth (Beauty)
7. Haniel: Netzach (Victory)
8. Raphael: Hod (Splendor)
9. Gabriel: Yesod (Foundation)
10. Metatron/Shekinah: Malkuth (Kingdom)

Let's meet some of the other prominent angels. Remember, if you don't want to call an angelic energy by name, you can call the essence of the energy instead.

Metatron (male aspect); Shekinah (female aspect)

(Also Metratton, Mittron, Metaraon, Merraton.) In non-scriptural writings, Metatron is a super angel. His names include the king of angels, prince of the divine face, angel of the covenant, and numerous others. He links the human to the divine. The meaning of his name is a mystery in itself. Some think the name comes from the Latin *metator* ("to guide or measure"); others think it is a purely Jewish invention.

When invoked, Metatron appears as a pillar of fire, as dazzling as the Sun. In some sources he is considered mightier than Michael. A great deal of lore surrounds Metatron, including that he may be a mortal (named Enoch) turned angel who now functions as the official heavenly scribe, who holds all written secrets, and keeps track of what humans are doing. Consider him both the creator and librarian of the Akashic records.

In the *Key of Solomon,* by S. Liddell MacGregor Mathers (Weiser, Inc.), the First Pentacle of the Sun—"The Countenance of Shaddai the Almighty, at Whose aspect all creatures obey, and the Angelic Spirits do reverence on bended knee..."—is the representation of Metatron. Around the disk is written: "Behold His face and form by Whom all things were made, and Whom all creatures obey."

Although enthusiastically supported by rabbis and mystical occult practitioners, Metatron is a thorn in the side of the Christians. Metatron is the writer of truth, and gives inspiration and knowledge to those humans who were much like himself before his ascension. The Christians have a problem with humans turning into angels, and continue to refer to Enoch as Enoch—no angelic title (Metatron) for him. Even worse, they associate Metraton with Satan, insinuating that Metatron is a bloodthirsty fiend who takes pleasure in slowly destroying disobedient people. Gulp. Needless to say, arguments between priests and rabbis zip around like a hard game of tennis.

In other lore, the prophet Elijah was transformed into Metratron's twin brother, called Sandalphon. His duty is to gather the prayers of all believers (much like the Seraphim in the Nine Choir system). From this fine web of energy he weaves a garland or tapestry of purple and red.

Most interesting about Metatron, however, is the association with the Shekinah, the Hebrew version of the Hindu Shakti, which is the female side of God in the human. The creation of the world is Shekinah's doing (according to the Zohar). The purpose of life, then, is to bring the two halves together, male and female, to create a balanced universe. Ah! A Pagan principle!

Shekinah is known as "glory emanating from the divine," and stands for liberation. Many see her as "the holy ghost." This is exciting to me, as I practice the magickal art of Pow-Wow and am not comfortable using the Christianized version of this art without indicating divine female deity. The association of the Holy Ghost as feminine helps balance the healing. In Jewish lore, the Shekinah stands between the creator and the human. On the Sabbath she drapes her veil of divinity upon the collective believers. At the end of the day she returns to her place with/of divinity.

In one tale, when Adam and Eve lost the rent on the Garden of Eden, the Shekinah remained. To me, this indicates humans turning to patriarchal ideas and leaving Goddess energies behind. Other lore indicates she sealed her fate with Adam and Eve and left the Garden of Eden with them. The purpose of the universe is to reunite Metatron (the Creator) and Shekinah (the Creatrix). In Metatron and Shekinah we see the Pagan concept of the God and the Goddess. This could be why the Christians disdain both Metatron and Shekinah, as the divine female has been ground under patriarchal foot. It is rumored that one of the main tasks of the Clan of the Seven is to bring Shekinah's energies back to humanity, so all may be in balance and harmony.

In the Lesser Banishing Ritual given previously, you will notice that I include the line: "Shekinah descend upon me now." This inserts the feminine mystery into an otherwise male-oriented prayer, bringing balance. I realize that some of you more scholarly types will have sudden heart failure over this addition; however, it works for me.

Raziel

(Also Ratziel, Akrasiel, Gallizur, Saraqael, or Suriel.) The angel of mysteries. In rabbinical lore, Raziel wrote the Book of the Angel Raziel, wherein all celestial and earthly knowledge appears for the perusal of the human race. The human author remains unknown; however, legend says the text has been modified by Adam, Enoch, Noah, then Solomon. We are basically talking about a grimoire—the megabook of magick.

Raziel seeks and knows everything, sort of like a divine snoop with compassion. He reminds me of a good concierge in a hotel. When invoked, he appears as a brilliant white fire. He commands the Hyyoth, better known as the four heavenly beasts associated with the female Shekinah. Their job centers on upholding the universe, and they function as the angels of fire.

Remiel

(Also Jeremiel.) He is the angel of "true vision," enabling those who call on him to ferret out the truth—of course, this may be at all costs. His totem animal is the eagle. Remiel and Uriel have similar attributes, and they appear to be the same in legend. This particular angel is also in charge of the soul integration process into a new human body, if one believes in reincarnation.

Angel Eyes

One of the best ways to work with angels is through the use of "angel eyes" in meditation. After you have learned the technique, you will find yourself using it in other places. Angel eyes allow you to look at yourself in a different way, or see how your decisions affect others or how you fit into any situation.

The angel eyes meditation can also help to attune your psychic energies for improving clairvoyance, psychometry, healings, or divinatory workings. Once you have learned and practiced the meditation, you can fall immediately into that state before a working.

Follow the basic angel meditation on page 68, but do not close up the chakras. Concentrate on aligning your essence with angelic energy. You may feel a quickening sensation, heat, tingling, etc. It comes to everyone differently. Some people feel enveloped by a sense of wonderment or love.

Consider your question, or the situation you need clarified. You may choose any topic—your career, a family matter, the health of a loved one, improving your self-image, etc. Don't try to think it out logically. Simply relax and let it float in your mind.

In your mind, say the following:

I ask for assistance from the angelic energies in [name the situation].

Relax. You may see an answer right away in your mind, or perhaps you will get a feeling of insight, a flash of "knowing," or you may see nothing at all. Just let yourself float and don't force the issue. Sometimes answers come after the meditation is over.

Thank the angels and close down your meditation in the usual manner. Don't forget to ground and center. Be sure to record your experiences in your angel journal.

Do You Hear Me?

Whether you are sitting in meditation or standing in the middle of a busy street, angels always hear you when you talk to them. They live by one basic rule in their interactions with humans—they cannot assist you unless you ask for their help. The gift of our level of existence is free will. Though we often take it upon ourselves to interfere with the choices of our fellow humans (and ignore that it is wrong to do so), angels cannot, and will not, become involved in our lives unless we explicitly ask them to do so.

Although each of us incarnates on this plane to work on specific areas of our being, we are all entitled to love and harmony—these are gifts from divinity to all creatures, beings, and spirits. Once we learn to bring this harmony into our lives, changes manifest almost immediately. It can begin with small things and work outward, like a flower opening from a bud to full bloom, or it can manifest with great impact from the beginning, like a firecracker, and continue to light our way until our mission in this life is over.

Any time is a good time to talk to the angelic beings. You don't have to be in trouble to seek their wisdom; however, if things are rocky, they are eager to help you. For example, the problem can be a minor one. On a warm February afternoon I went out with a friend of mine. She forgot to put gas in her car. As the needle slipped below "E," she realized her error. While we looked for a gas station, I called the angels in my head and asked them to help us reach the gas station in time. Although we sat through horrendous traffic, we finally glided into a station. A small bubble in the existence of the universe, but it was important to us. The angels always listen.

Angels, Meditation, and Poetry

One interesting way to find angels in meditation is to read a poem that you like very much, then meditate on the setting and energy of the poem. The poetry does not have to be angelic in nature to help you meet your angels. An excellent poem to begin with is the first few lines of "Kubla Khan" by Samuel Taylor Coleridge.

Be sure you keep track of your meditations in your angel journal. If you use poetry, jot down at least the title, if not the whole poem. You may wish to refer to the poem later.

Angelic Alignment Meditation

For this meditation you will need either a friend to orchestrate it, or tape it on a tape recorder. I suggest you tape it more than once until you get the feel of this type of meditation, and are comfortable listening to your voice. The angelic alignment meditation is designed specifically for magickal people, and those people who want to change their lives and work magick with the angels. When preparing for the meditation, choose a place and time where you will not be disturbed. You may play gentle music in the background if you like. I don't know about you, but I get cold during meditation, so I use a blanket to cover my arms, chest, and shoulders. You may like to use one, too.

Lest you think I came up with this alignment procedure all by myself, let me firmly tell you I did not. I got the idea from a book entitled *Commune with the Angels* by Jane M. Howard. She talks about angelic attunement in mediation. Since magickal people learn to align themselves with all sorts of divine energies, I just made the leap into the session that follows. The speech pattern in any hypnosis session should be modulated. The grammar in a hypnotherapy session is a little odd, so I suggest you practice before making a recording. If a friend is going to do this for you, please have him or her read over the text several times and practice a bit before getting started.

Relaxation

First I would like you to take three deep, cleansing breaths with your eyes open. Then I want you to stretch. That's right. Stretch every muscle. Now, close your eyes, and as you close them, feel yourself beginning to relax. Take a deep breath and relax. And another. Just feel the tension move out of your body. Take another deep breath. Good. That's very good. You are relaxing more and more, relaxing every muscle of your body from the top of your head to the tips of your toes. Just relax and begin to notice how very comfortable you are feeling. You are in a comfortable position, so you can simply relax and enjoy this feeling. Inhale and exhale, and as you exhale release any tension and any stress out of your body, mind, and thoughts; just let it go and relax. Feel those stressful thoughts begin to wind down and down and down. And as you relax you are becoming more aware of the God and the Goddess, and you are aware that the God and Goddess have sent your guardian angel to you. Feel the light and healing of your guardian angel all around you. Relax and let it go. Let go and feel the universal healing all around you. Notice how very comfortable your body is beginning to feel.

Angels will only help you if you ask them, so right now, in your mind, I would like you to ask the angels for their help while you undergo the angelic alignment. Do this now. *(Wait fifteen seconds.)* And now I would like you to reach out in your mind and ask for your guardian angel to be with you during this angelic alignment. Do this now. *(Wait fifteen seconds.)*

Take a deep breath now. Let it out. And another; let it out. Relax. You hear only the sound of my voice, no sounds around you will disturb you. You will hear only the sound of my voice. All other sounds will be distant. Breathe in and let it out. And again. Once more now, in and out. Relaxing, even breathing. I would like you to imagine the angel Raphael floating above your head, and the angel Raphael is going to touch the top of your head and send healing energy down through your body. Raphael is the angel of healing. This energy is going to push all the negativity, frustration, fear, and worry out of your body. Slowly pushing down, down, down past your eyes, relaxing the muscles around your eyes, your nose, down past your mouth, relaxing your jaw, and into your neck. And this energy moves the unhappiness, stress, and negativity down and out of your body. Down through your shoulders, your upper arms, your lower arms, out through your hands, into your fingers and out of your fingertips, out of your body. The energy moves down through your chest, your stomach, pushing all the negativity, fear, and frustration out of your body. Down, down, down through your pelvis, your hips, your thighs, your knees, your calves, into your feet and out of your toes. All the unwanted feelings are pouring out of your body.

And now the angel Michael floats above you. Visualize his strength and purity hovering above your head. The angel Michael is going to touch the top of your head, and when he does he is going to send loving strength down through your body, instilling you with honor and dignity, moving away any blocks you are experiencing. Now he touches the top of your head. Feel his warm energy trickling down through your body, down past your forehead, your eyes, down past your nose and mouth, relaxing your jaw. You feel safe and secure, loose and limp, hearing only the sound of my voice. You are sinking deeper into a state of relaxation. This energy makes you feel so comfortable as it moves down into your neck, your shoulders, your upper arms and your lower arms, into your hands and out your fingertips. Safe and secure, loose and limp. The energy moves down your chest, into your back; feel the soothing energy move down your back into your hips, your pelvis, into your thighs, your knees, loose and limp, into your calves, safe and secure, down into your feet and out through your toes.

Feeling heavy, floating; you are floating in angelic love, peace, and harmony. And now the angel Gabriel hovers above you. She is the angel of rebirth and transformation, and as she touches the top of your head she is going to send special energy into your body—the energy of change. She is going to touch you and give you the gift of happiness and balance in your life. Now she touches you; feel her gentle energy move down past your forehead, past your eyes, nose, and mouth. Hearing only the sound of my voice. This pleasant energy moves into your neck, past your shoulders, into your upper arms, your lower arms, into your hands, and out through your fingertips. Safe and secure, loose and limp. Feel the energy of Gabriel flowing down through your chest, down your back; soothing relaxation moving into your hips, your pelvis, down into your knees, regenerating your essence, bringing harmony into your life and body, down into your calves, down, down into your feet and out through your toes.

And now the angel Uriel hovers above you, waiting to instill in you the wisdom of magick and prophecy. The angel Uriel will bestow upon you the eyes of the spirit, those angelic eyes that will help you in your daily life. Now the angel Uriel touches the top of your head, sending this gift into every molecule of your body, every portion of your mind. You are safe and secure. Down, down, this energy travels into the very core of your being. Down past your forehead, your eyes, giving you the gift of second sight, past your nose, past your mouth, giving you the gift of prophecy, melting into your mind, instilling in you the wisdom of the elders, past your neck and into your shoulders. Loose and limp. Safe and secure. Accept the gifts that are being bestowed upon you. Down into your upper arms, lower arms, and into your fingers. Down through your chest, giving you compassion and loving healing, down your back, down, down into your pelvis, your hips, loose and limp, safe and secure, down into your thighs, your knees, your calves, down into your feet and into your toes.

Floating; you are floating in a vortex of angelic energy. Feel the peace and harmony of the universe around you. And now your guardian angel will help you align your spiritual, mental, and physical body. The angel first touches your physical body. Feel it tingling, growing warm and in harmony with the universe. And now your guardian angel touches your mental body, bringing it into alignment with your physical body. And now your guardian angel touches your spiritual body. It is like expensive silk, rustling over your mental and spiritual bodies, coming into alignment with both, into harmony with the universe.

Chakra Cleansing

And now I would like you to envision a small red cloud. You are going to breathe in, and your inhalation is going to pull the red cloud toward you. And as you breathe out, you will go deeper, into a deeper state of mind. Your breath will push the red cloud away. We will go through the chakra system with colored clouds. You will breathe them in toward you, then push them away. Do it at your own pace, no matter where we are in the sequence. You won't forget any of the colors. Breathe in now, pulling the cloud toward you, closer, closer, and breathe out, pushing the red cloud away. And you are going deeper and deeper, into a deeper state of mind.

And now envision an orange cloud. Breathe in the orange cloud, pulling it toward you, closer, closer, and breathe out, pushing the orange cloud away. Good. Watch it go. And you will go two times deeper than before.

And now breathe in a yellow cloud. Breathe it in, pulling the yellow cloud toward you, watch it drift closer, closer, and now push it away. That's right, watch it drift away. Just relax and let it go and you are going three times deeper than before, and now you are going deeper and deeper.

And now breathe in the green cloud, pulling the green cloud toward you, closer, closer, and breathe out, pushing the green cloud away. Watch it travel gently away from you. And you are going three times deeper than before, relaxing.

And now breathe in a pink cloud, pulling the pink cloud toward you; that's right, watch it coming toward you, and breathe the pink cloud out, pushing it away from you, going three times deeper than before, down, down. Feeling safe and secure, loose and limp.

And now breathe in the blue cloud, pulling the blue cloud toward you, closer, closer, and breathe the blue cloud away from you, going three times deeper than before. Relax and let it go. That's right. Very good.

And now breathe in the purple cloud, pulling the purple cloud toward you, closer, closer, and breathe the purple cloud out, pushing it away from you, going three times deeper than before, down, down. Feeling safe and secure. Loose and limp.

And now breathe in the golden cloud, pulling the golden cloud toward you, closer, closer, and now push it away; you will go five times deeper than before, feeling safe and secure, loose and limp.

Deepening

And now a white cloud comes toward you, and on this white cloud is your guardian angel. You are ready now, says your angel, and the angel takes your hand and you mentally step on the cloud and it is floating, floating. Floating in a beautiful universe full of love and harmony, and your cloud floats to a beautiful summer field and lets you and your guardian angel step into this summer field full of flowers and love. This is a sacred space made just for you. And every time you see a flower you will know that the Goddess is in your life and that the angels are willing to help you. The flowers smell so good. Take a deep breath and smell the beautiful flowers, and as you do, you go ten times deeper than before.

And now you look up into the blue sky and you see little clouds, as white as driven snow. And these little clouds move together and spell your name in the sky. See your name in the sky. Yes, see your name. The angels are ready for you; they are spelling your name in the clouds. They are happy and so are you. And now a puff of wind comes through the field and rustles your clothing. It passes across the sky and blows away your name. Your name is gone and you are safe and secure, loose and limp.

And now your guardian angel takes you by the hand. You feel so good and at peace. You are comfortable and protected and safe, and now you are going to walk down through this beautiful field. It gently slopes down, down, down. And there are ten hills we will walk down, down hill number ten, walking down, down hill number nine, down, down, down, safe and secure, total harmony in every step you take, down hill number eight, going deeper and deeper, down hill seven, strolling down deeper and deeper, down hill number six, down hill number five, down, down, down hill number four, down hill number three, in total harmony, down hill number two, down, down, down, hill number one. Safe and secure, ten times deeper than before.

The Alignment

The temple of the Goddess awaits you. See it at the edge of the field. This is a very special place for you. You float toward the temple of the Goddess. It is so peaceful here. Off in the distance you can hear the sounds of birds chirping and the rustle of the grasses in the field. You float down a path, past a burbling stream of sparkling clear water. This water is blessed by the Goddess. Stoop down and take a drink of this holy water. This water cleanses your body of all past difficulties and renews your soul. It is so peaceful and serene here. Move closer to the temple. See how glorious it is. And do you see the angels? Yes, yes, they are all about the temple. Some are floating, some are tending the temple gardens, some are sewing, some caring for animals; you see them, shining. They are the shining ones.

The wide doors of the temple are in front of you. They are gold and taller and wider than anything you have ever seen, and they glow in the sunlight, pulsate; this is a place filled with power. The doors swing open and you walk through, into the huge Hall of the Angels. It is here where you will meet the Goddess of the angels, and she will bestow the gift of angelic alignment upon you. You look up and the Goddess approaches you. She is as beautiful as you anticipated. Her aura shines so brightly you can hardly focus on her caring face. She reaches a hand out toward you in greeting. She smiles and kisses you on the forehead. Your aura glows with healing energy.

The Goddess now asks you the important question; you must answer Her in your mind. "Are you prepared to receive the alignment that will change your life forever?" *(Wait ten seconds.)*

She nods her head and angels from all over the temple surround you with their loving, caring essence. One brings a beautiful cloak and gives it to the Goddess. Then all the angels gather 'round. Some hold hands in a circle around you. Others float above your head. They are all so happy for you and they are very excited. The Goddess smiles at you reassuringly and places the beautiful cloak around your shoulders. You can feel its energy start to transmute your essence. Your shoulder blades itch, but you dare not scratch them. And as quickly as the itching begins, it stops.

The Goddess lays her hands upon your shoulders. "From this day forward," she says, "your life will be in harmony with the universe. You will function as one of my angels on earth. You will operate for the good of all. I bestow the gift of harmony and psychism upon you and no one can ever take it from you, save myself. Be it known you will lose the gift should you intentionally work magick to harm another for the simple joy of it." Answer her in your mind that you understand.

She presses lightly on your shoulders, and you feel the energy vortexes of your body begin to align. First the lower chakra, which is the color red. Then the orange chakra in your pelvis. It aligns, too. You body is so harmonious. Now the yellow chakra at your navel. Moving into alignment with the universe. And now the green chakra at your heart. Feel your whole essence becoming one with the universe. And now the pink chakra, bringing universal love into your body. Now the blue chakra at your throat, pulling gently into harmony. Now the purple chakra at your temple, where the gift of second sight and wisdom rides. And finally the glowing white crown chakra, pulsing in tandem with the others, bringing you into total alignment.

And now the Goddess asks you to kneel at her feet. You do so. She stands above you holding a beautiful silver crown. The angels begin softly saying: "Align, align, align, align." And their voices grow louder. "Harmony, harmony, harmony, harmony." "AwwwwwwwwwwwwWWWWWWWWWWWWWWWWWWWWWWW!" *(Begin softly and increase the sound for a few seconds.)*

The Goddess places the crown upon your head and the alignment has occurred. The angels raise you to your feet and congratulate you. Everyone is so happy. You feel different. Changed. Special. You can now go out into the material world and help others, feeling confident, safe, and secure.

The Goddess removes your cloak and guides you to a mirror. And there you see yourself, transformed and beautiful. You are a shining being and you have wings! Enjoy this place for a few moments and listen as the Goddess gives you a special message. *(Wait five minutes.)*

The Return/Emergence

And now it is time for you to return. Bid farewell to the angels. You may come back to this temple anytime during your private meditations. It will always be here. You and your guardian angel now leave the temple and go back into the field. I want you to relax a moment, just float and relax. Good. That's right. And now I'm going to count from one to five; when I reach the number five you will come back to full consciousness, and you will feel refreshed as if you have had a long rest. You will come back feeling wide awake and wonderful. You will have no side effects from this meditation.

One—begin to come back now. Two—coming up; three—remember you will be wide awake and feeling very good. Four—you are almost there; begin to open your eyes. Five—open your eyes now. You are wide awake, alert, and feeling well. Wide awake.

What you have just experienced is a full-blown hypnosis session with the angels. Drink a cup of tea, eat a cookie, and record your experiences in your angel journal. I'm sure you will never forget it.

Discovering Past Lives

The angels will help you uncover past life experiences that may be useful to you in this incarnation. You will follow the same procedures as you did in the angelic alignment. This means you will need a place where you will not be disturbed, and either a partner (whom you feel you trust implicitly) or a tape recorder. Remember, if you use the tape recorder, run through the session several times until you feel you are ready to tape it.

Begin the session with the relaxation, chakra cleansing, and deepening sections found in the angelic alignment meditation. Take yourself all the way into the angelic temple, into the Hall of Angels. Continue as follows.

And now I'm going to talk to you, and as I talk to you, you will relax even more deeply. I will be asking you to imagine certain scenes. This imagining will relax you more and more. You will feel safe and secure. You feel in absolute harmony in the Hall of Angels. This is a safe and secure place. You will be able to observe any scene you envision in an unemotional and detached manner, just like watching a picture show. And you will remember everything you see.

Imagine yourself at the top of a golden staircase. You are dressed in the flowing robes of an angel. Your hand is upon the gleaming railing, and as you prepare to descend you can feel the love of the angels all around you. As you descend these blue-carpeted stairs, you will relax even more deeply. I'm going to count from five to one, and as I do, you will be able to step outside yourself to see new aspects of your being. We start at five now. You begin to step lightly down the stairs, and each step will relax you deeper and deeper. You are amazed at how wonderful and light you feel. And now we are at four, and you grow more harmonious with the universe at each step; the carpet feels like soft, cottony clouds. Down, down, down, to three; you look down at your feet and they are not even touching the steps, you are so relaxed, floating down, relaxing deeper, and deeper, and deeper. Down to two, you can see the bottom of the stairs below you now, and you float softly toward it, down, down, relaxing into the soothing sensation, free of gravity, and now your feet touch ever so gently to the ground. You are completely relaxed and harmonious in every aspect of your being. *(Wait fifteen seconds.)*

See yourself standing on a large, circular patio. It is like a big gazebo with beautiful white columns and all sorts of lovely plants growing around the perimeter. In the center of the patio is a big round pool. The tile of the pool is a deep, restful blue. Nothing disturbs the water in the pool. Step over to the pool; feel how light your steps are. Look at your own reflection. You are amazed at how beautiful you are when you look so relaxed. As you look into the pool the water ripples distort your image, and you see a reflection of yourself as you were five years ago; you remember what you were doing then. The image is so strong that you try to touch it, but when you do, you disturb the water and it shifts and disappears. *(Pause.)*

Another image appears and you see yourself ten (or fifteen) years ago. Look at your hair, your clothes. Remember what you were doing then. *(Pause.)*

You touch the water again, and the image shifts to yourself as you were in high school [or elementary school, if you are still in high school]. Notice the clothes again. Your face. Your shoes. Your hair. What memories does it show in the pool? *(Pause.)*

Remembering relaxes you even more deeply than before. You touch the water again, and the image shifts and changes, and you know that the pool is letting you see the events that have shaped your life and your being as you are now. The image blurs again and there you are on your first day of school. What are you wearing? How are you feeling? *(Pause.)*

You touch the water again and the image shifts. Breathe deeply. So relaxed, safe, and secure. These images help you relax; the pool is now filled with gentle, swirling colors and another image begins to form. You touch the water. The image is coming from very, very far away. It is not from your present life. You watch the image as the ripples get smoother and smoother. You watch this new face smooth out in the pool. You touch your nose; so does the reflection, but this is the you of another lifetime. The face may not be the same. You will remember everything you see in the pool and all impressions you receive.

(Make sure you allow enough time to answer each of the following questions.)

Is your reflection that of a man or a woman?

What type of clothing do you see?

Does the person appear to be happy or sad?

Is there anything striking about the image?

What time period do you think the image is in?

What was the most significant event in that lifetime?

What was the greatest accomplishment?

The greatest disaster?

What was not resolved in that lifetime that is being carried over to the present?

What talents did that incarnation have that you could access now?

Reach out and pull those skills and talents toward you now. As you look at the image you will be deeply relaxed.

Is there anyone in that incarnation who is with you now in this one? If so, who is this person, and how does he or she fit into the lessons of your present?

As you look upon the images now playing across the pool, you realize that further significances to you will reveal themselves in the days ahead of you. You will find that you are still relaxed, safe, and secure. Reach out now and touch the water. The image blurs and you see yourself again, looking at your present incarnation's reflection. Breathe deeply, relax; you are comfortable, safe, and secure. *(Pause.)*

You are now looking at the place where you were between lives; in fact, right before this one. Right before you entered your mother. What lessons were you planning to work on in this life? What accomplishments were you supposed to try to achieve? What is the signal for you to begin these works? Do you remember the signal given to you for the next stranger who will be important in this incarnation? Is there something you have forgotten that you need to remember? *(Pause.)*

We are going to leave the pool of remembering now. We will go back up the steps and into the Hall of the Angels. We smile at the angels and wish them well. Into the field you walk with your guardian angel. Take a few moments and relax now. Relax and float. You will remember all that you have experienced, and you will gather more insight into this incarnation, and others, in the days ahead. You will feel healthier and happier, in harmony with the universe.

*C*onclude the meditation with the return/emergence procedure given earlier. As with the angelic alignment, you may want to have a cup of tea, relax, and eat a cookie or two. Write down your experiences in your angel journal. If you worked with a friend, you may want to talk about your experiences with him or her.

Six

Angels and Ritual

*T*here are two kinds of ritual: the act of honoring divinity and the act of creating change in the universe (often called a working ritual). Honoring divinity usually occurs on religious holidays.

All ritual is a familiar set of motions, thoughts, and exercises designed to celebrate divinity in our lives, as well as put us in tune with universal energies. The working ritual is usually shorter and performed for a specific purpose—for example, to help a friend heal after an operation, or to bring a new job for yourself. Angels love both types of rituals, and are more than willing to assist you.

Some ceremonial magicians will not work any magick unless they have first contacted their guardian angel. They work as a team—human and angel. It is possible for you to do that, too, no matter what your religious belief or magickal practices. I've structured this chapter to assist you in working in such a manner. The spirit who works with you in magick can be your guardian angel, a specific angel that you call by name to assist you for a particular type of working, or a positive energy essence that you do not call by name. (For example, the essence of healing, prosperity, etc.)

The Basic Format of Angel Ritual

There are several variations in ritual format; for our work, we will stick with those procedures that flow well with angel magick. You are free to change the format in any way you desire. The purpose of showing you the following outline is to give you an idea of how I do it. Please understand that this is not the last word on ritual format, but is simply an example for you to try.

Angelic Ritual Outline

    I. Opening
        A. Ground and center
        B. Altar devotion
        C. Purify the room
        D. Call your guardian angel
    II. Circle casting
        A. Cast circle
            1. Perform the Lesser Banishing Ritual
            2. Cast the free-form angelic circle
        B. Call quarters
        C. Raise your vibratory frequency
        D. Invoke deity/angelic energies
        E. Name working
            1. Healing
            2. Talismans
            3. Psychic work
            4. Other
        F. Perform working
        G. Meld with angelic energy
            1. Song
            2. Dance

3. Visualization
4. Chant
5. Drumming
6. Rattles/bells

III. Closing
    A. Dismiss quarters
    B. Thank angels and deity
    C. Closing prayer
    D. Pull up the circle (counterclockwise)
    E. Ground and center

Ritual Overview

One of the most sacred performances in life is ritual designed to honor or work with deity. These are special times, between you and the Creator/Creatrix, where you give of yourself to move in tandem with the universal energies.

All parts of ritual are important. The ritual becomes a beautiful symphony, where each movement reflects upon those that go both before and after it. Before you begin any ritual you need to plan what you wish to accomplish. Is your ritual for honoring divinity and connecting with the universe, or do you wish to add some sort of working to help someone you know in need? The purpose of the ritual dictates what words you will use (if any), what supplies you will need (perhaps a specific candle), and how long it will last.

I've designed the angelic ritual form (see page 89) to help you plan your rituals. You may want to copy it so that you can use it many times, and set up a notebook just for your angel rituals.

The Ritual Opening

Most rituals begin with a procedure called grounding and centering. This can be contemplative or meditative. Grounding and centering is when you step away from your busy life and prepare to invite divinity into your heart.

Some individuals wish to start with a prayer or a chant. Others may like soft music, drumming, or singing to themselves. You can begin by reciting a poem, or simply closing your eyes and visualizing perfect peace and harmony in the universe. It doesn't matter how you begin your ritual. No one has to approve of what you are doing, and it is no one else's business how you do it. Here is one poem I like:

In sacred hour I touch the altar
I know the love of my Goddess will not falter
And the God manifests to exalt Her.

The positive energies coalesce, unite
In my sacred temple of brilliant light.
Air and earth, water and fire
I watch the holy flame stretch higher.
And here about the shimmering glow
Poised, a symphony of magick grows.
Angels hover, guttering candle with mighty wings
To fan the magick my Goddess brings.

The Altar Devotion and Devotional Hours

Use the altar devotion both in ritual and in devotional hours. Most religions have times, or hours, of devotion, usually occurring at morning, noon, sunset, and midnight. You don't need a great deal of planning to design devotional hours. Some people I know simply take a break from their busy schedules, close their eyes, ground and center, and meld with the divine essence. I realize we all live busy lives and sometimes it just isn't possible to drop everything, turn to a compass direction, and get down on bended knee for the next twenty minutes. I also understand that you are not always near your altar during your devotional hours. Although I will show you an altar devotion you can use for both ritual and devotional hours, you are free to change it in any way you see fit.

The Angel Altar Devotion

Take three deep breaths. Ground and center. Light your illuminator candles or lamps.

Hold your hands over the altar and say:

As above so below
Energies circle, the Goddess glows.

In clockwise fashion, touch each of the four corners of your altar four times.

Hold your hands over the center of the altar and say:

Angelic forces on wings of dove
I conjure harmony
Insight, will, and love.

Feel your hands build power over the altar. When you are ready, remove your hands and seal the altar first by making the sign of the equal-armed cross over the center of the altar, then tap the side of the altar four times with your knuckles.

From this point you can purify the room or add any type of beginning ritual actions that you desire, such as purifying salt and water, cleansing and consecrating tools or supplies, or simply going further into the ritual and purifying the room.

Angelic Ritual Form

Date of ritual: _____ Moon phase: _____

Day: _____ Hour: _____

Reason for ritual: _____

_____

Opening: Poetry, music, sing, chant, visualization, drumming, other _____

_____

I will begin by: _____

_____

Altar devotion: Standard, other _____

_____

I will call my guardian angel by: _____

_____

Circle casting I will use: _____

_____

Quarters I will call: (list names you will use or how you will do it) _____

_____

I will invoke deity or call angelic energies: (list who and how) _____

_____

The working I will be doing: (list what and for whom) _____

_____

The minor magicks I will employ: _____

_____

Supplies I will need: _____

_____

I will meld with deity by: _____

_____

I will dismiss quarters by: _____

_____

I will thank angels and deity by: _____

_____

My closing prayer will be: _____

_____

Call Your Guardian Angel

The next step in ritual is to call your guardian angel. You can use the incantation provided here, or you can make up your own. It is your choice.

Universal light circle nigh
Bring my guardian angel by.
Silver wings about me protect
All negative energy they will deflect.
Amid this dancing universe I move
My life safe, secure, and perfectly smooth.
From holy enchanted grove I came
Among Earth's terrors I walk again
Haunted ever of Summerland's lore
And the magick I know that went before.
I raise my arms in solemn oath
To heighten humanity's spiritual growth.
Together we work, angel and I
To focus the magick, to stop pain's cry,
We move in tandem, as above, so below
Melded as one our power will grow.
The Goddess smiles at the work we have done
When she looks down at me, she sees two, not just one.

If you see divinity as male in nature, you can substitute *God* for *Goddess* and *his* for *her.* Here is another incantation you might like to try:

Guardian angel I call thee here
To vanquish any hate or fear.
Together now I work with thee
As I will, so mote it be.

Angelic Circle Casting

The point of casting a magick circle is to give you working space devoid of negativity, to allow you to gather your energy and the energy of the universe into a focused area, and to enable you to increase your vibrational rate with the goal of melding with divinity and angelic forces. There are all sorts of ways to cast a magick circle, but here we are going to concentrate on casting only the angelic circle. If you prefer another method of circle casting, use that procedure. However, when working in ritual, remember that as many sections as possible should be in tune with each other. This is why I have designed every element in the ritual to coincide with the primary purpose—that of using the angelic forces for your work.

Cast free-form angelic circles with your dominant hand. You may begin either at the north or the east—it is your choice. You may walk around three times in circle fashion, pointing your dominant hand out, with your index finger slightly directed toward the floor, or you may choose to make only one circle. It is up to you.

Here is a standard circle casting:

I conjure thee, O circle of angelic art
So that you will be for me
A boundary between the world of human and the realm of the angels
A meeting place of perfect peace and joy, love and trust
Containing the power I will raise within thee.
I call upon the angels of the east, the south, the west, and the north
To aid me in the consecration of this circle.
In the name of divine and universal energies
Thus do I conjure thee, O great circle of power.
And the legions of light await my call.
So mote it be.

Stamp your foot and then say:

As above, so below
This circle is sealed.

The main difference between an angelic circle casting and other traditional castings is that you do this type of casting with your guardian angel. This means you work as a team; visualize your guardian angel working by your side. The details of the visualization are up to you. You may see yourself holding hands, or the guardian angel's hand extended over yours as you cast the circle. You will need to determine what works best and is most comfortable for you.

It is a good idea to learn the altar devotion, circle casting, and quarter calls by heart. It takes something out of the ritual to have to refer to a book all the time. Also, you may be so busy reading that you are not concentrating on visualizing the right energies. When working on the altar devotion, you should be visualizing pure white energy enveloping your altar and yourself. When circle casting, you should envision a sphere of blue or white fire, a glowing light that encircles yourself and the room like a bubble. In quarter calls you need to open the veil and allow the angelic energies of that quarter to come through to work with you.

There are few rules with circle casting. Basically, never walk out of a cast circle without cutting a door first. In an angelic circle, simply stand at the perimeter and open your arms, envisioning a curtain parting. Walk through, turn, and close the circle as you opened it. When you wish to return to it, follow the same procedure.

You must take a circle down in the opposite way in which you put it up. This means you will be walking counterclockwise, drawing the angelic circle back into your hand. When you get very, very good (this requires practice), you can simply stand in the middle and clap your hands, envisioning the circle's energy dropping back into the earth.

Here is another circle casting:

Angels of north, stability circle 'round
Angels of east, wisdom abound
Angels of south, passion surround
Angels of west, transformation be found.
I circle thrice, the shape of the plan
Invoke the light to where I stand.

Quarter Calls

The angelic energies of the quarters bring protective and harmonious energy as well as strengthen the boundaries of the circle. As with circle casting, there are many types of quarter calls practiced for many different reasons. However, because we are working with angelic forces, we will stick with the standard quarter calls. If you would like to elaborate or use your own calls (summonings, stirrings), you are free to do so.

When working with quarters, you are dealing with a passageway to another realm. In this case, it is the angelic one. Envision it as a door, an opening, a curtain parting—it doesn't matter, as long as you understand the concept of "to open." Likewise, close quarters at the end of a ritual; the most important action here is "to close." While calling an angelic quarter you may feel hot, cold, calm, excited, etc. Remember these emotions so that you will understand what these energies mean to you, and when you feel them again, you will recognize what is happening.

Always say your altar devotion, circle casting, and quarter calls slowly. This isn't a race; nobody is going to earn a medal for being the fastest-talking ritualist. Take your time. Savor the words, thoughts, and feelings you are trying to impart, and the energies that you are manifesting and drawing toward you.

Finally, dismiss all angelic energies precisely in the manner in which you called them. Since you have called angelic energies, you hail and farewell them as well as thank them for their time and energy.

Below you will find quarter calls for an angelic ritual. As you stand at each quarter, open your arms wide to allow the angelic energies into the circle.

Hail, angelic guardian of the east
Thy name is Raphael.
Healer, protector, nourisher of Gaia's children.
Angel of love, joy, and laughter.
I call thee forth to protect this circle and guard this sacred space.

Hail, angelic guardian of the south
Michael is thy name.
He who brings balance into our world.

Angel of justice, strength, and protection.
I call thee forth to guard this circle and protect this sacred space.

Hail, angelic guardian of the west
Gabriel is thy name.
She who brings transformation to the children of mystery.
Angel of resurrection, mercy, and peace.
I call thee forth to guard this circle and protect this sacred space.

Hail, angelic guardian of the north
Ariel is thy name.
He who is the bringer of dreams and prophecy.
Angel of nature, psychism, and instruction.
I call thee forth to guard this circle and protect this sacred space.

To dismiss, go counterclockwise around the circle, beginning with the angelic force you called last. In this case, that would be Ariel:

Angelic essence of the north
Ariel is thy name.
I thank you for your gifts of nature, psychism, and instruction.
Go if you must, stay if you please
Hail and farewell.

Angelic essence of the west
Gabriel is thy name.
I thank you for your gifts of resurrection, mercy, and peace.
Go if you must, stay if you please
Hail and farewell.

Angelic essence of the south
Michael is thy name.
I thank you for your gifts of justice, strength, and protection.
Go if you must, stay if you please
Hail and farewell.

Angelic essence of the east
Raphael is thy name.
I thank you for your gifts of love, joy, and laughter.
Go if you must, stay if you please
Hail and farewell.

When you called the angelic forces, you opened your arms as if to open a portal. To dismiss, you might try closing your arms and bowing your head to signify both closure and honor.

Remember, if you perform the Lesser Banishing Ritual you do not have to cast the circle and call the quarters, because you have already done so with the LBR procedure. However, I know people who like to do both, and it doesn't hinder the ritual.

Raising Your Vibratory Frequency

The electrical force of the angelic presence in your circle can enhance your energy field, allowing it to vibrate at a higher frequency. You can assist by helping these energies enter your body. As we are creatures of free will, we must first indicate our desire to the angels that we want to do this. We must also ground and center before the procedure begins, so that we don't feel ill or jittery after the ritual is over.

You can work primarily with your guardian angel or the quarter energies you have called, or you can do both. This takes practice. You may feel a rushing sensation, fluctuations of body temperature (too hot or too cold), or feel like your nerves plugged themselves into a light socket. Visualize your vibrational frequency transmuting to pure, white light. Some individuals visualize each quarter angel touching them lightly on the shoulder, helping them raise their energy pattern. Other people envision their guardian angel hugging them. The choice is yours.

Invoking Deity/Angelic Energies and Naming the Working

Here is where you need to have done your homework for the ritual. What energies do you wish to call for your working? First, you will need to call divinity—your visualization of God or Goddess. Next you will call upon the specific energies needed for the working you have planned. We talked about invoking in Chapter 2, but to remind you briefly: Invoking means calling something into your circle. That means you want to call only good things, meaning divinity and positive angelic energies. There is never, ever a danger when you invoke beings of light. If you will be doing a healing, you will need to focus on these energies. You may call an angelic force by name or simply ask for the essence of that force.

You can begin with a Goddess invocation like this one:

I salute you, O Goddess
Maiden, Mother, and Crone
Treasure of the universe
Deity of the eternal flame
Crown of the enlightened ones
Scepter of my faith
Indestructible temple
I bring thee forth

Into my body
To work the magick of this night.

Or:

To bring the healing energies into this working
I invoke thee, Holy Mother
To surround me with the essence of the angelic beings
So that I may [state the purpose of your ritual].

This part of the ritual is very important, so you will want to be sure you have worked out what you are going to say and why you will be saying it. As you have seen, magickal workings allow for variations. Here again, you have a choice during the invocation. You can draw the essence into your body or around you with the intention of helping you. Either way is fine. It is what you feel most comfortable doing that is important. Remember, the angels will not interfere with your free will, nor will they give you any assistance that you cannot consciously or subconsciously handle. They are much better at following universal rules than we are.

As you can see, I combined the invocation and the naming of the working, but you can do those separately, especially if you are planning on invoking a very strong deity or angelic force. For example, perhaps you like working with Isis. You may wish to invoke her first, drawing her essence into your body, then state the working.

Heavenly hosts, gather 'round
As I draw the energy of the Mother down.

Now it's time for the angels:

Earth and sky, water and fire
I pull to me angelic power.

Here is another way of invoking angelic forces:[1]

I charge you [name of angel], *who are an angel of light, and bound in the service of the God and the Goddess, who are above and before all things, descend into this magick circle.*

Perhaps it bothers you to invoke anything. I can understand that. After a while it won't disturb you, but let's just say for now you are terrified that you are going to do something wrong and blurt out a bizarre string of words (you won't, but let's humor you anyway). In that case, just invoke the light.

Performing the Working

This is precisely what it sounds like. If the working is a focused prayer, then so be it. If you are making a talisman, empowering a guardian angel pin for a friend to

---

1. Wording by Donald Tyson in his book *New Millennium Magick.*

promote protection and healing, or if you plan to do a meditation to increase your psychism—here's where you should do it. It is wise to have all your supplies ready so you don't keep walking in and out of the circle. Every time you cut a door in your circle energy, you weaken it (unless you have practiced and practiced and practiced).

Melding with Angelic Energy

Melding with angelic energy is a form of raising power. We call this the cone of power, because it looks like a cone as you focus the energies at your disposal to a point, then send the energy outward to cause the change you desire. If you raise your own power and do not meld with divinity or the angelic forces, you will probably feel tired. This isn't the idea of raising power at all. There are forces at your disposal; use them. For centuries magickal people have been "raising energy" by song, dance, visualization, chanting, drumming, rattles, bells, etc. There is even an old folklore practice of using one white stone and one black stone, and clapping them together. This sound puts the individual into alpha (and hopefully into theta) where connection with divinity and angelic essence occurs. You will need to choose the method that is best for you.

A simple chant would be:

In this night
In this hour
I call angels
To raise power.

It is best if chants rhyme, but if you are comfortable doing it another way, that is just fine. Some people simply repeat the name of an angel or deity. It works for them; it may work for you, too.

With any of these methods you start out slowly and quietly, then raise tempo and volume. When you reach the peak, release the energy you have been raising, focusing it directly at the intended change you desire to make. It is that simple.

After you have raised the energy, you may wish to relax. Magickal people often consume "cakes and ale" in the circle environment. This is a communion with divinity. You may prefer to have a glass of juice and some cookies or sweet bread. Carbohydrates are very good in assisting you to ground your energy. If you have any excess energy, you can place your hands on the altar and feel the energy drain into it, or you can place your hands on the ground and do the same thing.

You may also wish to meditate at this time. Simply sit back and relax, allowing the angels to minister to you and assist in bringing peace and tranquillity into your life.

Closings

We have already gone over quarter dismissals. Please remember to stand in the middle of your circle and thank both deity and the angelic forces that have assisted you.

Don't forget your guardian angel, either. I'm sure some thanks would be appreciated. Many people like to utter a closing prayer or benediction at this time. Pull up your circle, then ground and center.

Angel Communion

In communion you honor divinity. That's the idea of the ceremony. In the angel communion you will honor divinity and thank the angels for their assistance. You can incorporate communion within a ritual, or you can hold a ritual of communion by itself. For example, if you work magick often, I doubt you will use communion every time. It takes a while for you to perform. I perform the ceremony once a week, and it is not always on the same day due to various family activities.

You will need some sort of cake or bread, and either an alcoholic beverage (such as wine) or juice. Most of us these days opt for the juice. Keep both the bread and the juice container covered before the ceremony. Have everything prepared before your ritual so you won't have to go scrabbling for it at an inopportune time.

Uncover the bread. Fold the cover neatly and set it on the left side of your altar. Consecrate and bless the bread by making a banishing pentagram over it, saying:

> *From heaven above and earth below, I call forth the angelic hosts.*
> *I stir the energies counterclockwise 'round, and banish all negativity in this bread.*
> *I stir the energies clockwise 'round to bring forth peace, harmony, and love.*
> *I invoke the blessings of the Lord and Lady, consecrating this bread*
>   *for divine communion.*

Lay your hands over the bread and feel the essence of divinity pouring through the top of your head, down through your hands, and into the bread. Tear off a piece of the bread (don't cut it). Before you eat it, say:

> *I put this bread into my body as a sacrament to* [name your divinity here].
> *May I be blessed throughout this day and evermore with peace, harmony, and love.*
> *So mote it be.*

Uncover the juice. Pour it into a consecrated and blessed cup. Cover the container and place it on the left side of your altar. Consecrate and bless the cup by making a banishing pentagram over it, saying:

> *From heaven above and earth below, I call forth the angelic hosts.*
> *I stir the energies counterclockwise 'round, and banish all negativity in this liquid.*
> *I stir the energies clockwise 'round to bring forth peace, harmony, and love.*
> *I invoke the blessings of the Lord and Lady, consecrating this liquid*
>   *for divine communion.*

Lay your hands over the cup and feel the essence of divinity pouring through the top of your head, down through your hands, and into the cup. Say:

I put this liquid into my body as a sacrament to [name your divinity here].
May I be blessed throughout this day and evermore with peace, harmony, and love.
So mote it be.

Drink the contents.

Spend a few moments in meditation, contemplating the gifts of divinity.

Summary

In this chapter we have covered basic ritual format, and reviewed the intricate details involved in angelic ritual. Now it's time for you to start practicing. The more you do ritual, the better you will become at it. That doesn't mean the first workings you do will not succeed, but you will get more fluid and confident as you practice.

Seven

Guardian Angel Express

Be thou a bright flame before me,
Be thou a guiding star above me,
Be thou a smooth path below me,
Today, tonight, and forever.[1]

Trying to convince someone that he or she has a guardian angel is not an easy task. Our society exists in a material realm. Our lives depend on material items—food, shelter, clothing, heat, running water, etc. Surrounded by so many earthly needs,

1. *Carmina Gadelica Hymns and Incantations* by Alexander Carmichael, page 47.

sights, and sounds, we fail to recognize the subtleties of the universe—those things felt, but not seen.

I live in a small, rural town, where my clients are not normally open to mystical beliefs. Many of them have lived in a self-imposed prison most of their lives, catering only to their physical needs and desires. When I first began mentioning guardian angels during my sessions, my clients would look at me in utter disbelief. A witch who believes in angels? What was the world coming to?

I began incorporating angel messages with my Tarot card readings through the Temperance card. It's a logical choice, since this card depicts an angel encouraging the querent (the person for whom the reading is done) to mix and match his or her talents to the situation, to have patience with a matter, and to learn to seek divine intervention. I got many a raised eyebrow when I incorporated a message about contacting the querent's guardian angel.

Belief in angels, like religion, rests entirely on personal experience. Although the testimonies of others are interesting, the reader cannot interact with them. It is rather like reading *The Night Before Christmas*—"and what to my wondering eyes did appear, but ... eight tiny reindeer." You read it, but you know you don't believe it. Still, you love it just the same.

No book, discussion, television program, or movie can convince you that angels exist. You need to take the initial step to invite them into your life, to acknowledge their presence in order to experience their wondrous gifts and assistance. I've found that by interacting with angels, my life goes more smoothly, coincidences turn into everyday occurrences, and I have a better outlook on life. I can't prove to you that they exist, but I can prove that my life is fuller and more harmonious because I believe in them.

Guardian angels are how you perceive them to be. Some people see their guardians as warriors, others as mild and beautiful women, and still others as aged sages with authoritative demeanor. The diaries of the German mystic Mechtilde, known as the Ancilla Domini, who died in 1919, enjoyed wide circulation because she described a visual relationship with her guardian angel and many of the angels of the celestial court during her lifetime. Her writings tell us that the guardian angels of those who experience intense suffering on earth wear a crown and clothing of crimson. The guardian angels of innocent souls wear white. The guardian angels of children are often dressed in blue.[2] It is quite possible that Mechtilde picked up on the auras around specific individuals, which does correspond to what occultists know about auric colors.

---

2. *Angel Power* by Janice T. Connell, page 100.

Guardian by My Side

As with other mystical concepts, many legends surround guardian angels. Some people believe we have only one guardian angel at our side throughout this lifetime to help us make important decisions and protect us. Others believe each human has thousands of guardian angels. Still others hold the belief that, although we have one angel assigned to us, others come to our aid when we are in deep trouble or when we begin various projects where their help can be of assistance. As one progresses spiritually, various angels may visit us at intervals, helping us along and teaching us what we need to know. Finally, some individuals believe that angels are our higher selves—the part of us that is spiritual in nature and attuned to the universe.

When people look at me as if I have a screw loose because I tell them to ask their guardian angel for guidance, I just say, "Try it. What can you lose? Nobody is going to hear you—except the angels."

Over the years, many tales of angels have come my way. For example, while writing this chapter, a Wiccan from Idaho called me, asking about an organization I run. We got to chatting and I told her about this book and my work with the angels.

"You know," she said. "I had the strangest experience last night. Things have been really bad around here. I almost got shot by poachers on my land. They leveled a gun at me and everything! I thought I was a dead woman, but for some reason right when I thought I was gonna get it, they lowered their weapons, got back in their truck, and drove away. I was so upset that I walked down to the creek. I love my land and I've been having a lot of problems with poachers. I sat down on the creek bank and cried my heart out. After a while, I got real sleepy and lay down on the bank. I dozed off. An hour later, someone started shaking my shoulder. Opening my eyes slowly, I looked around. There she was, standing right over me—a raven-haired, green-eyed beauty. She said, 'Wake up, wake up. If you lie here all night, you'll freeze to death in your sleep. You've got to go home now.' Then she disappeared. She was right; February nights can kill you out here."

When I asked the woman about the raven-haired beauty, she said, "I've been seeing her since I was a little girl. She wears leather and carries a double-edged ax." Although this is not the standard delicate, soft image of a celestial being, this force is truly a guardian angel. Oh, I forgot to tell you what this lady does for a living: she drives trucks and hauls explosives. Can you think of a better guardian for her? I can't.

Angels are what you perceive them to be. They are helping hands, loving thoughts, and bits of wisdom formatted precisely for you. They meet your energies atom for atom, molecule for molecule. A good friend of mine describes her guardian angel this way: "He has a killer body, long dark hair, and black wings. I don't think of him in a sexual way, but he is there when I need him. He's so stable. When I reach out to touch him in my mind, it is those massive wings that make me feel so comfortable." Think about the word guardian, which means protector and helper.

The guardian angel of one of my hypnotherapy clients surprised both of us by popping up during a past-life regression session. "There she was, standing in the middle of a field. At first, I didn't realize she was my guardian angel. She was a Native American maiden with long, black braids. I loved the impish grin on her face. She didn't have wings, but she could fly anyway. Her dress was brown with a colorful, beaded design of red, yellow, and black. She told me she'd been with me since the day I was born. I received the impression that she was an ancestor of mine. She can heal, and she said she would be with me until the day I die."

Taking Charge

When you actively seek to contact your guardian angel (or any angel), you are stating in a positive manner to the universe that you are prepared to change your life. You are eager to take responsibility for your own actions. You're not going to blame your problems on your parents, your teachers, your friends, your spouse, your boss, your children, etc. "I'm prepared to clean up my act" is the motto we begin with when we contact the angels. We are seeking divine intervention in our lives, and are ready to change to bring ourselves into balance with the universe.

Angelic energies are kind. They will move as fast, or as slow, as you personally need. Their decisions on how to help you do not rest on corporate back stabbing, money, sex, family jealousy, or overall greed. Their actions are pure and dedicated to raising your spiritual being. Angels are special because they hold no hidden agendas.

Your first task in working with a guardian angel is to allow yourself to take an inventory of your life. Begin clearing out old hatreds and sorrows. Get rid of those crusty, yucky experiences. Ask your guardian angel to shine his or her light on them, so you can deal with the issues one at a time. Humans carry too many unnecessary burdens. Often these psychological bonds lead to dysfunctional behavior. As you unlock yourself from the prison of condemnation, your outlook on life will be fresher, cleaner, and more exciting than before.

You can start by writing a weekly ritual for yourself. Tailor the words to fit your lifestyle. It doesn't have to be long and involved to get the point across and change your vibrational frequency. When it comes from your heart, it is perfect.

Meeting Your Guardian Angel

How you choose to establish contact with your guardian angel is entirely up to you. Here are some ideas:

In meditation. You can meet and commune with your guardian angel at any time during your meditation process.

In prayer. Talk to your guardian angel. Tell him or her what you need. Here is a lovely little prayer, which is a variation of one taught to Catholic children:

Angel of the Goddess, my guardian dear,
To whom Her love commits me here;
Enter this day (or night), be at my side,
To light and guard, to rule and guide.

In a letter. Sit down and write a letter to your guardian angel. Explain why you would like to contact him or her. Don't be shy. No one but an angel is ever going to read this letter. Let go. Write as if you wished to tell your thoughts to your best friend. When you are finished, take the letter to your altar and burn it. Scatter the ashes to the winds. Soon you will hear from your guardian angel.

In a want ad. I have talked about this earlier in the book. However, I'd like you to know that the want ads I wrote brought results in less than two weeks.

In a poem or other expression of art. One of the nicest ways to commune with your guardian angel is through your own natural talents. This includes anything you do well—drawing, painting, sewing, crafts, poetry, writing, etc.

Simply start talking. Feeling down? Lonely? Talk to your guardian angel. Are you excited, happy, thrilled to be alive? Guardian angels enjoy hearing about the great things in your life and how you feel you are progressing. They will also listen to the weighty thoughts you have. What is divinity? How do I fit into the universe? What is my mission? Do I have one, or several? By engaging in dialogue with the angels, you are allowing the angels to relate back to you. You may get flashes of insight, wise answers to your question via that calm little voice in your head, images of things, etc.

A friend of mine recently went through a nasty divorce. "When things got tough," she said, "I would talk to my angels." She has two who served as both bodyguards and spiritual strength points. "They're big dudes. I feel them around me all the time. I'm so glad I met my angels. They make me feel a lot better—more confident."

All it really takes is for you to open your heart and your mind. Take a few moments right now and ask your guardian angel to become known to you. I am sure you won't be disappointed.

Helping Establish Contact

In magick we learn that the universe carries correspondences—items, places, visual and non-visual images—that are in sympathy with each other. Let's discuss a few items that can help you connect with your guardian angel.

Statues

By placing a statue of an angel where you live or work, you can draw angelic energies toward you. A statue is a reminder that you are not alone in the universe, and that loving and caring energies are always around you. Empower statues with divine energy. The energy in the statue constantly focuses on transmuting negative energies into positive ones.

I do many Tarot readings for abused women. Several women (and men, too) come to me on the brink of divorce, trying to make the right move for both themselves and their children. During these sessions we talk about mundane items—local attorneys who have good track records, how these women should conduct themselves in court, how to deal with family members and friends who are either for or against their decision to leave the abuser, and so on. We also talk about spiritual things, such as where they can draw strength during this difficult time.

I always suggest that they purchase an angel statue and place it in the room where most of the arguments occur. I instruct them to cleanse, consecrate, and empower it to protect the room, and transmute negative energy to positive energy, love, and light. Although it does not "solve" the problem, the ladies report the room contains a more soothing atmosphere, and brings a quicker resolution of the problem—usually through getting the abuser out of the house permanently. When all the fireworks cease and the client is moving forward in her life, I visit the house and do a proper cleansing ritual.

Jewelry

One of the nicest gifts you can ever give anyone is a guardian angel pin. They range from inexpensive ($1.50) to elaborate. When I have the extra money, I visit a local store and purchase a bag of these pins. As you pin it on the person, say, "All you need to do is ask, and your angel will help you. This little pin reminds you that you are loved and not alone in the universe. So mote it be."

As soon as they get the pin, some of the people clutch their clothing and say, "Help me, help me, help me!" shaking the pin and shirt in their hands. All these individuals have been happy with the assistance they received.

One Friday evening I made a special dinner for my children and my dad (my husband, dutiful man that he is, had to work late). We ate dinner by candlelight. With dessert I told everyone at the table I had a special gift for them. I reached in a bag and pulled out a guardian angel pin for each person at the table. As I pinned it on each of them, I told them all how much I loved them, and that any time they were in trouble and I wasn't around to help them, they should call on their guardian angel. "Even if I'm right there," I said, "you can still talk to your guardian angel in your head. The angels will listen to you." All the children thought this was a wonderful idea. Each night they lay their pin on my desk (so it won't get lost) and every morning they pin it on before they go to school. That way they consciously take both my energy and the energies of the angels with them to school. My father keeps his pin in his pocket. Each night he puts his change on the dresser, then gently sets the pin on top. In the morning, both the angel and the change go into his pocket.

Artwork

Paintings of angels can help us access the angelic realms. Hang one over your altar, or in the room where you do most of your meditation exercises. I have a friend who carries a copy of an angel painting in his wallet for both peace and prosperity.

Angel Clothing

This does not mean you have to parade around with angels stitched all over your clothes, though you could if you wished. When you start working with angels, I warn you now, there are things about your personal appearance that will change. Perhaps it is your taste in clothing, or perhaps you will change your hair, even redecorate your house. I have found that when working with angelic forces one's self-esteem rises, and you urge yourself into creativity. Often our first attempt at change is a personal one. You look into the mirror and think, "Yuck! I don't believe I've been looking like this! What can I do to improve myself?" Hence you change something about yourself—and you like it. This encourages you to change something else, and the creativity keeps rolling into other areas of our lives. You may find yourself improving both your personal appearance and your environment to create harmony. The act of creation, and the results, urge others to do the same thing.

For example, some acquaintances who began working with angel magick started dressing in more flowing garments (nothing outrageous, however). These classy gals chose to sew some of their own clothing, and picked colors they felt were more harmonious to their being. I noticed the men wore their clothing in a more easy manner. Those who were slightly unkempt began to take pride in their appearance. Both women and men working with angel magick have lost unwanted weight and found themselves interested in physical fitness programs. Angels like individualism and creativity, and will assist you in finding your own space in the universe where you are not ashamed to be yourself.

After you have first made contact with your guardian angel, you will find many messages coming through to you. Sometimes a message is subconscious, then surfaces later when triggered by an event. The more you work with your guardian angel, the more information and enlightenment you will receive. As with any spiritual study, the more you practice, the better you will get.

Guardian Angel Junk Jar

Turn this exercise into a ritual if you like, added to a morning devotional hour once a week or done before bedtime. I have designed this ritual to assist you in clearing out the dirt and cobwebs in your life, whether you perceive it as an old hurt or something that is happening right now.

You will need a jar, several slips of paper, and a pencil or pen. Choose a time when you know you will not be disturbed for at least an hour. Go to your angel altar and perform the angelic devotion, including the Lesser Banishing Ritual (see page 30).

Ground and center. Sit down with your slips of paper and pencil. Write down all the negative thoughts and events you can't seem to release. You can write why this negativity still hangs with you, or simply write "I don't know why I'm still dealing with this, but it hurts," or whatever you are feeling. You may like to play a tape of peaceful music, rev up the CD player, or even hum to yourself.

Fold each paper so you can't see what you have written on it, and place it in your junk jar. Leave the junk jar on the altar. Ground and center. You're done for this session.

When you feel ready to deal with the junk jar, continue as follows. You will need a lighter and a fire-safe bowl.

At your angelic altar, do your altar devotion and the Lesser Banishing Ritual, then take one of the papers out of the junk jar. Don't root for any one in particular.

Read the paper. Then ask your guardian angel to help you deal with this crusty thing. Hold the paper by the corner like it smells like you-know-what. This is definitely something you want to get rid of, right?

Ground and center. Visualize your guardian angel by your side, helping you to discard the grime in your life. Hold the paper over the bowl and say:

> *I commit thee to the angels. I transmute all negative energy attached to this situation into positive, life-affirming loving energy. Now!*

Burn the paper.

Ground and center. When the fire goes out, return the ashes to the earth, saying:

> *Blessings upon you Earth Mother*
> *Who absorbs pain and sorrow*
> *And transmutes it to positive energy*
> *For the use of all your children.*

You are done for this session. Wait a few days before you do another junk jar burning. If you like, you can make a "junk jar day" once a week. When your jar is empty, you can refill it as life progresses. You will find that the number of papers in your jar will decrease as you work with the angels in your life. Someday it will be time to put the junk jar away. Keep track of the success you have in your angel journal. For example, indicate how you felt after you burned that paper about your ex-spouse, and the pain you've been experiencing since the breakup. Or perhaps you lost a close family member or friend and never quite got over it. That's a junk jar thing, too.

Many people like to decorate their angel junk jars. It can have any design you choose, though I suggest it be pleasing to the eye, so that the moment you put the trash in the jar you know that the process of transmutation has begun. If you are not into arts and crafts, you may like to plan an angel day to find your special jar.

Angels and Perception

As you work with your guardian angel, your perceptions on life will change. For example, I used to have a boss who would not allow his employees to walk in his office and say, "I have a problem." I had to say, "I have a situation that needs to be addressed." Then I was to outline the situation briefly and offer possible solutions. It took a while to get used to remodeling my behavior. I learned to think about a situation first and consider its possible reasons for existing, followed by various steps that could be taken to resolve it.

I've found that angels see our experiences in the same way. When you talk to your guardian angel about difficulties you experience, you need to think of them as situations, not problems. A problem means you have already decided the occurrence is a bad thing, when possibly it could be a learning experience, a situation that needed to happen to help you further your career, or another beneficial turn of events. Even though they may be hard to deal with emotionally, sometimes problems are really gifts in disguise.

When something happens to you, step back and say: "Why did this happen right now in my life? What is this experience trying to show me?" Learn not to panic. Fear stops you from thinking rationally about the situation. Handle good times the same way. For example, what if you meet someone who is very different from yourself, and you spend a great afternoon together? You know you will probably never see this person again. You might want to look back on the experience and pose those questions to your guardian angel. Why did I meet this person? What should I learn from this day? You may not get a bells-and-whistles answer right away, but eventually the pieces will fall into place.

Over the years I've been enlightened more than once by my Tarot clients. I've learned that everyone perceives the world differently. Even things that I thought were "standard" in society are not. Let's take the idea of love as an example. To me, love is caring, nurturing, honor, and respect. But I found that not all people see love the same way I do. Some see money and love as inseparable entities. Many clients equate sex and love. Others see love as security and safety in their lives. Indeed, every human has a different criterion for defining love, perceiving where loving feelings come from, and how love needs to be manifested for them.

When working any type of magick, you need to be aware of your own perceptions. What do you need to feel loved? What do you need to feel secure? How do you perceive money? Success? Friendship? Is quality or quantity more important? Once you've thought about it, you may want to change your thinking on certain issues. Perhaps you have set up some negative blocks, not allowing yourself to see the whole picture, or have gotten stuck in a rut rather than looking ahead.

Ask your guardian angel to help you evaluate your perceptions. What issues do you need to work on to bring harmony into your environment? What can you enhance? What do you need to get rid of? Have you allowed others to control your perceptions of yourself and life in general? Your guardian angel will assist you in housecleaning your brain. All you have to do is ask.

And It Harm None

Angelic work will keep you on your ethical toes. Help from the angels always manifests in the highest good for everyone concerned. This is an advantage when working magick with them and communing with the universe. None of us really wants to hurt anyone when working magick. Sadly, some people stop studying magick because they are afraid that they will change the course of events by accident and may harm someone in the process, even though what they thought they were doing would help everyone. When working with angels, this concern is a moot point. Magickal students who are prone to meddling in others' affairs won't get far if they are only taught angelic magick. When they are ready to learn other disciplines, the angels will know and move them along. If they never learn the values and principles necessary to continue their training, the angels will eventually shut them down. The person will turn to other pursuits and no one, including the student or teacher, will be hurt by the experience.

I've trained quite a few people in the last ten years, and have come to the conclusion that the first type of magick introduced to a new student should be angel magick and contact with their guardian angel. In this way you can work both with student and angel, making the best choices on training for everyone concerned.

Guardian Angel Dialogue

This exercise is designed to get you talking to your guardian angel. You will need some paper, a pen or pencil (or your computer), and about ten minutes of your time.

Create two characters: a guardian angel, and the human for whom the angel is responsible. The human doesn't have to be yourself, if you don't want it to be. Think about this as a scene in a play. You are going to let yourself go wild with this one.

Close your eyes. Take a deep breath. Then another. Imagine your two characters sitting across from each other. The setting is your choice. The human and angel are smiling at each other. The angel shakes the human's hand and introduces him/herself.

Open your eyes. Write a dialogue that takes place between the two characters. You don't have to delineate on paper who is speaking, because you will already know that. Later, you can go back and put an "A" beside the angel thoughts and an "H" to represent the human thoughts. Just let yourself go. You can be as bizarre as you want. No one is going to know, right?

After ten minutes put your pencil down and close your eyes. Relax and take a deep breath or two. Thank your guardian angel for helping you with this exercise.

Twenty-four hours later, read your dialogue. Does the dialogue make you feel better? Is there a message there for you?

Here is my dialogue. The angelic being is Murphy and the human is Sherman.

Murphy: Greetings, Sherman.

Sherman: Greetings.

Murphy: How can I help you today?

Sherman: I'm stuck on this manuscript. There is so much I want to put across about angels but I seem to be falling flat on my face.

Murphy: One man's floor is another man's ceiling.

Sherman: I understand that, but I want to make people's lives better.

Murphy: You've been doing pretty good so far. They like your other books. They will like this one.

Sherman: *(whine)* I need more material.

Murphy: No problem. We just did the angel brainstorming together. That worked.

Sherman: Yes, it did. Thanks for giving me that.

Murphy: I know—how about an angel check?

Sherman: What's that?

Murphy: Oh, an idea I had for people to bring prosperity into their lives.

Sherman: How does it work?

Murphy: Easy. Draw a check on a piece of paper, big enough for you to write in. It will be a check from the First Angelic Bank of the Universe. Got it?

Sherman: Yeah. I think so. So what do you do with the check?

Murphy: Fill it out, of course. You could write down the amount of money you need, or you could draw out health, peace, sincerity. Anything you want. The First Angelic Bank is limitless and it doesn't discriminate. If you are more modern, you could make yourself a credit card—ha, ha!

Sherman: Hey! Cool idea! I'll try it! Thanks, Murphy.

Murphy: *(smile)* That's what angels are for.

Thanks to Murphy, a sample of a guardian angel check appears below.

The Angels
Halo Way, Infinity

Pay to the order of

$

Dollars

First Angelic Bank
Universe Lane
Anywhere or Everywhere

For

Your Guardian Angel

:0120000034: 567890123456

Your Guardian Angel and Magick

Before you came to the earth plane, you were the center of attention. There was a big conference about you. Your guardian angel wasn't chosen by spinning a roulette wheel, or drawing numbers out of a golden hat. Guardian angels and humans are paired much more carefully than that. You see, the universe knows you are a very special person. You are a part of that small group of people who desire to go beyond the material realm, and seek to manifest spiritual light, love, and laughter on the physical plane through the gift of magick. This requires a very special guardian angel indeed.

All your life your angel has been whispering to you in dreams, feelings, coincidences, visions, and impulses, trying to help you remember your tasks here on Earth. Your guardian angel is not superstition or fantasy. If you don't believe me, ask him or her to prove it to you, and be specific on what it will take for you to believe. My comment was: "I need bells and whistles." I got precisely that. Hitting me over the head wouldn't have been any clearer.

Your guardian angel, whether you know it or not, has been recognized as energy of the highest importance in Western magick for several centuries. All is believed possible when one converses with his or her guardian angel, as this being is an individual guide to many levels of existence. Although your guardian angel links you to divinity, it is not divinity in and of itself, nor will it stand as an intermediary in your direct communication with God/dess (such as a priest in a confessional in the Catholic religion).

Those who teach magick today do you a great disservice by saying that angels (and in particular your guardian angel) belong to a particular religious sect, and since they don't believe in that sect, there are no such things as angels. Boo. Hiss. Cutting off the angels puts you on a leash that belongs to someone's boxed belief system. I don't care what anyone tells you, once you have worked with your guardian angel in ritual, there is nothing else like it. To shut this power source off deliberately is to cut you off from a method of learning and helping others. Every time I see a magickal person who throws a tantrum because I believe in angels and work with them, I see a spoiled little magician who won't go beyond the realm of possibility, and I sadly know this person will never become a true adept.

With your guardian angel in tow, you become exceedingly efficient in magickal acts. Things that were difficult or took more work can now be accomplished with ease. The guardian angel helps you to learn about and gain insight into any situation, and thereby gain harmony in your life. The guardian angel helps remove psychic and mental blocks leading to success. Your guardian angel is both messenger and instrument of the divine light.

You cannot manipulate angels. They have orders that go beyond your comprehension and follow the rules of the cosmos. That's why they are angels. You can ask them for help, you can seek guidance, you can work with them, but you can't tell them what to do, when to do it, and how it should be done. That's not your territory. Spirits can be manipulated; angels cannot (if they are really angels).

False Angels

While cruising on American Online® one night I read a message from someone who insisted there were false angels. What an oxymoron, I thought. It rather reminded me of people calling Witches bad. What a joke. Real Witches are not minions of Satan (they don't even believe in that guy). Real Witches take an oath to protect and serve humanity. Here I saw the same sort of thing. A true angel wouldn't be, couldn't be, false. There's simply no such thing.

This "thing" the person talked about told them to drink poison. Now, I ask you, what angel, what being of light, would tell this poor person to drink poison? None.

No real angel would even entertain such an idea. After this person's story, several others added messages—yes, yes, they said, there are false angels. My first reaction was: "Where are these people's heads?" Not in the angelic realms, that's for sure.

There are many dabblers in the spiritual, new age, and occult worlds. This person, and those who agreed with him, were dabblers. They hadn't done any real study on the subject of angels, but were willing to do something dumb (or agree with a foolish action) because they thought of it themselves. We must all learn to take responsibility for our own actions and not build excuses on shaky foundations. Yes, there is evil in the world—everyone knows that—but it doesn't manifest with the angels.

Guardian Angels and Receptivity

When working with your guardian angel, you have to learn to stop thinking that things happen by coincidence. Actually, I don't believe there is any such animal as coincidence. Most things happen for a reason, and we're just too closed and blocked to realize it. To work with angels you must acknowledge from the beginning that you need to be receptive to all sorts of communications. Angels can be very subtle, especially if you don't pay attention to them most of the time. If you have tried to contact your guardian angel and don't trust the calm voice in your head, or are sure angels can't talk to you that way, it is okay. You can use other means to get messages.

When we read things, we have a habit of believing them. I'm not saying this is always a good thing, but situations and information in print seem to penetrate our thoughts easily because our brain is in the physical; it is something we can touch and see (in a manner of speaking). In the case of the media—radio, books, television, movies—we can see, hear, and touch. Using our physical senses puts more of an impression on our minds, and we then think this is reality.

There are several simple techniques that magickal people have been using for a long time to obtain immediate answers to big and little problems. They are all very easy and start with the same sort of wording:

Dear guardian angel,
Let the third song on the radio after this one contain a message for me
concerning [state your issue].

Wait for that song and I'm sure you will be enlightened. This also works for the television:

Dear guardian angel,
I'm running out of ideas. Let one word, or a sentence, or perhaps a picture of something
spark my creativity, and send me in a good direction for this project while I watch this
television program.

The movies:

Dear guardian angel,
I don't know which movie to see tonight. Lead me to the movie that will give me the most information, or the right emotional input for my spirituality.

Who knows; you guardian angel might feel you need to lighten up and send you to the most uproarious comedy you've ever seen. A book/magazine/newspaper:

Dear guardian angel,
This is my problem/question [state the problem/question; be specific]. I will open this book and let the pages fall where they may. Please guide me to the right sentence that will help me.

On a computer network:

Dear guardian angel,
I need information on the following [state specifically what you need]. Please lead me to the right person or area on the network to help me get my answer.

Being open to the unknown allows your mind to open to the energies of the angels. The more receptive you are, the faster you will get information, the more spiritual you will become, the stronger your faith will be (getting tired yet?), and so forth. The next step is to learn to be responsive to the messages you get. Angels never send negative messages or put evil thoughts in your head—then they would not be angels.

Team Angels

It is thought that as we reach higher and higher levels of spirituality in life, we are assigned additional angels to help our guardian angel, sort of like a specialized team chosen for each specific individual who goes beyond the ordinary humdrum of human existence. This team is drawn from any of the Nine Choirs (see Chapter 2). When you work magick with the angels, you are immediately assigned these team players to help you manifest positive energies that are beyond what you could do alone. Although some angel believers think that you can't access the various groups of angels unless you have more than one human present, I don't agree. However, working with angels with groups of humans is beneficial to human consciousness, and I do not negate the power of many minds together. First, though, you have to learn to work with the angels by yourself, so you are confident. You also need to clean up your own life, make it more hospitable to angelic energy, before you can work with other people. You will know when you are ready.

The Angels and the Income Tax Fiasco

My father worked faithfully for many years. The year after he retired, he came to me in quite a quandary. It seems his tax preparer up and died the week before his taxes needed filing. My husband suggested a particular business, but said he didn't know how good they were. Off my father went, clutching his papers. He returned a few hours later, highly agitated. The tax preparer told him he would have to pay an extra $2,000 on his return. I thought this was odd, but didn't really know what to do about it. I'm no mathematical genius.

I took a few moments from my hectic day and quietly asked my guardian angel to help my father. I didn't think it was fair that he should be penalized just because he finally reached that golden stage of retirement. As I opened my eyes, the phone rang. It was a girlfriend I hadn't talked to in over three months, asking me to go to lunch with her. Impulsively I asked her if she knew of someone reliable who could help senior citizens with their taxes. She immediately gave me the name and number of a reputable fellow, and even offered to call him for me and make the arrangements not only for my father's taxes, but mine as well. In twenty-four hours my father's taxes were computed correctly, saving him more than the $2,000 amount. Furthermore, the person my friend had recommended found an additional error made by the first preparer, saving him even more money.

When my father returned from the man's office, he was all smiles. He told me about the meeting and how well it went. I grinned and said, "That's great!"

He stepped back for a moment and got an odd look in his eye. "You knew all the time it would work out, didn't you? I bet my news isn't a surprise at all!"

I looked at him carefully and said, "The angels never cease to amaze me."

Eight

Angels and the Element of Air

*A*ir, fire, water, earth—these elements of creation function as an integral part of our plane of existence. Whether we are aware of their presence or not, our energies mix with these holy elements every day. We need the air to fill our lungs and bring us rain for healthy crops. We use fire to heat our water for bathing, and warm our homes when outside temperatures plummet. We need the water to sustain not only our bodies, but provide nourishment for plants

115

and animals. We build our homes on the Earth and enjoy the fruits of her soil. To keep our world functioning properly through the structure of these elements, is it any wonder that specific angels have been assigned to each element?

If these angels are so busy with their elemental tasks, would they be interested in working with you? Absolutely! The angels of the elements know how important human interaction and magick is to the cosmos, and will be delighted if you decide to work magick with them or ask for their assistance. By studying and working with air, fire, water, and earth, you naturally pull balance and harmony into your life. You become more aware of the physical world around you and how much care that world requires. These elemental angels are eager for you to harness the gifts of the elements.

When working with these angels (or any angels), keep in mind the following:

One calls angels (do not summon or command them).

Work for positive ends only—angels will not do no-nos.

You can call the essence of the energy, not the angelic name, if you want.

Always work with your guardian angel.

Be creative with your magickal work.

Be sure to acknowledge the essence of the element, as well as the angelic force.

I like using the element of air in magick because you can't see it, but you know it is there; sort of a testament to things unseen. Used in magickal applications for centuries, this element can be either a friend or terror of humanity. Powerful, swift, strong, and invisible, it displaces things quickly, blows away negativity, and ushers in a fresh outlook on all things. The angels of air move in the same fashion. Strong, compelling creatures, they assure purity and peace with the breath of divinity. By working with this element and its angels, you can achieve all sorts of beneficial magicks.

Air represents intellect, communication, knowledge, concentration, the ability to know and understand the mysteries, movement (usually swift), the unlocking of secrets, telepathy, memory, hypnosis, altered states of consciousness, and wisdom.

Regulated breathing is also very important in magick. Messages from the angels come through to you more easily if you are in a relaxed state of mind and body, and this means slow, even breathing. One way to improve your breathing is to meditate every day. Remember, good meditation skills make a happy, balanced, peaceful person.

Angels of Air Meditation

Choose a time when you will not be disturbed. You will need at least fifteen minutes. Get in a comfortable sitting or lying position. Try not to cross your arms and legs, as this can disrupt the flow of energy in your body.

Breathe deeply at least three times. In and out; nice and slow. Ground and center.

Close your eyes and relax; let everything go.

Relax. Imagine a summer breeze moving down your body from head to toe. Let it remove the day's negative experiences, leaving you feeling safe and secure.

Visualize yourself protected by a golden bubble of light. Allow yourself to feel warm and loved. Call on your guardian angel for assistance in this meditation.

Visualize various things associated with the element of air, such as a feather, softly swaying willow trees, or rippling summer grasses. Let this element surround you. Feel the peace and harmony of the universe extend and encompass you.

Now visualize the angel of air. If you cannot see anything right away, don't worry that you aren't doing it right. Everyone perceives the world differently, so what you see is right for you. Ask the angel of air to bring the gifts of air to your life.

Continue to relax; drift if you like. When you are ready to come out of your altered state, take three deep breaths, drawing happiness and energy into your body. Open your eyes and say: "I am wide awake and alert."

Ground and center. Keep track of your progress in your angel journal. Repeat this meditation any time you wish.

Elemental Air Correspondences

Air energy is projective in nature. Here is a selection of correspondences to assist you when working with the element of air, and the angels of air.

Astrological signs: Gemini, Libra, Aquarius

Colors: Yellow, gold, the soft colors of dawn

Herbs: Fennel, hops, marjoram, parsley, sage, mint, dill, basil, oregano

Metals: Tin and copper

Musical instruments: Wind instruments

Places: Elevated areas such as mountains, towers, and airplanes; libraries, travel agencies, psychiatrist/psychologist/hypnotherapist's offices or places of mental healing (such as a gathering of like-minded individuals), schools, beaches

Rituals and requests: Mental healing, divinatory and esoteric study, to learn the truth of a matter, to remove negativity, recovering lost or stolen property or people, safe travel to anywhere

Scents: Highly fragrant flowers including roses (preferably white, pink, or yellow), essential oils (especially lavender or lily of the valley)

Sense: Hearing

Sports: Snow skiing, running, archery, sky diving, bungee jumping, hang gliding

Stones: Citrine, moss agate, rose quartz, quartz

Time: Dawn

Types of magick: Divination, self-improvement, mind, wind

Visualizations: Feathers, smoke, incense, floating leaves

Angels Generally Associated with Air

Angels of air (general): Chasan, Casmaron, Cherub, Iahmel

Angels of altitudes: Barachiel, Gabriel, Gediel

Angel of announcements: Sirushi (Persian)

Angels of birds: Arael, Anpiel

Angels of the clouds: General, unnamed (created on the first day of creation)

Angel of communication and protection: Ambriel

Angel of the dawn: Hlm hml

Angel of doves: Alphun

Angel of dreams: Gabriel

Angel of free will: Tabris

Angel of grace: Ananchel

Angels of hurricanes: Zamiel, Zaafiel

Angel of intellectual achievements: Akriel

Angel of inventions: Liwet

Angel of memory and tolerance: Mupiel

Angel of moderation: Baglis

Symbol of the Element of Air

Angel of noonday winds: Nariel

Angel of the north wind: Cahiroum

Angel of pure wisdom, knowledge, and learning: Dina

Angel of philosophers and meditation: Iahhel

Angel of positive thoughts: Vohumanah

Angels of prayers: Akatriel, Metatron, Raphael, Sandalphon, Michael

Angel of protection for libraries, archives, and places of learning: Harahel

Angel of purity: Taharial (cleanses both thoughts and surroundings)

Angel of secrets and hidden knowledge: Satarel

Angel of sky: Sahaqiel

Angels of storms: Zakkiel, Zaamael

Angels of thunder: Ramiel, Uriel

Angel of truth: Armait (also harmony, goodness, and wisdom)

Angel of those who seek the truth: Haamiah

Angel of twilight: Aftiel

Angels of the whirlwind: Rashiel, Zavael

Angels of the wind: Moriel, Ruhiel, Rujiel, Ben Nez

Angel of writing inspiration: Ecanus

Angels of the Four Winds

The angels of the four winds are Raphael (east), Michael (south), Gabriel (west), and Uriel/Ariel (north). We have already talked about these angels in detail (see Chapter 2), but let's talk about the winds and how they mix with magickal study.

When working with the angels of the four winds, be sure to turn in the proper direction to hail them. For example, to call the angels of the east wind, face your body east, open your arms, and speak clearly. Wind angels don't like humans who mumble. The angels of the four winds are assertive and want you to learn to be proud of yourself and stand your ground.

To find the best times to work with these angels, you may want to purchase a wind sock. Although the weather channel on cable television is a great guide, you may live in a valley or hollow and the direction could be different. You could even decorate your wind sock with angels if you are handy with needle and thread.

When hanging it, ask that the angels of the four winds guard your property and keep your family safe from harm. Be sure your windsock is visible from a window, unless you want to run outside and hang it up every time you wish to use the angels of the four winds. (I don't know about you, but you won't catch me outside when it is twenty below zero.)

If you can't afford a wind sock, don't worry. Take a dowel and tie a strip of cloth to it, then stick it deep enough in the ground so it won't blow over, yet high enough so you can see it from a window. Use a yellow or white strip, and embroider or paint magickal symbols on the cloth that correspond to the angels of the four winds.

Angels of the East Wind

When you think of the angels of the east wind, think of spring breezes and the cold winter removing its icy claws from the land. This is a lightly scented, warm waft of air that tickles the nose and gets the sluggish blood singing through your veins, or that tingle you get when you learn something new or get a concept right. Angels of the east wind bring promise, new ventures, exciting beginnings, and the hope that tomorrow will be a better day. These angels love to work with people who have great ideas and are willing to put them into action. They guide the movers and shakers of the universe. If you have a humanitarian project, ask for guidance from the angels of the east wind.

These angels are very good at mass communication on a personal level. As angels of friendships, they can carry your messages to an entire family (whether by blood, soul, or mental connection). Call on the angels of the east wind for finding lost items or people, to find out the "real" truth on a matter, and to give yourself an intellectual boost or a head start on mental training.

Angels of the east wind concentrate on expansion. They adore positive affirmations. Before writing or practicing an affirmation, call on these angels to carry your messages to the divine source.

Ask these angels for help in any type of communication, including phone calls, letters, important documents and contracts, faxes, e-mail, television, newspapers, magazines, even the Internet! These angels work best when the wind blows from the east.

Sunrise magick lies under the auspices of the angels of the east wind. You can compose an angelic ritual for the dawn that includes a purification rite. Other magicks associated with dawn are study, employment, breaking addictions of all kinds, travel, releasing guilt and jealousy, the alert mind, and business success.

Invocation

Hail, angels of the east wind
Warm energies of the hopeful morning
Winds of action and communication
Enter here this sacred space
And lend your propulsion to my magick.

Angels of the South Wind

Think of the heavy fragrance of summer days, blazing afternoons and delicious sunset glories, when the air kisses your brow and the nights fill you with burning desire. Think of spicy, thick air, and you have the angels of the south wind—muscular, compassionate, creative creatures who sear the soul with divine illumination. These robust angels love firm decision-making and the pursuits of creativity. Of all the angels of the four winds, they love to laugh the most. They like jokes and amusements, hobbies, and a stress-free environment. They are definitely the angels of good clean fun.

The angels of the south wind are also associated with fire. Magicks that include candles, fire pits, lanterns, campfires, and flames in general are well attended by these angels. Naturally, they work best when the wind blows from the south.

Artists, musicians, dancers, and those involved in one-to-one combative sports are favorites of the angels of the south wind. They also enjoy any type of cooking venture, from the outdoor barbecue to elaborate French cuisine. Definitely the angels of daring-do, they work at assisting you in transformation, success, refinement, and purification.

Noon magick lies under the auspices of the angels of the south wind. This is a wonderful time to perform a ritual for renewed strength. Other magicks that fall under noon correspondences are protection, money, courage, and general success.

Invocation

> *Hail, angels of the south wind*
> *Fiery energies of noon creativity*
> *Winds of laughter and compassion*
> *Enter here this sacred space*
> *And lend your desire to my work.*

Angels of the West Wind

Think of the pungent odor of autumn leaves and the mist at sunset, stealing through the cooling dusk. This is the time of twilight enchantment, when crisp draughts of air dance through vibrant fall foliage. Think of cool, shapeshifting energy; beings who can undulate through any situation, no matter the odds—these are the angels of the west wind. Whenever spiritual healing and soul transformation are needed, you will find these angels.

Angels of the west wind are associated with the element of water. Magicks involving intuition, emotions, love, spirituality, and healing are their responsibility. Guardians of caregivers, marriage vows, and soul mates, the angels of the west interest themselves in the easy flow of life and the steady stream of harmony. Naturally, winds that blow from the west assist magickal work in the element of water. Angels of the west love religious rituals of all kinds, and lend sparkling energy and cleansing vibrations to your magickal endeavors.

These angels guard the gates of death, and will attend any funeral to ensure that both the living and the deceased find solace. Call these angels when you have lost a pet or person dear to you, as they will provide comfort and healing while spirit and human deal with the transformation of death.

Sunset magicks are a wonderful time for performing rituals of personal transformation. Other sunset correlations are transforming negative habits and patterns, breaking addictions, journeying within the self to find answers to important questions, weight loss, and grief transformation.

Invocation

> *Hail, angels of the west wind*
> *Cool energies of twilight enchantment*
> *Winds of healing and transformation*
> *Enter here this sacred space*
> *And lend your gentle flow to my magick.*

Angels of the North Wind

Think of the mighty jaws of a winter blizzard and the crackling cold of towers of glittering ice. Harsh, biting blasts of frigid, barren air coursing down through lonely, stark hollows at midnight—these are the angels of the north wind, with muscles of iron and the presence of overpowering giants.

Angels of the north wind are destructive in a positive way—this is a stern, forbidding wind that will gut any situation of negativity. They delight in ripping anger from the planet, in destroying those energies that seek to harm the universe. These chilly angels concern themselves with protection and balance, and although associated with the element of earth, they do not find entertainment in magicks of fertility or prosperity. You will find them in combative situations where you are trying to do what is right, or defending yourself from evil.

Excellent in court situations, guardians for police officers and armed service personnel, these angels don't take any guff and grind injustice beneath their mighty heels. Their time is midnight.

Midnight magicks are excellent for rites of psychism and spirituality. Other magicks associated with midnight are those involved with dreams, meditations, beauty, purification, friendship, stability, and fertility in all things.

Invocation

> *Hail, angels of the north wind*
> *Icy energies of midnight protection*
> *Winds of balance and justice*
> *Enter here this sacred space*
> *And lend your iron strength to this working.*

Guardian Angel Bells

One delightful idea for a family activity is to conduct a ritual involving the hanging of guardian angel bells outside your home. Each person blesses a bell that can withstand the weather at least for one full turn of the year. You choose the day that you think is most propitious for this activity. For example, everyone can do it at Spring Equinox or Easter, or it can be done on each person's birthday. The gentle ringing of the bells carries through the seasons, reminding you that your guardian angels are always nearby.

Take the bell(s) to your angel altar. Cleanse, consecrate, and empower them to ring true harmony, peace, and health into your life. Ask your guardian angel to bless them.

Take the bell(s) outside and hand them on a tree in your yard or on the eaves of your back porch.

Ground and center. Call the angels of the four winds and ask them to bless the bell(s).

Ceremony of Angel Lights

You can perform this ceremony at any time during the year. If you are Christian, you may wish to perform it around Christmas. If you are Wiccan, you may choose Candlemas (February 2) or Yule (December 21). Those of the Jewish faith may prefer Hanukah. However, if you like to do things outdoors, then Summer Solstice would be an ideal time.

Supplies:
 Twenty lunch-size paper bags
 Twenty votive tea candles
 Sand/non-flammable cat litter (at least one cup per bag)
 A pair of scissors
 The pattern of an angel (see next page)

Trace the pattern of an angel on each paper bag, then cut out the angel. Put one cup of sand/cat litter in the bottom of each bag. Place the candle on top of the sand. Arrange the bags so that they make a path to the altar—ten on either side.

The theme of this ceremony is to learn to walk with the angels. The officiator of the ceremony goes through first, lighting each candle, then lighting the illuminator candles on the altar. As each candle is lit, he/she says:

Guardian angel, take my hand, I am ready.
Angels of air, creating words and thoughts
Spreading the sweet air of wisdom with each candle flame
I walk with you on the path of light—

123

Angel bag pattern

124

> *Out of the darkness and into the radiance of the spirit.*
> *I now guide the way.*

Each person follows after, saying:

> *Guardian angel, take my hand, I am ready.*
> *Angels of air, creating words and thoughts*
> *Spreading the sweet air of wisdom with each step I take*
> *I walk with you on the path of light —*
> *Out of the darkness and into the radiance of the spirit.*

Stop at each set of candles and ask for some sort of help, or say something that carries an expression of honor and joy. For example, you could say: "I seek wisdom," "I thank the Goddess for my health," etc. You need not say the requests or words of honor aloud. Only divinity and the angels need to hear. When each individual reaches the altar, he or she should perform some sort of devotion, then step aside.

When everyone is finished, the officiator of the ceremony walks back down the path, extinguishing each candle. At the end of the path, he or she says:

> *Guardian angel, thank you for walking with me.*
> *Angels of air, stay if you like, go if you must.*
> *May I always walk with you on the path of light —*
> *Out of the darkness and into the radiance of the spirit.*
> *Hail and farewell.*

He or she then hands the angel candles to those who participated in the ceremony, so that they may take them home and use them on their altars.

Angel Dream Pillow

Having trouble remembering your dreams? Sew up three sides of a small cloth square, and fill it with mugwort and rose petals. Stitch it up; add a ribbon if you like. Place the sachet under your pillow. Draw the banishing pentagram on your pillow to rid it of any negativity. Before you go to sleep, place a pad and pen (or a tape recorder) beside your bed. Say the following before you close your eyes:

> *Angels of dreaming, angels of air*
> *Angel Gabriel, most beautiful and fair*
> *Angels watch over me with kindness and care.*
> *Dreams I now catch and hold them close*
> *I desire to remember what I need to know most.*

When you wake, immediately write down anything you can remember about your dream. If you can't interpret it right away, don't worry about it. Look at your notes a day or two later. It may take time for the meaning to sink into our conscious minds.

Angels and Online Services

Have you ever been in a chat room and somebody really unpleasant is there, disrupting the room? Here's a little ditty I made up one night and it worked wonderfully to change the atmosphere.

I hold the power in my hand
I raise my arm, I make my stand
Speed of air, swift of wind
Harmony I'm about to send
The angels sing, I whirl about
I throw the energy up and out!

Upon experimentation, I've found that it works wonders when you are under stress, or simply dealing with nasty, mean people, even if you are not a BBS freak like me. It sure makes surfing the Internet easier!

Sending Angel Messages

I've gotten many angel messages over the years from kind and generous people who read my books. Invariably, these letters and gifts come when I least expect them from people I don't even know, on days when I think my life is in the toilet. I am so grateful for these random acts of kindness. If you hear that a friend or an acquaintance has had a bad day, or some other unhappy event, why not send an angel note to them? You don't have to be long-winded about it. Just a short poem like this one will do:

A little note to let you know
I love your work, your kindness shows.
So go outside, take a big deep breath
And pray that all your needs be met.
I know the angels will listen to you
That's because I asked them to.
May love and light wing your way
May your spirit soar throughout the day.
May your troubles fly on a wing and a prayer
May your every day be sunny and fair.

If you don't like poetry, write a short note, letting the person know that he or she has made a difference in your day. I have a special box of note paper and a roll of stamps I keep on my desk, just to give someone a smile when I think they need it. It doesn't cost a lot, and spreads harmony and good cheer.

Nine

Angels and the Element of Fire

Fire—it seduces us with its inviting warmth, yet bares snapping fangs if we venture too close. An element of comfort or chaos, it eats the air we breathe and consumes anything that gets in its way.

Fire—the sacred element of temples and parlors must be controlled to exist harmoniously with humans. Yet in magick, we unleash its fury, from the gentle flicker of a magickal candle to the force of a volcanic eruption, to achieve positive ends. Like the element itself, angels of fire are brash and exquisite in form and countenance. Brave and bold, they enjoy anything robust and exciting.

Fire angels seek to assist humans in the passion of creativity. The element of fire represents purification, courage, the will to succeed, the higher self, refinement, the arts, and transformation. It can be seen as the benevolent Sun during a soft summer afternoon, or the scorching heat of an uninhabitable desert. Fire is passionate, and so are its angels.

Angels and Creativity

To make a change in your life you have to first desire the change. You must not merely want to make things different, but desire it so deeply that you can hardly stand it. You need to prime your conscious mind and let it know that you are going to make this change, regardless of the blocks you've subconsciously put into place. Calling on the angels to help you does make it easier, but you have to do your part as well. Unfortunately, change doesn't happen just because you want it badly.

The harder you strive toward creativity, or any goal, the more fleeting it becomes. To keep a constant creative flow, you must see things differently all the time. Total harmony does not increase creativity. We need the chaos of life to simmer until a thought rises from the pandemonium, transformed from muddy concept to glistening idea. Primary in this process, however, is the ability to relax and be patient—two part-ners that don't always dance well together. It is hard to be creative, patient, and relaxed when those around us don't understand the creative process. They seek to define and control creativity through deadlines, useless rules, or scholarly snobbism.

When I'm writing and I can't seem to make headway (no, it does not automati-cally roll out of my brain and into the computer), I shut everything down and go in my room. "Going to sleep on me?" is the standard comment I hear from my husband.

"Nah, just resting for a while." At that point I relax and do the Lesser Banishing Ritual in my mind. Then I'll do an altar devotion in my head. From there I let myself drift, releasing the stress from my body. I have two lines of defense for not being dis-turbed. First, my husband waylays the children before they can disturb me. If they slip past him, my sheltie (he's a big sheltie—I think he has some bizarre growth hor-mones) runs them out of the room.

When all is calm, I sometimes talk to my guardian angel in a sort of a dreamy communication. Other times I'll breathe deeply and close my eyes, feeling comfort-able and secure. This method allows me to steer away from creativity squashers such as fear ("I can't get this." "What if I fail?") and self-criticism ("Who do I think I'm kidding, I can't do this." "My work isn't as good as so-and-so's.") and criticism from others ("What are you doing that for? You're not any good at it." "Stop wasting your time."). It also breaks the need to focus on the subject so intensely that I come up with nothing but frustration. Once I overcome these, the creative muse takes over.

For example, when I get over the frustrating mechanics of a chapter (whether it is fiction or non-fiction), away I go, totally absorbed in the creative process. I have no idea what time it is or what's playing on the television in the next room. I'll put off trips to the bathroom (no kidding) and Goddess help the person who calls me on the phone to chat.

However, you've got to accept the fact that creativity requires unproductive periods. During this time you can do other things, like (gulp) clean the bathroom, wash those dishes, concentrate on the laundry, mow the lawn, change the oil, run errands, or balance your checkbook. Sometimes I will take a break and look through a magazine, watch a favorite movie, take a walk, or call a friend—anything to take my mind off the project. I'll also work on small creative projects in the house, like repainting a room. (It took me from October to March to repaint my dining room.) I did little bits at a time. Sand this window today. Paint one coat tomorrow. Wait a week or two, and do the second coat, etc. It is a relaxing way to move from the computer and into a project that takes my brain miles from my writing.

Angels of fire love to help in the creative process. Call on them when you are dealing with creativity inhibitors—fear, self-criticism, criticism from others, and times of frustration. Fire angels love to laugh and play, so you may get some surprising help, like an invitation to go swimming, or a chance to see a movie that you thought was sold out. I gave you the example of writing, because that's what I do; however, all creativity is the subject. For example you could be a whiz at fixing classic cars; you may paint, dance, sculpt, write computer software, etc. Creativity can be in every facet of life, if you just open yourself up to it.

Angel of Fire Visualization

Ground and center. Close your eyes and take three deep breaths. If you feel jittery, breathe deeply several more times. Relax. No one is going to run off with your project and make a success of it while you take a few moments to become secure in the creative process.

Visualize yourself in an open, summer field with the noon sun above you. An angel with iridescent wings appears before you, offering to take you to a place where ideas are unlimited. However, there is one condition. You must dig a hole and bury all your doubts, fears, and criticisms. You agree and follow through.

Suddenly, the ground shakes and from your buried negativity rises a golden tree of knowledge. The angel pats you on the back and tells you that the tree will help another traveler very soon. The angel takes your hand and you soar into the blue sky, feeling the air swirl about you in gentle waves. This is what it is like to be free.

Soon it is time to land. The angel chooses a clearing surrounded by a forest of supreme beauty. In the center of the clearing is a blazing fire. The angel instructs you to relax by the fire, promising that the images and ideas you seek can be found within the dancing flames; he or she then tells you that you will remember all the images and ideas. Relax and look into the flames. Don't push yourself; let the images come into your mind.

When you are through, allow the angel to take your hand again and fly you back to the summer clearing. Relax under the shade of the golden tree of knowledge. When you are ready to return to a waking state, count from one to five and open your eyes.

℞ecord your impressions in your angel diary, or on a piece of paper or index card. If you get some good ideas, use them. If nothing jumps out at you right away, don't worry. Carry the card with you for a few days, referring to it occasionally.

The more you practice this meditation, the easier the creativity will flow. It is necessary to believe that the angels will help you, and trust that idea germination is a growing process—most great ideas need time to percolate in your subconscious before they manifest in your conscious mind. If the information on the cards does not help you, put them in a box and check them out about a month later. You may be pleasantly surprised at what you wrote. There have been times when I've had ideas that didn't apply to the current project, but a few months later, fit right in with what is happening with something else.

Elemental Fire Correspondences

Fire energy is projective in nature. Here is a selection of correspondences to assist you when working with the element of fire and the angels of fire.

Astrological signs: Aries, Leo, Sagittarius

Colors: Red, orange, burnt sienna

Herbs and flowers: Sunflowers, marigold, dragon's blood, cayenne pepper, garlic, onion, rue, bay, broom

Metals: Gold, brass

Musical instruments: String instruments

Places: Deserts, volcanoes, ovens, fireplaces, sports fields, hot springs, saunas, beaches, arenas, beauty parlors, dance studios, movie sets, theater stages, bedrooms

Symbol of the Element of Fire

Rituals and requests: Creativity, sexual passion, courage, strength, energy, authority, banishing, vibrancy, destroying cancers

Scents: Highly stimulating fragrances such as bougainvillea, citrus, lilac, patchouli, clove, frankincense, nutmeg

Sense: Sight

Sports: Hunting, sharpshooting, football, soccer, triathalon, boxing, kickboxing, martial arts

Stones: Red jasper, bloodstone

Time: Noon

Types of magick: Protection, creative pursuits, candle, storm, star

Visualization: Any type of flame, hot objects, stars, comets

Angels Generally Associated with Fire

Angel of the burning bush: Zagzagel

Angels of comets: Zikiel or Ziquiel, Akhibel

Angels of constellations: Kakabel (Kochbiel), Rahtiel

Angel of creativity and vivid imagination: Samandriel

Angels of the disk of the Sun: Chur (ancient Persian), Galgaliel

Angel of good cause: Nemamiah (warrior angel)

Angels of fire: Nathaniel (Nathanel), Arel, Atuniel, Jehoel, Ardarel, Gabriel, Seraph

Angel of flame: El Auria, a name equated with Ouriel (Uriel)

Angel of inspiration in art and beauty: Hael

Angels of light: Isaac, Gabriel, Jesus, Mihr (Parsi religion), Parvagigar (Arabic)

Angel of the light of day: Shamshiel

Angels of lights (general): Raphael as regent of the Sun, Uriel, Shamshiel

Angel of love, passion, romance, and soul mates: Anael

Angels of song: Uriel, Radueriel, Israfel, Shemiel, Metatron

Angel of success and good fortune: Barakiel

Angels of the north star: Abathur, Muzania, Arhum Hii

Angels of the stars: Kakabel, Kohabiel

Angel of the star of love: Anael

Angels of the north star: Abathur, Muzania, Arhum Hii, and four angels in Mandean lore

Angel of the Sun's rays: Schachlil

Candle Magick and Angels

One of the most popular minor magicks is candle magick. Candles are romantic, non-threatening, comforting, and colorful. Candles are easy to use and don't attract much attention. No one thinks twice if you like to burn candles—after all, it adds to the atmosphere of any home and creates vibrations of security.

Candle magick is simple. Candles absorb your personal power quickly, release power without your having to hover over them, come in a variety of colors to make choosing magickal correspondences easy, and are an immediate reminder that you are doing something to make your life better. You are working to cement the idea in your mind that you want something in your life to change. Candles are also signals to the angels that you are ready to work. Angels adore candle magick.

Unlit, a candle represents the element of earth, but when the flame touches the wick it becomes a vehicle of the four elements. Its undulating smoke is associated with air; its melting wax corresponds with water; the dancing flame is associated with the element of fire; the candle itself represents earth. Although there are times in history where candle burning was considered unacceptable and evil, candles have been generally accepted as a form of religious practice and honor for several hundred years, so don't be shy about working with them.

To "light a candle" for someone represents respect for that person and his or her needs, a desire within yourself to help someone, an active response to the need of the individual, a sense of honor in oneself and one's beliefs, and an act of faith.

If you stop to think about it, these are pretty serious reasons. The simple act of lighting a candle brings more positive action into play than most people think about. Since no one will know you are doing it (providing you don't blab it all over your apartment building), no one will laugh at you.

Candles are also easy to work with because they take little time to "dress" and empower. Dressing means rubbing a light coat of scented oil or holy water on them. Before you begin, ask your guardian angel to help you. State your desire clearly so that there is no mix-up in communication. We humans have a bad habit of not saying what we really mean, or worse, not really understanding what we want in the first place. Yes, our guardian angels are good at ferreting out what our minds are churning over, but we need to be clear to ourselves, so we can focus more precisely. Of course, honesty in everything is always the best policy.

To bring things toward you, begin from the top of the candle and rub the oil down to the middle of the candle, then rub the oil from the bottom of the candle up to the middle of the candle. To send things away from you, do the opposite: start at the middle and rub up. Then start from the middle and rub down. If your candle has been poured by the manufacturer into a glass cup, use holy water instead of oil on the outside of the glass and let it dry, or draw a banishing pentagram over the top of the candle with a light tracing of oil. You can also draw a banishing pentagram in holy water on the underside of the glass cup or container.

Hold the candle firmly in your hands (or hand, however you are comfortable) and allow your energy to circulate around the candle. Envision your guardian angel holding the candle with you. Think of your desire and implant it into the candle. Some people like to hold the candle tightly while doing this; others simply allow their thoughts to flow into the candle. Do what feels most comfortable for you.

Candle and sigil magick work well together. Carve your favorite sigils on the candle before lighting it. You can place your personal sigil on it, the sigil of your guardian angel or an elemental angel, an astrological correspondence, or the symbol of your desire. Use the point of a heated darning needle or a nail to carve your sigils and symbols. (For more information on sigils and symbols, see Chapter 14.)

Although you can use any type of candle holder, I suggest brass. Wooden candle holders have a tendency to catch on fire, and glass holders can (and do) split, creating a fire hazard as well. A good old brass candlestick on a metal tray is the safest way to go, though I advise not leaving a candle burning if you are not in the immediate area.

When lighting your candle, try not to use a match. Angels don't care much for sulphur. Use a lighter instead. Focus on your desire; you can say it aloud if you want (and keep your words positive), then slowly lower the flame to the wick.

There is also an art to extinguishing candles. Folklore holds that one never blows out a candle because you are extinguishing the light of the divine with your own breath (sort of like spitting in divinity's face). Many magickal people use candle snuffers. They are inexpensive and come in a variety of styles to suit your taste. By either pinching or snuffing out a candle, you are sealing the power of your intent as well as showing honor to divinity. Also, one theory says that blowing out the flame inadvertently scatters the magick you worked so hard to perform.

Limit your focus to one intent per candle. By concentrating on a variety of situations you are not focusing in a single direction, which will weaken your magickal work. I burn a candle in honor of my guardian angel while working other candle magicks. Candles used only to honor your guardian can be relighted. However, it is best to let candles used for specific circumstances burn completely. If you can't hang around all day while a candle burns, use a small one instead. Bigger is not better in candle magick. In emergencies, a birthday candle will do.

The number of candles you use in one magickal application is also not of the utmost importance. Yes, I know some magickal activities require various colored candles to be lit in one sitting, but you will often find this is not necessary for simple magicks. More than one candle can be used effectively in ritual, but for a simple act of honor or one specific request, a single candle will do. You don't need to light up your parlor like in the movie *Carrie*. That is a definite fire hazard!

Finally, if you cannot get the candle color you want, use white. White is the all-purpose color in any type of magick, due to its relation to purity and divinity.

Letters to the Angels

This is a simple magick that can have a profound effect on your life. Write your needs in a letter to the angel you have chosen, then burn the letter, asking the angels of fire to carry your message to its desired recipient. This also works for human communication. Say you really want to hear from someone, but don't have the nuggets to call. Write a letter to him or her (be sure it is positive in nature), then ask your guardian angel to contact the person's guardian angel and send your message through. You must also indicate that, if this is not the proper time in your spiritual paths to communicate, the message will be held until the time is right. Remember, you must always think of your motives and the results of your action on others. To contact someone because you want to seek revenge won't work through the angels.

Angels and Liberation

All of us have occasions where we feel that we've been run over by a fleet of tractor-trailers. In these times we need power. Try this little invocation at your altar the next time you feel you've given just about all you've got, and have no more.

I take the power in my hands
From air and fire water and land.
Power of the of the angels and divinity
Moves and pulsates, the energy in me.
I build, I birth, I bring to form
I raise with might an energy storm.
I shape, I build, the ultimate power
From within me blooms the perfect flower
Of strength
Of healing
I reign.

Ten

Angels and the Element of Water

Water, like our emotions, surges, patters, cascades, and ripples through our lives. Always moving, it sustains us and shows us how to flow through difficulties or crash down mental blocks. It can drown our sorrow, or lift us on rolling waves of pleasure. Water, like emotion, is ever-changing.

Water nourishes and cleanses. It is the sacred element of purification. Angels of water are pleasing of face and form. These angels may appear gentle and feminine, but don't let them fool you—their energy runs deep and strong. These angels seek harmony in the universe through healing and internal transformation.

Water angels can be seen in the undulating currents of a deep stream or the gentle ripples at a river dock. They constantly move through our lives, bringing healing wherever needed. Water magick is accomplished with anything flowing, such as the sea, fog, rain, creeks, rivers, sacred bowls of liquid, or mirrors.

Angels and Self-Esteem

We seldom notice that we are suffering from poor self-esteem. Others may notice it or think our behavior is irrational, but we cruise merrily along, sinking deeper and deeper. If we are lucky, an event or a person gives us a wake-up call and we work to change things. If we are not so lucky, eventually we will hit the bottom of the proverbial human barrel.

The major cause of poor self-esteem lies in negative programming. How does negative programming begin? Do we catch it like the flu? Actually, sometimes we do. Negative people tend to bring you down into their muck. The angels of water will help remove these people if you ask them to, and if that is what you really want. Sometimes we need to take an inventory of where we are and what we are doing—not simply worry about it in passing, but look closely at people in our lives. Why am I around this person? Is he or she a healthy and positive influence on me? How do I feel when I'm around this person? Why do I care what this person thinks?

Humans have a nasty habit of judging one another unfairly. An act of condemnation may be fueled by jealousy, egotistical thoughts, or fear. Learn to see these unfair judgments clearly, then let them roll away from you.

We also need to take the responsibility for our own negative programming. Self-criticism is a good thing, if it keeps you doing good things for yourself and others, but it is the pits if it inhibits your creativity, stifles your personality, or creates fears and phobias. If we carry a poor perception of ourselves, that is what we will project.

Low self-esteem can sneak up on you when you are least expecting it. An undeserved reprimand from a boss, a rude comment from your significant other, not getting a contract you worked night and day for, not passing the midterm that was to raise your grade, or a wake-up call when your friend videotapes your mother's birthday and it dawns on you that the overweight person with the bad hair and circles under the eyes is you—all of these could be linked to self-esteem problems.

Everyone on this planet suffers from low self-esteem at one time or another—that's why we do so many dumb things. We show off, cut corners, make decisions without considering their impact on others (or the planet), or gravitate toward people of low moral character only because they are popular. Although we can't be on top of the world every day, we can hit a happy medium by changing our life patterns to flow harmoniously with the essence of the universe. Who ya gonna call? The angels of water, naturally.

First, you need to get rid of all those negative comments you've been saying to yourself, and dispose of the nasty junk people have poured into your ears since you arrived on the planet. Sure, you've heard this before, but did you know that self-esteem work is an ongoing thing? As humans, we often like to have things in the "once and done" category so we can go on to new things. Like a car you dearly love, your self-esteem needs maintenance. Self-esteem is also like your garden, because it grows if it is well maintained. I'm not encouraging you to become an egomaniac, but feeling good inside allows you to treat others with respect and courtesy. Angels, if you haven't guessed this already, appreciate manners, and will do all they can to help you if you learn to cultivate them.

Ask the angels of water to help you reprogram the comments you make to yourself. Listen to your thoughts and change the negative chatter in your head to positive dialogue. If you are having trouble doing this, choose some favorite passages from a book of enlightenment and repeat one or two when the negative-thought boogies intrude on your space.

Improve your self-image. Change your hair, clothes, posture, etc. You don't have to become Cinderella or Prince Charming overnight, and this doesn't require forty charge cards and a wad of bills in your pocket because this time you're going to pick what is you. Don't worry about the hottest fashions; those are for vapid folks who have low self-esteem and enjoy judging others because their fear keeps them from looking at themselves. Your higher self knows what type of physical accessories will raise your self-esteem and enhance your spirituality. Ask the angels of water to help you choose clothing, furniture, etc., that is pleasing to your energy or that will enhance your feelings of self-worth. Take your time and enjoy the process.

Eat right and exercise. This doesn't mean you have to become a calorie counter or buy expensive gym equipment, but you do need to learn to take care of your body. It is the only vehicle you have in this lifetime and it will serve you well if you take care of it.

Work on your self-confidence. Find things that you like to do, even if it is only a walk in the park, and spend time doing them. You don't have to have something material to show for your time, but you do need to feel good about how you use it. If you think you aren't good at anything, ask the angels of water to help you find something to boost your self-confidence. You may be surprised and pleased at the opportunities that come your way. Consciously try to keep yourself from getting in a rut. If you see things repeating themselves, make an effort to change the routine.

The Angel Board

To raise your self-esteem, you may want to create an angel board. Children particularly like this activity as it allows them to be creative.

Supplies:
>A piece of lined paper and a pencil or pen
>Construction paper (a variety of colors)
>Angel wings pattern (see below)
>Scissors
>One sheet of poster board (any color)
>Tape or glue
>A black felt-tip pen
>Artsy-craftsy things (sequins, lace, ribbons, etc.)

Ground and center. Breathe deeply three times (or more if you've had a stressful day). Write down on your paper all the positive things you would like to bring into your life, or things in yourself you would like to change or make better.

Choose which correspondences match your desires. Check the angel names, timing, colors, etc. Make these notes beside each desire.

Cut out angel wings from construction paper for each desire, matching the colors of the paper to the colors on your list.

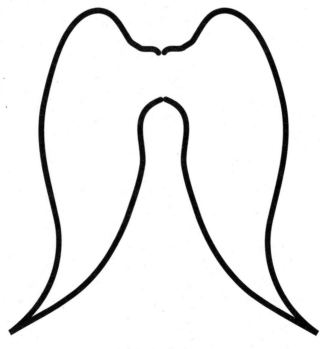

Angel wings pattern

Sample decorated angel wings

On the front of each pair of wings, write down the desire. On the back, draw the appropriate sigils, angel name, etc. If you don't want to make it detailed, you don't have to. Decorate the wings if you like.

Write your name in big letters across the top of the poster board. Glue or tape the wings you made onto the board. Hang it up in your bedroom, or in the kitchen on the fridge. As each desire manifests, take the wings off and thank the angels. Burn the wings and scatter the ashes in the wind. Reward yourself with a little something special, such as that CD you really wanted or perhaps those new shoes. On the same day you do something special for yourself, do something special for someone else — a random act of kindness.

Elemental Water Correspondences

Water energy is receptive in nature. Here is a selection of correspondences to assist you when working with the element of water, and the angels of water.

Astrological signs: Cancer, Scorpio, Pisces

Colors: Blue, aquamarine, turquoise; the colors of a muted sunset

Herbs and flowers: Seaweed, cactus, water lilies, lettuce, apple, thyme, vanilla, yarrow, sandalwood

Metals: Silver, mercury

Musical instruments: Singing bowls, cymbals, resonant metals

Places: The sea, creeks, docks, rivers, ponds, streams, wells, fountains, swimming pools, showers, bathtubs, Jacuzzis, health spas, steam rooms, foggy places, ships, boats, rafts

Rituals and requests: Physical healing, divinatory pursuits, purification, psychism, dreams, sleep, friendships, family matters, grief release

Scents: Softly fragrant flowers and essential oils such as chamomile, myrrh, night-blooming cereus, hyacinth, iris, jasmine

Senses: Taste, psychism

Sports: Swimming, diving, boating, skating, any type of racing, water ballet

Stones: Amethyst, lapis, blue tourmaline

Time: Dusk

Types of magick: Divination, self-improvement, healing, spirituality

Visualizations: Seashells, waves, a sparkling pond, fog

Angels Generally Associated with Water

Angel of aquatic animals: Manakel

Angels of wiccanings and baptisms: Raphael, Barpharanges

Angel of beauty: Camael, who also presides over joy and happiness (Essene prayer: "Camael, angel of joy, descend upon the earth and give beauty to all things")

Angel of birth prophecy and conception: Gabriel

Angel of childbirth and breast milk: Ardousius

Angels of compassion: Rachmiel, Raphael

Symbol of the Element of Water

Angels of the deep: Tamiel, Rampel, Rahab

Angels over fish: Gagiel, Arariel, Azareel

Angel over wild fowl: Trgiaob

Angel of gratitude: Shemael

Angels of hail: Bardiel (Baradiel, Barchiel), Nuriel, Yurkami

Angel of healing body, mind, and spirit: Shekinah

Angel of intuitive powers: Sachiel

Angel to overcome jealousy: Balthial

Angel of liberation and independence: Colopatiron (unlocks prison gates)

Angels of longevity: Mumiah, Scheiah, Rehail

Angels of love: Raphael, Rahmiel, Theliel, Donquel, Anael, Liwet, Mihr

Angels of mercy: Michael, Gabriel, Rhamiel, Rachmiel, Zadkiel

Angel of peace and balance: Gavreel

Angel of platonic love and friendship: Mihr

Angel of positive and loving thoughts: Hahaiah

Angel of protection for travel over water: Elemiah

Angels of rain: Matarel, Mathariel, Ridia, Matriel (say them in chant sequence); also Zalbesael (Zelebsel), Dara (Persian)

Angels of the River Jordan: Silmai, Nibdai

Angels of rivers: Trsiel, Rampel, Dara (Persian)

Angel of running streams: Nahaliel

Angel of science and medicine: Mumiah

Angel of the sea: Rahab

Angel of showers: Zaa'fiel

Angels of snow: Shalgiel, Michael

Angel of the waters: Phul

Angel of water insects: Shakziel

Angel Waters

Folk customs throughout America include several recipes for holy water. These blends of water, a pinch of alcohol, and pulverized herbs were strained through cheesecloth and used as floor washes, or sprinkled about in an effort to cleanse and/or heal people, places, and things. The basic formula is:

8 ounces spring water
¼ ounce isopropyl alcohol
Selected herbs

To pulverize your own herbs you will need a mortar and pestle, or you can buy essential oils and dispense with the mess of grinding and straining through cheesecloth.

General angelic floor wash: Wisteria and honeysuckle. Call on the angels of the lights.

Angelic peace water: Jasmine and lavender. Call on Itqal, the angel of affection who works for human harmony.

Angelic blessing water: Frankincense and myrrh. Call on Gabriel, the angel of baptismal waters.

Angelic healing water: Eucalyptus and pine. Call on Raphael, the angel of healing.

Angelic banishing water: Clove and angelica. Call on Michael or Uriel, the terminator angels.

Angelic purification water: Lilac and pine. Call on Gabriel and Michael.

Consecrate and empower these waters on your angelic altar in the same manner in which you learned to make holy water (see Chapter 2 for a simple procedure).

The Housecleaning Angels

Angels bless this house
From site to stay
From beam to wall
From end to end
From attic to basement
From foundation to summit
Foundation and summit.

I kid you not, the angels will help you clean your house, both physically and psychically. Remember when Mom and Grandma cleaned the house every six months— you know, spring and fall cleaning? Most of us got sucked into the procedure. Idle hands were wasteful hands, and all that. Personally, I think they just wanted us kids to work so they'd have company and could shout orders—the "in-charge" mentality. However, as my grandma used to say, poor doesn't mean dirty. Get over there and clean those venetian blinds—ugh!

Rather than waking up one fine morning and saying, "I think I'm going to clean today," plan to do your housecleaning. Watch the weather reports and pick a day when the sun will be shining. Before you go to bed the night before, drink some chamomile tea. Make a list of what you want to get done. Don't overdo it; you can clean on more than one day.

Twice a year most magickal people do an all-out cleaning of their homes both physically and psychically. You know what supplies you will need for the physical cleaning, but how about that psychic stuff? That's easy. Make one of the waters above, and buy some clove oil. Choose an incense that appeals to you. (Check the magickal correspondences in Chapter 4.) Purchase one white taper candle or a votive candle in a cup for each room in the house.

As for the physical cleaning equipment, try to choose environmentally safe products and buy yourself a new bucket and sponges, a new broom or mop, or whatever. Then treat at least one room in the house to an "angel pretty"—something special (it doesn't have to cost a lot) that will remind you that the angels are with you all season long.

On angel cleaning day (kids love this, by the way; it makes the drudgery easier), begin your morning with an altar devotion. Ask the angels to help you clean today, keep you from getting overly tired, and bless your home. Take everyone out for an angel breakfast. If you don't have much cash, a fast food restaurant will do. The idea is to get out of the house, enjoy the sunshine, and breathe the fresh air.

Clean each room physically. Then open the windows and imagine the angels of air coming into the room and clearing out all the negativity. Close the windows and sprinkle your pre-made water around the room in a clockwise direction. Ask the angels of water to cleanse and bless the room. Next, light the incense, asking the angels of fire to cleanse and bless the room. Carry the candle around the room in a clockwise direction. If you have a votive in a cup, place it on a safe surface and let it burn out. Finally, take a pinch of salt (I know, you just cleaned) and sprinkle it around the room in a clockwise direction, asking the angels of earth to cleanse and bless the room. If you like crystals, you can charge one and carry that around the room (less messy), then leave it beside the burning candle.

The last task is to seal all the doors and windows. Dip your finger in the clove oil and draw a pentacle above and below each window as well as above and on the door. Don't get sloppy; you don't need a lot. Ask the angels of spirit to guard and protect your home from all negativity.

At noon, do another altar devotion thanking the angels for all you have accomplished so far, and for their continued strength while you clean. You may like to plan a picnic lunch to get away from the cleaning job, or make a sandwich and eat it outside under your favorite tree.

At sunset, repeat the altar devotion. Plan an easy dinner that you like. Let's face it, most people don't like to cook a big meal after cleaning all day. Think about ordering an angel pizza or angel Chinese, something that requires no cooking at all. Before bedtime or at midnight, thank the angels for their assistance in cleansing and protecting your home.

A Box of Angels

This project will probably take you a while to complete, but it is well worth it. It is a great gift for children and adults alike, or you can use it for yourself.

Supplies:
> Construction paper in various colors
> A black marker
> A list of "good thoughts"
> A box
> Glue/paint/various craft supplies (glitter, ribbon, sequins)
> Sheets of laminated plastic
> Hole puncher
> Yarn
> A small stamp of an angel

Cut the construction paper into two-by-three-inch slips. If you are inventive, you may want to cut the paper into the shape of angels, or you can use a stamp of an angel and stencil it on each piece of paper.

With the black marker, write one good thought on each slip of paper.

Laminate the slips of paper.

Punch a hole in each slip of paper.

Thread a small piece of yarn through the hole. Tie the ends to make a loop.

Decorate the box.

Write the following on a nice piece of parchment paper:

> *You hold in your hands an angel box*
> *Blessed by love and Goddess thoughts.*
> *When you are feeling down and blue*
> *Or want the angels to talk to you*
> *Open the box and read the message*
> *Hang it where you'll see its blessings.*

When the day is through
Thank the angels for helping you.
Return the message to the box.
Sleep with sweet and pleasant thoughts.

Angel Frustration Cord

I have to thank my friend Annie for the many hours she spent with me in hypnosis sessions. When Annie first came to me she was plagued by intense pain in her left shoulder. She had suffered an injury on the job quite some time before that, but as we delved into Annie's psyche many other issues surfaced, including old injuries that had never been dealt with properly, as well as emotional issues. The pain began to abate as we worked through each issue, until finally, she had full and pain-free control of her arm. During this process we used both her guardian angel and healing angels to speed her recovery.

When the arm was better, her leg began to act up. Her physician suggested I work on her diabetes (which at this time did not need medication). During the weeks of physical therapy with her physician, I worked with her mind. Eventually we reduced her leg problems as well.

During one session I asked to speak to Annie's higher self. "What does Annie need?" I asked.

"So much," came the reply.

"Tell me a few things." I waited patiently through a moment of silence.

"She's all knotted up. She needs to relax."

"Can you help Annie relax this week?"

"Yes, but she doesn't listen to me very well."

I thought for a minute. "Let's do this. What is Annie's favorite color?"

"Blue."

"Good. Does Annie like pretty things?"

"Oh, yes."

"I'm going to make Annie a very pretty cord—all blue. I'm going to put lots of knots in it. When Annie feels stressed, I want her to untie one of the knots. Can you help Annie do this?"

"Yes."

After the session, I reminded Annie about the cord. I gave it to her the next week. In my private time I had cleansed, consecrated, and empowered the cord, asking both Annie's guardian angel and the angels of water for assistance in resolving the stress in Annie's life.

Annie didn't bother to use the cord during the first week. "Things were busy," she remarked absently. I knew that part of Annie was in denial and wanted to hold on to those knots. I smiled politely and told her to try again the next week.

The following session I found that Annie had still not used the cord. She held fiercely to those old habits, fearing that if she gave them up, she wouldn't be needed or loved by her family any more. It took several more sessions to work through this with Annie, but eventually she untied those knots and released herself from a negative pattern.

Later, Annie hung the unknotted cord on her lamp beside her bed to remind herself of the healing gifts from the angels.

Angel Birthday Ceremony

Angels love to celebrate birthdays, especially when you do it in a spiritual way. Your birthday was the day you chose to enter the earth plane and begin your lessons of this life. Everything was designed specifically for you—your environment, your parents, your body, and the time of your birth. All fit into the grand plan of the universe. No one on the face of this earth has not been provided for in this way. Therefore, each of us, regardless of circumstances, is truly a special person.

If you know the precise time of your birth, all the better, but if you do not, don't worry about it. Know that the time you choose for this private ceremony is fine and meant to be. In planning your ceremony, take into account your favorite colors and what passions belong to you and you alone. You may wish to put something special on your altar, a gift for yourself perhaps, or find a piece of poetry or favorite passage that you would like to read during the ceremony. Consider all the good things that have happened to you this year and formulate goals for yourself to apply to the year to come. Write these goals down on a piece of paper and set them on the altar.

When you are ready, ground and center, then light your illuminator candles or lamps. Cast your angelic circle and call the angelic quarters. This is a ceremony of reverence, no words really need be said, but if you have your special passage ready, read it now. You may wish to thank divinity and the angels for the life you have had, and the life you intend to live. You can ask for their help, guidance, and wisdom in the coming year. Many individuals like to relax and meditate during the birthday ceremony. When you are finished, cleanse and consecrate a bowl of water and anoint your body, hailing divinity. Finally, release the quarters and draw up the circle.

Angels and Anger

No one really likes to be angry. Years ago a friend of mine told me to do the following, and it has worked for me ever since. Carry a few small packets of salt (the kind you find in fast-food restaurants) in your pocket or purse. Write your favorite angel's name on each packet as well as a symbol of your choice. Itqal is a good choice, as this angel works for harmony among dissenting individuals. When you find yourself facing angry people, open the packet and put a bit on your tongue. Throw the rest on the ground or over your shoulder. Visualize the anger falling away or transmuting into positive energy. The salt on your tongue helps remind you of your own angry feelings and will help you keep those feelings in check.

Emotions are approximately ten seconds in duration—no kidding. If you can hold that negative thought and transmute it to something positive during those ten seconds, you are way ahead of the game.

When you are dealing with difficult people, immediately call your guardian angel for help. Keep your temper. Don't argue if the issue really isn't important to you. During the confrontation, keep you voice low and continue to lower it. That will help take the heat out of the air. Don't make vague requests of people. Be straight and to the point. Try to discover the real issue. Sometimes arguments pop up because you literally aren't on the same wavelength as the other person.

If someone accosts you verbally and makes out-of-the-blue threats and you don't understand what is going on, ask your guardian angel to interpret what is really happening. Take a deep breath and open your ears. The answer you need will come to you as quickly as you need it. Sometimes threats come from people because they are feeling depressed and floundering in life or on a particular issue. They are at the end of the proverbial rope, so to get someone to feel as they do (misery loves company), they will let unfounded accusations and empty threats fly. Don't panic. Instead, keep your cool and calmly consider why this is happening and how you can work it out. Sometimes there is nothing you can do at the moment but listen.

Angels and Equality

Angels are very good at assisting you in making "all things equal." Have you ever felt that someone has some sort of power over you or your life, and you don't like it? The angels will help balance things if you ask them. You will need a small white pillar candle, a regular old cooking pot, and some ice. Melt the bottom of the candle so that it stands firmly in the pot. Place plenty of ice around the candle. Ground and center, calling upon your guardian angel and the angels of water. Ask them to extinguish, in a positive way, the control that others hold over your life. As the ice melts, visualize the blocks and coldness flowing from your life. When the candle flame reaches the ice (or water), it will sputter out. Watch it sputter, knowing that your freedom is at hand. After the candle is out, pour the water in a hole in the ground or add it to a body of living water. Bury the candle. Remember to thank the angels of water for their assistance.

This little magick works well for any sort of block in your life, whether it be another person, circumstances, a block in creativity, health, etc. Choose the color of candle that is most appropriate for the situation, as well as the appropriate angelic hour that applies to your circumstance.

Here is a neutralizing passage for you to use if you like:

Angels of water
Wanted friends
Treasured hosts of light
Come to me
Cast the blocks in my life into the waters of transformation
Burn the blocks in my life in the flames of harmony
In the name of the God and Goddess/Father, Son, and Holy Ghost
So mote it be.

Angels and Healing

Most health problems are a result of stress, an accident, or an inherited condition. Some physicians and researchers feel that stress is the primary cause of many physical and mental ailments. The more stress you are under, the more predisposed you are to illness. Ill health caused by an accident is fairly straightforward. You were hurt; now you have a problem. Illness due to an inherited condition may manifest itself at birth, during times of stress, appear at an advanced age, or never appear at all. In all these cases your mental attitude can make or break the healing or remission process.

Anytime we speak of healing and magick we never infer that magick "does it all." One should seek a physician when needed, follow a pattern of good nutrition, cut back on stimulants (such as caffeine), reduce stressful situations and negative patterns in your life, and schedule periodic leisure activities. However, asking the angels to help us doesn't hurt, and can assist in speeding up the healing process.

This fact came into focus with an unfortunate event experienced by one of my clients.

"What's the matter?" I asked Amanda as she blew in my front door, accompanied by a biting winter gust and a few errant snowflakes.

"You wouldn't believe it," she said, throwing off her coat and joining me at the dining room table.

I poured her a cup of tea and watched as both the cold and stress visibly drained from her face. "What's the scoop?" I asked.

"My best friend shot himself last night!"

"No!"

She nodded sadly. "But he's still alive and he may make it. What can I do?"

We discussed the situation and decided that it was imperative that she first contact her friend's guardian angel in either prayer or meditation. After that she called the hospital to find out what she was allowed to put in her friend's room. The next day she went shopping. She found a little angel to hang over his bed, as well as a guardian angel pin to put on his hospital gown. Every night she burned a white candle, intoning the following Pow-Wow chants I'd given her and ending with Gabriel's prayer.

Hast thou recovered health and Goddess
I will lead thee again to the Maiden, Mother, and Crone
Therefore so help thee our Goddess readily
And thou shalt be blessed as well as the cakes and ale
Which Aradia offered to her followers before she left them.
Therefore so help you
Maiden, Mother, and Crone.
So mote it be.

And these signs shall follow those that believeth in my name
They shalt cast out demons and they shall speak in new tongues
And if they drink anything deadly, it shall not harm them
They shall lay hands upon the sick
And they shall recover
In the name of the Father, Son, and Holy Ghost.

Hail Lady, full of grace, the God is with you.
Blessed are you among women and blessed is the fruit of your womb,
    the Consort and Son.
Holy Goddess, Mother of Earth
Work your mystery for your children
Now and in the hour of our need.
So mote it be.

In less than two weeks her friend was out of intensive care and on the road to recovery. I cannot describe to you the amazement of the doctors. Of course, the friend had to work through both mental and physical issues in the following months, but I can think of little more deeply touching than Amanda, who went beyond the role of a grieving friend and decided to do something about the unfortunate situation in the best way she knew how. Her friend fully recovered. To this day, he wears his guardian angel pin proudly on his jacket.

Angel Smiles

It's true. Smiling can alter your immune system efficiency.[1] When research subjects were trained to smile, their physiology immediately changed. The hormones in their

1. "The Power of Your Own Thinking to Strengthen Your Immune System" by Paul Pearsal, Ph.D., *Going Bonkers Magazine*, March 1995, page 22.

bodies altered drastically. Whether you like it or not, you should practice smiling often every day. By doing this you will alter your blood chemistry. Practice giving these angel smiles to other people. Simply call your guardian angel first, then smile, sending loving energy to other people. Not only are you keeping yourself healthy by smiling, but your friends, family, and associates will receive the benefits of both your positive energy and that of your guardian angel.

When working with any client in hypnotherapy, I always give him or her a "smile" suggestion to help speed the healing process. It works every time.

Angelic Invocation for Wiccaning and Baptisms

The ceremony of wiccaning/baptism was practiced prior to any of the religious structures currently in place on our planet. It is, indeed, a Pagan practice. Here is an all-purpose Celtic blessing for any child:

I sprinkle the grace of divinity on this child
Give thou to him/her virtue and growth
Give thou to him/her strength and guidance
Give thou to him/her financial stability and possessions
Sense and reason void of guile
Angel wisdom always
That he/she may make a difference in this world
And find his/her mission in life.
So mote it be.

Eleven

Angels and the Element of Earth

Earth is our home. If Earth did not exist, if we had a different habitat, we would be totally different beings. An element of both strength and nurturing, the earth freely shares her mysteries, should we be open to accepting them.

Earth, the sacred foundation of our being, provides us sustenance. Her heart beats at a steady rhythm. The angels of earth are pillars of stability. They are there for us to lean on when we need strength and endurance. Experts on the mystery of life and magick, they speak to us every day through the flora and fauna of the planet.

Patient and kind, the angels of earth primarily concern themselves with the survival of the planet and the enlightenment of its human population. Earth angels find interest in fertility, nourishment, seasonal cycles, stability, and prosperity.

Angel Charm Bag

This is a fun project for the whole family and makes a wonderful gift for a special friend. Find (or make, if your fingers are nimble) a small cloth bag that appeals to you. It can be decorated or plain. From a piece of felt, cut a pair of angel wings and sew it onto the bag. Use the color correspondences in Chapter 4 to personalize the bag.

Hold the bag over your angelic altar and ask the angels to bless and consecrate the bag. If it is for a friend, be sure to state specifically whom you want the bag to go to. Ask that, in the next few days, you find some very special items to put in the bag.

In the next few days look for things to put in the angel bag—a feather, a pretty stone, a bauble from the department store, decorative beads, etc. Place the bag on top of the altar. Put each item you have collected on top of the bag. When you have finished your collection, ask the angels to bless and empower each item. Put them all in the bag. Hold the bag to your heart and fill it with good will. See it glowing in your mind.

When you are finished, thank the angels for their help and give the bag to your friend, or if it is for yourself, place it in your pocket or purse. The rule of the angel bag is never to show the contents to anyone. They are private, for the owner alone.

Elemental Earth Correspondences

Earth energy is receptive in nature. Here is a selection of correspondences to assist you when working with the element of earth, and the angels of earth.

Astrological signs: Taurus, Virgo, Capricorn

Colors: Green and brown

Symbol of the Element of Earth

Herbs and plants: Moss, ferns, trees, straw flowers, ground cover, cypress, mimosa, mistletoe, holly

Metals: Iron, lead

Musical instruments: Drums, all percussion instruments

Places: Forests, gardens, caves, parks, farms, markets, kitchens, plant nurseries, caves, any business underground, basements, mines

Rituals and requests: Stability, growth, prosperity, fertility, grounding, finding employment, finding a home, charities

Scents: Tangy fragrances including pine, musk, bayberry, frankincense, patchouli, honeysuckle, myrrh

Sense: Touch

Sports: All winter sports

Stones: Jade, quartz, obsidian

Time: Midnight

Types of magick: Self-improvement, knot magick, gardening, stone magick, marriage and criminal magicks

Visualizations: Stones, trees, salt, dirt, clay, wheat, corn

Angels Generally Associated with Earth

Angel of abundance: Barbelo (female—goodness, faith, and integrity as well as success and abundance)

Angel of agriculture: Risnuch

Angel of alchemy and mineralogy: Och

Angels over tame beasts: Thegri (Thuriel), Mtniel, Jehiel, Hayyal

Angel of commerce: Anauel (success, commerce, prosperity; protection for those who own or want to start their own business)

Angel of deserts: Unnamed

Angel of domesticated animals: Hariel (in charge of protecting dogs, cats, other pets, and farm animals)

Angel of the dust: Suphlatus

Angels of earthquakes: Sui'el, Rashiel

Angel of farmers: Sofiel

Angels of fertility: Samandiriel, Yushamin

Angel of food: Manna

Angel of gardens: Cathetel (increases the growth and yield of vegetables and fruits and assists in keeping them healthy)

Angel of nourishment: Isda

Angel of forests: Zuphlas

Angel of fruition: Anahita (female—protector of those who care for nature and keep the earth fruitful)

Angels over fruit and fruit trees: Teiaiel or Isiaiel, Adad (Assyro-Babylonian)

Angel of herbs: Unnamed

Angels of the hills: Unnamed (often thought to be fairies and devas)

Angel of mountains: Mehabiah

Angel of plants: Sachluph

Angel of protection for small children and young animals: Afriel

Angel over tame beasts: Behemiel

Angels over trees: Maktiel, Zuphlas

Angels of vegetables: Sealiah, Sofiel

Angels of the wild beasts: Mtniel, Jehiel, Hayyel (will also help in stopping the extinction of wild animals)

Angel of wild birds: Trgiaob

Angel over creeping things: Trgiaob

Angel of the wilderness: Orifiel (protects the wilderness and those who care for it)

Angels of Gaia: Michael, Jehoel, Metatron, Sar ha-Olam, Mammon

Finding a New Home with Angel Magick

Where we live affects us deeply. Our home represents our safety and security in life. Naturally, when circumstances require us (either by accident or design) to find a new home, the choice of where we will live is very important. Regardless of whether you are moving by choice or necessity, working magick for your new home follows the same procedure.

Write down everything you need and want regarding a place to live. Do you want a big house, a small apartment, in the city, in the country, near your work, near a good school? What kind of house or apartment do you want—Victorian, igloo, split-level? Do you want land to care for, or not? Take your time and page through a few magazines or real estate publications. Do you need appliances? If so, which ones? Spend a few days forming in your mind precisely what kind of environment you wish to live in. When you think you know, check your list to make sure you have everything you feel is necessary.

Next, find a little wooden house. Many of them are sold as tree ornaments around Christmas, but if it is not the season, check toy stores or craft shops. With white paint, write your name, apostrophe *s* house (I would write "Silver's house") on the little house. Leave enough space to put a house number.

Check your correspondences and determine when would be the best time to work for your house. Choose the appropriate candle colors, day, hour, etc. From what you have learned so far, choose a specific angel to help you, or simply ask the angels of earth for their assistance.

Begin with an altar devotion. Cleanse, consecrate, and bless your little house. Hold the house in your hands and ask your chosen angels for help in finding the right place for you. Set the house on top of the list you wrote and leave it on your altar.

When you find the right house or apartment, paint the number of your choice on the little wooden house. Do another altar devotion. Hold the house in your hands and ask your chosen angels for help in procuring the house that you found, if it is right for you. (Sometimes you may think you have found the right house, but do not have all the facts. Always leave an escape mechanism for the magick so that it will work in your best interests, should the house or apartment not be right for you.)

When you've definitely found the right place and find yourself immersed in the financial transactions, again go to your altar and ask the angels for assistance. Keep in mind you are looking for a smooth, legal, and honorable transaction. Be sure you indicate this, as well as leave yourself that escape route should something be wrong with your choice.

When you have moved in, be sure to set up your sacred space, do the necessary magickal housecleaning, and thank the angels for their help in procuring your new home. Leave the little house in a safe place. You can use it later in any number of situations, such as protecting your home, increasing harmony in your environment, or assisting with making repairs or new purchases for your home.

Let the Angels Help You Find a New Job or Plan Your Career

If you are not happy with your work, no amount of money will bring harmony into your home. The best situation is to enjoy what you are doing and make enough money to satisfy your needs, with a little extra "joy money."

When seeking what career will satisfy us, we need to answer some tough questions. If you don't answer these, you won't get far in career magick.

Sit back and think (I mean really think) what it is you want to do with your life. What do you desire? What type of career will make you in harmony with your surroundings and yourself? This isn't a question you can answer overnight. You may wish to meditate on the subject. The most important ingredient in your soul-searching experiment is the suspension of belief. This means you can't worry about all the blocks and dead ends you may think are in your way. (For example, "I can't go to law school because I don't have any money.") If you start thinking that way, you've just slit your own throat. Imagine that you live in a perfect world and whatever you want or need is open to you. With that in mind, feel free to choose anything you dearly want to do.

Begin working toward that career both magickally and mundanely. Write on an index card specifically what your career goal is, and set it on your bedroom dresser, on the refrigerator, or any prominent place where you will see the card at least once a day. Find out, calmly, what steps are necessary for you to obtain the career that you would like. If you would like to become an attorney, how much college will you need, how much does it cost, etc.? Don't talk yourself into believing that you cannot reach your goal. Keep your internal dialogue positive and upbeat.

What if you are not sure what steps are needed to reach your dream job? Start talking to people. This isn't as hard as it sounds because people love to talk about their careers, and usually no one wants to hear about them. They will open up and give you all sorts of interesting information if you show you really care about what they are saying. Often they will outline, in detail, how they got to where they are, and tell you likely pitfalls along the way. Listen closely. They usually know what they are talking about. Take notes if you feel the need.

Draw a flowchart, laying out the logical steps to your career path. For example, if you want to be a nurse, find out what forms you have to fill out to begin career training and make a box for that, then make a box for the next step, etc. This flowchart is important because you can also use it to work your magick in steps, following your plan of accomplishment. Beside each box, write the name of the angel you wish to ask for help in accomplishing what is in that box. If you don't want to name a specific angel, then write "angels of earth" or the attributes of angels that may help you with your choice. For example, Raphael or "healing angels" would be helpful for a career in nursing. If you learn to break up large goals into smaller pieces, they are easier to accomplish. Each time you finish one of the boxes on your flowchart, treat yourself to something special—whether it be the book you always wanted, the movie you've been dying to see, or a long-distance phone call to a friend you haven't contacted in a long time. The rewards don't have to be big ones as long as they represent accomplishment to you. Be sure to thank your angels each time. At no time should you worry about money, or how you will get to the next stage. Self-talk yourself into confidence and into your new career.

Work on bringing your goal toward you in meditation and visualization. See yourself as an attorney. See yourself smiling, being busy with what you want to do. Practice this every day. Imagine yourself enrolling in college, see yourself smiling as you sit in class, talking to your classmates, and so on. See your tests being handed back to you with high grades. Visualize yourself enjoying the study and excitement of the new venture.

Begin working angel magick. Cut out pictures of someone in the line of work you desire. If you want to be an artist, find pictures of an artist, or if you want to be an attorney, find pictures of attorneys. Even better—dress up as what you want to be and have a friend or family member take an instant picture of you in that career dress. Write down specifically what type of career you want. Be sure to include details such as salary, location, perks, insurance necessities, transportation, etc. Be thorough. Check which correspondences would be good for the type of employment you want. Write them down, too, as you will be using them often in the future.

As with the house magick we talked about before, put your picture and your list on the angelic altar. Perform an altar devotion. State specifically what type of career/job you are working toward, and ask for help in obtaining that goal. If your career will involve several steps, such as training or apprenticeship, take that all into account, and work magick one step at a time. Don't expect your success to happen overnight. And, as with the house magick, leave yourself an escape clause should the career you chose not be right for you. Sometimes we don't think about all the facts when weaving dreams. For instance, I'd love to be a doctor, but I can't stand blood and guts. If I can't get over that revulsion, then perhaps something else within that area would be better for me. Above all, leave that option to change your mind so you can stay on the right path to your success. With the beginning of each new step in the career process, perform another ritual.

When it comes time to apply for jobs, be sure you have a professionally done resume. Take the resume to your altar, do the altar devotion, and again indicate your specific needs for that career choice. Ask the angels to bring the right job opportunities toward you. Leave a copy of the resume on your altar.

Start looking for the right job and filling out the necessary applications. Each evening after job-hunting, return to your altar, continuing to ask for assistance. At no time should you become disappointed that things aren't moving as fast as you may like. Keep it foremost in your mind that the best job opportunity that will meet your specific needs will come your way. Because you have the escape clause, you will do fine.

When you have scheduled the dreaded interview, artistic showing, or whatever, go to your angelic altar the night before and ask for assistance in obtaining the right job that meets your requirements. In meditation, see yourself going through the interview successfully. See yourself at ease, intelligent, and interesting. When you reach the building where the company is housed, ask your guardian angel to assist you. Then tell the guardian angel of the business you are about to enter why you are there and what you are seeking. Remember the chapter on the Nine Choirs? Every business establishment, government agency, etc., has its own guardian angel. They will help you find what is in your best interests, and the best interests of the company. Believe me, I wish I'd known that tidbit of information before I took some of the jobs I've held! It would have saved me a lot of unhappiness and bother. If the job interview, showing, etc., doesn't pan out, don't lose faith. Remember, your suspension of belief is necessary.

When you do reach your goal, reward yourself and remember to thank the angels for their assistance.

What are the most important issues in this process? Suspension of belief, a plan of achievable actions, and trust in divinity. No matter what type of magick you are using or what you are working for, try always to keep these three necessary points in mind. They are your keys to success.

Be creative in your planning sequences. Here are some other examples:

Design a business card with your name on it and the occupation you wish to do.

SILVER RAVENWOLF
Angel Counselor and
Clinical Hypnotherapist
HOURS BY APPOINTMENT ONLY
(010) 555–HYPNO

Write a newspaper article detailing your rise to success, or simply write the headline.

The Angel Times

Jenine E. Trayer Hits #1
on Best Seller List with Latest Title

Design a certificate that says you have reached your goal.

This is to certify that

_____

has reached the goal of

_____

on this day, the ___ *of* _____ *19* ___

Signed _____

Congratulations!

Practice signing your name with the title you wish to gain after it. Don't feel silly; no one will know.

Silver Ravenwolf—Best Selling Author

Silver Ravenwolf—Best Selling Author

Bill Gets a $35,000 Job

This is truly an out-of-the-blue story. A young woman called me one afternoon indicating that her boyfriend would like to talk to me. I had other commitments, but she said she was really concerned for him. Would I be around for a phone call the following morning? I finally agreed to take the phone call the next day, when he would be available.

True to her word, he called me in the morning. His first questions dealt with his daughter, who lived in Texas with her mother. Was she okay? I threw the cards and read through the layout—a normal read, no significant problems. During the conversation he mentioned that he was going for a job interview that day. He expressed concern that he wouldn't get it. The salary ranged between thirty and thirty-five thousand dollars.

"I really need this job," he said.

"Why don't you try contacting your guardian angel and asking for help?" I asked.

"Out loud?"

"Sure. Ask your guardian angel to help you, and then as you walk into the building where the interview is taking place, ask the guardian of the business to help you, too. Everything will be okay," I told him.

I forgot about this conversation. Indeed, I figured I'd never hear from him again. That evening, another phone call came in.

"This is Bill. I just wanted to thank you so much for telling me about my guardian angel. I did exactly what you said, and guess what—I got the job!"

Turning Fear Around

There is no end to what your mind can create. Anything positive in nature will help you reach your goals. Naturally, you have to know what your goals are before you begin. This means eliminating fear from your life.

For example, I was scared to death to go on television and talk about my beliefs. My father felt sure my life would be ruined if everybody knew I was "into" alternative religions and healing. He respects my religion and knows that it is not harmful, but he was frightened that I would be making a big mistake if I went public. His fears were not unfounded, as many of my fellow Wiccans do experience persecution on the job, where they live, even within their own families. I ought to know; I work with these discrimination cases often. He feared for my welfare and the safety of my family. When I got my first chance to go on national television, I blew it. My fear made me unappealing to the people who pre-interviewed me, and I knew it. The fiasco left me feeling inadequate and stupid. It was time to think about, I mean *really* consider, what I wanted out of life—and why.

I came to the realization that you can't sell books and not do some sort of publicity work. If you buy into the career, you've got to play the game. The idea is to make the game work for you, not against you, and in no way should you feel forced to do what others think you should. For example, I refuse to carhop all over the country to sign books because my primary responsibility is to take care of my children now. I'd like to make it clear this isn't a particular company's requirements, it is an acceptable thing that most authors do. It's part of the game. If people show up at your book signing, it does raise your self-esteem. However, I know I have to make some concessions—choosing only those few places where I want to go, and not worrying about the care of my children while I'm away. This means I don't go very far for very long. When my children are older, I'll be able to enjoy this aspect of the publishing business, but I choose not to do so until that condition is met. In your career, it is your decision how you will handle its aspects and ramifications, and you must never forget that you are the major player. Slowly, very slowly, I worked toward better public relations. It didn't happen overnight. Finally, I was asked to appear again on television. Yes, I was afraid. I went over and over in my mind the worst things that could happen, then realized my mistake. I was creating negative circumstances and drawing problems toward me.

I switched my plan of attack and turned my fears around. The television spot went off very well, and I had a great time. My world did not come crashing down about me. Those who saw me on television were very excited. I'll never forget walking into my bank two days after the television show, and as soon as I stepped through those glass doors one teller yelled out, "I saw you on television the other day. How exciting!" She wasn't angry at me at all. The other tellers were excited, too. "Oh, I'm sorry I missed it!" said one, and her words came from the heart—I could hear it in her tone of voice. When I went to a local restaurant, I got the same excellent treatment.

Through this experience I learned the valuable lesson of not giving in to my fears. I also learned how to turn my fears toward a positive resolution of my internal conflict. This is no easy task for anyone. When you have succeeded, learn to pat yourself on the back. Be proud of your accomplishments. Too often we belittle ourselves because we don't want people to think we are being snots. To be humble is good—to destroy your self-esteem is stupid. Not only does poor self-esteem bring you down, it grabs onto everyone around you and pulls them into the abyss of despair, too. Remember that every action you do has an equal reaction somewhere else, on someone other than yourself.

How to Handle Jealousy

Although we would consider jealousy an emotion (of course it is), it usually deals with earthly subjects: work, home, possessions, and of course viewing other people as property (which we subconsciously know is wrong, but humans have a bad habit of doing it anyway). Therefore, I've chosen to cover this subject under the element of earth because it is directly related to our stability and security in life.

Obviously jealousy is not an angelic thing and is harmful rather than helpful to us. However, angels can help us work on our jealousies if we have the courage to air them out and look at them for what they are.

Everyone has a different "jealousy button." This means that what makes me jealous may not affect you in the same way. Therefore, each person should determine precisely what makes him or her jealous, and why. Again, as in dealing with our fears, this is not an easy task. Fear and jealousies are excellent bedfellows and horrid harmony smashers. Add our insecurities to this bubbling cauldron, and you've got a spoiled mess that occasionally threatens to erupt. The more it spews into our lives, the greater the muddle, the unhappier the person. Like a row of dirty dominos, these negative energies can bring everything you've worked for tumbling down so quickly that sometimes we don't know what the heck happened, or why.

Eradicating negative energy from our lives requires courage and honesty with ourselves, so before you start digging into your psyche, make peace with yourself. Determine that whatever you discover cannot possibly be that bad and could be changed for the better. If you see a dark, yawning hole, you've not eliminated your fear in dealing with the bad stuff within yourself. Instead, look toward the light, and know that every human on this planet must travel the same road of looking within to become a balanced and harmonious person.

Answer the following questions. How often do you get jealous? (Several times a day? About once a week? Once in a while?) The more you tango with jealous feelings, the greater amount of work is ahead of you. What sort of jealousies do you have? (Do you covet possessions of others? Do you get jealous in affairs of the heart?) Is your jealousy targeted at one specific person, or situations in general?

Most jealous feelings come because we somehow feel our security and safety are threatened. Logically consider the answers you gave to the questions above. Do your answers indicate the fear of losing something or someone? Do the answers deal with your self-esteem and the feeling that there's "no way out"? Some people get jealous after they have been harmed. Sometimes this is the worst sort of jealousy because it can fester into hate if we are not careful. As you can see, we are working to find the root of the problem.

Once you determine the underlying reason for your jealousy, you can begin to work toward eradicating it from your life. Every time you get a jealous or bad thought, counteract it with the words "angels bless." This turns a negative thought into a positive one.

On a full moon, write your jealousies on a piece of paper and take it to your angelic altar. Do your altar devotion and ask the angels to help you overcome your negative feelings. Mundanely work toward removing jealousies from your life by trying new things, congratulating yourself when you succeed, facing your fears, and learning not to be too critical of yourself or others.

Angel Abundance Affirmation

I am a big fan of affirmations. Affirmations are positive statements designed to help you lead a more productive, harmonious life. You can say them or write them down, it doesn't matter, as long as you keep them short and positive for everyday work. A short affirmation would be:

The angels bring harmony into my life.

Here's a longer one for when you get up in the morning or before bedtime:

I am one with the universe
I am one with the riches of my conscious and subconscious mind.
I am one with divinity.
It is my right to be prosperous, happy and successful.
Money flows to me freely, in profusion, and endlessly
I am truly worthy of universal richness
The angels bless me with financial wealth and security
And in turn, I bless others with my talents and love.

Angels and Lost Pets and Lost Objects

In our society, pets are very important to us. They help bring us closer to the earth and teach us the lesson of unconditional love. When a pet is lost, great sadness fills the household. The angels will help you find your lost pet. You will need a green candle, a green ribbon, a picture of your pet, its favorite toy, and anything that has its fur (or scales or feathers) on it. The angel of tame beasts is Behemiel. Light the green candle, call your guardian angel, then ask for the assistance of Behemiel to help you find your pet. Loop the green ribbon on your altar and tie the ends with one knot (and one knot only). Place all the items associated with your pet in the center of the loop. Ask for your pet's safe return. Leave the items on the altar until you find your pet. When your pet returns, thank both your guardian angel and Behemiel.

To find a lost object, change the candle color and ribbon color to match the object. For example, should it be a diamond ring, the color would be brown or green, as diamonds are tied to the earth. You may wish to check your correspondences further, choosing the appropriate angelic hour to call for assistance. Pick the angel that has the greatest association with the lost item.

Protection

Protection magicks belong to all the angels, depending on the form of protection needed. For property, one would ask the angels of the earth. For protecting your health, call upon the angels of water. For protecting your passion and creativity, contact the angels of fire. For protecting your mind and any type of knowledge of communication, one would ask the angels of air. Most protection magick is done either on the full moon, on Monday (which is a Moon day), or in the angelic hour of the Moon. Protection magick is best done in a magick circle in ritual.

To call the angels of protection, try this passage:

Sword and lightning, swift the flash
By powers of Mars, my enemies smash.
Turn back the attack, focus on them
Give their pride a rightful trim.

Go sweet Michael, by the light of your fire
Accomplish my protection, my firm desire.
Go sweet Michael, by heaven's employ
No more shall they speak lies that remove others' joy.

I break the bonds, I sever the friendship
I invoke the powers of my own kinship.
Blood and bones and seething fire
Michael circles, higher and higher.

I work the magick for my protection
I call the angels of divinity's selection.
Upon the screaming winds they fly
Protection I hail, the evil will die.

For those of you who work magick often, this passage is a normal one. For those of you who do not work a great deal of magick, you may feel this is too strong. If it bothers you, don't use it. It is appropriate to call for justice and protection, no matter what religion you follow.

Twelve

Angels and
the Zodiac

Astrology is the study of heavenly
cycles and cosmic events as they are
reflected in our earthly environment.[1]
What happens in the heavens is a
direct mirror of what is happening on
Earth. The angels of the zodiac, combined with the art and science of
astrology, can move you further along
in your spiritual life than you ever
thought possible. Yes, it will take
some study on your part, but if you
truly want to get a grip on your life,

---

1. From *Astrology for Beginners* by William
Hewitt, page 4.

investigate the realm of the zodiac angels. They can assist you in determining what is going to happen (or has happened) at any moment. Astrology moves forward and backward in time, allowing you to perceive things in a non-linear fashion. The angels of the zodiac will help you work "out of time," so that you do not feel the controlling effects of linear energies.

Although astrological natal charts are the most popular magickal tools, astrology can be of particular interest to those who counsel, divine, or work magick. It can also be useful in general study as well. For example, if you enjoy history, you can check out a chart for the Battle of Gettysburg or the day of an earthquake. There are endless uses for astrology and the wisdom of the zodiac angels.

You don't have to be a mathematical genius to work with astrology or the angels of the zodiac. In this chapter we will not talk about casting charts, but discover the energies of the zodiac angels. You can apply these energies to various aspects of your life. After studying the angels of the zodiac and the angels of the planets, you may wish to review your natal chart (or the charts of others) with the information contained in these two chapters. This chapter will concentrate on the basics of the angels of the zodiac, and how these angels apply their energies to the universe.

The Signs of the Zodiac

The zodiac was originally constructed as a method of measurement, showing the amount of time it takes for the Sun to pass through the constellations. Although this movement is really representative of the Earth revolving around the Sun, from the Earth it appears as though the Sun transits the heavens. The zodiac takes the form of a circle, and its divisions number twelve equal parts. Each part is called a sign. The Sun appears in each sign, or part, at approximately the same time each year. Each part or sign bears the name of a constellation. Over the centuries, each part gathered unique qualities, energies, and histories. Each zodiac sign also has angelic associations, including "angelic rulers."

Angels of Aries (March 20 / 21 to April 19 / 20)

Color: Crimson

Ruling planet: Mars

Angelic hour: Camael

Herbal associations: Black pepper, clove, coriander, cumin, frankincense, ginger, pennyroyal, pine, woodruff

Sigil: ♈

In ceremonial magick the angel of Aries is Aiel or Machidiel. In the Cabala, the two spirits governing the sign of Aries are Sataaran and Sariel. The angels of Aries represent raw energy. They are angels of action, swift and instantaneous. Courageous, wild, and passionate, these angels literally tread where other angels fear to go. As Aries represents the first sign of the zodiac, Aries angels are always the first on the birth of any situation. They are the angels of beginnings and impulses. These angels influence leadership, enthusiasm, strength, and strife.

Aries angels are adventurous and enjoy the outdoors, and any sports associated with that realm. Aries angels will help you with big and little things. For example, there are times in our lives where we need to use force. I stopped at a grocery store one evening just so my youngest son could get something out of one of those quarter machines. He'd worked very hard for his seventy-five cents, and knew exactly what he wanted. His oldest sister took him inside. They reappeared a few moments later, tears streaming down my son's face.

"What's the matter?" I asked.

"The machine is stuck," replied my daughter. "He didn't lose any money, but he didn't get what he wanted."

I sighed. "Get in the truck; I'll be back in a minute."

At the machines I put the quarter in and tried to turn the knob. No go. I tried again. Stuck. "Angels of Aries," I muttered, "unstick whatever got stuck and help me turn this knob, please." I gripped the knob and turned. Presto!

I came back to the truck with the treasures in my hand.

"How did you do that?" asked my son.

My daughter rolled her eyes. "How do you think she did it? The way she always does! She used magick."

"Cool," said my son.

Angels of Taurus (April 20/21 through May 20/21)

Color: Turquoise or green

Ruling planet: Venus

Angelic hour: Uriel

Herbal associations: Apple, cardamom, honeysuckle, lilac, magnolia, oakmoss, patchouli, plumeria, rose, thyme, tonka, ylang-ylang

Sigil: ♉

In ceremonial magick, the chief angel over Taurus is Tual or Asmodel. The governing spirits of Taurus are Bagdal and Araziel. Taurus angels are quiet and stable, beings of intense and well-honed focus. Often associated with agriculture and things that grow, these angels love "pretties" (things and energies that are aesthetically pleasing). Taurus angels are not random in action or thought. They are excellent planners, good with structure and hierarchy. These angels are renowned for their strength, and are considered the "heavyweights" of the universe. Their passions include singing, playing instruments, and other forms of entertainment. However, they can be stubborn and persistent when necessary.

Taurus angels oversee income and assets. When asking for assistance to draw a new career to you or shopping for that new freezer, Taurus angels will assist you. They are also good in assisting you to get people to pay you money that is legitimately owed you. It is easy to get angry when people owe you money and won't pay up. If you have a temperament like mine, you'd rather walk up to them and slap them in the face. Of course, this is not the best course of action and won't get you anywhere, least of all closer to your money. You want to do it in a loving way. People who act with love are a great deal easier to work with.

My best friend's husband is a great guy, but people always take advantage of him. He sometimes has difficulty getting people to pay him for the work he does. They think that because he is a nice guy, it is all right to make him wait while they pay other bills to keep their you-know-whats out of hot water. If my friend were independently wealthy, she wouldn't care; but, like most people on the planet, she's not. If her husband doesn't get paid, the whole family suffers. I'm sure many of you can relate to this. What to do?

The moment her husband tells her he has "one of those" customers again, off to the altar she goes, green candle in hand. First, she inscribes the sigil of Taurus on the candle. Then she writes down the "deadbeat's" name on the left side of an index card, and her husband's name on the right side of the index card. She draws the Taurus sigil on the top of the card. She draws an arrow from the deadbeat to her husband. Along this arrow she puts little dollar signs, and the amount of money owed. She also considers the timing. For example, if she can wait a week for the money, she gives it a week. But if she needs it within twenty-four hours, she'll use that timing. On the back of the card, she writes the angel abundance affirmation (see page 163).

The best days to do this working would be Thursday or Friday. The best angelic hours would be Sachiel or Uriel. Light the candle, then hold the card in your hand while focusing on your desire. Ask your guardian angel and the angels of Taurus to help you. Leave the card on your altar until you receive the money owed to you. Be sure to thank the person who pays you the money, and the angels for their assistance.

Angels of Gemini (May 21/22 through June 20/21)

Color: Silver

Ruling planet: Mercury

Angelic hour: Raphael

Herbal associations: Benzoin, bergamot mint, caraway, dill, lavender, lemongrass, lily of the valley, peppermint, sweet pea

Sigil: ♊

In ceremonial magick, the primary angel is Giel (also Ambriel). The two governing spirits of Gemini are Sagras and Saraiel. The angels of Gemini are concerned with mental cycles and energies such as communication, ideas, and understanding intangible concepts. These angelic energies are very much a part of our information age. They are also "the informants"—not seekers of knowledge, but the disseminators of it. The angels of Gemini are always around when partnership is in the air, whether it be in business, love, or play.

Gemini angels oversee travel, relationships with siblings, activities in the neighborhood, friends, memory, self-expression, and neighbors. They are fascinated with the media, especially the technologically sophisticated information superhighway. Gemini angels are guardians of travelers, lecturers, writers, designers, composers, and anything to do with public relations. If you need excellent publicity for anything, call the Gemini angels.

Because these angels are so interested in the transfer of data, they are familiar with the need for protection of its vehicles. For example, if you wish to send a letter to someone, put the symbol of the Gemini angels on one corner of the envelope. If you are worried about your computer crashing, take a permanent marker and draw the symbol of Gemini at the top of your monitor on the plastic. Keep your books from being stolen by placing the Gemini sigil on the inside cover. If you need to find information, call on the Gemini angels for assistance. Protect computer disks with the Gemini symbol as well.

Angels of Cancer (June 21/22 through July 21/22)

Colors: Turquoise and dark blue/green

Ruling planet: Moon

Angelic hour: Gabriel

Herbal associations: Chamomile, cardamom, jasmine, lemon, lily, myrrh, palmarosa, rose, sandalwood, yarrow

Sigil: ♋

Ceremonial magicians call upon Cael, Manuel, or Muriel. The governing spirits of the sign of Cancer are Rahdar and Phakiel. The primary goal of Cancer angels is to gather and dispense emotional energy, and assist you in holding on to things that you have already earned. They are interested in the home base of family. These angels are best at manipulation of circumstances. Those things of lineage and gifts passed from mother to child, or father to child, are also the territory of Cancer angels.

Cancer angels govern intuition, sensitivity, and the need for public recognition. Property ownership also falls under the realm of the Cancerian angels. They represent the home in the mystical sense as well, including warding off negative energies, protecting family secrets, and ensuring the security you seek in old age. Employ the Cancerian angels any time you are making something for your home, protecting keepsakes from the ravages of time, or remodeling the homestead.

An Angelic Guard to Protect Your Home and Family

Supplies:
Angel patterns (see facing page)
One large square of white felt
One large square of gold felt
Glue and a glue gun
Scissors
An eight-inch piece of gold ribbon or thin gold cord
One gold pipe cleaner
Two small black beads (and any other craft supplies)
A small amount of Spanish moss
Five flat magnets (or one six-inch strip of magnet with adhesive backing)

Using the patterns as a guide (you might want to enlarge them), cut out the angel body from the white felt. Cut the wings from the yellow felt.

Glue the gold cord (ribbon) around the neck so that the ribbon ends hang down the front of the angel.

Glue the angel body on top of the wings with the glue gun.

Sew on the two eyes (or you may wish to purchase ready-made glue-on eyes found at your local craft store).

Form a small handful of Spanish moss into a loose ball. Glue the moss onto the head, arranging it to frame the face.

Form a halo out of the pipe cleaner and glue it to the back of the head. Cut the magnetic strips and stick them to the back of the angel: one at the head, one on the top of each wing, and two at the bottom of the skirt (one on each side).

With a pen, write on the back of the angel's body "Angel House Guardian" and the sigil of the Cancerian angels. Take the angel to your altar and ask your guardian angel and the Cancerian angels to assist in protecting your home and family. Hold the angel firmly in your hands, visualizing the safety and security you want for your home. When you are finished, thank the angels, then hang the angel on your refrigerator. Renew your angel once a year.

Angel wings pattern

Angel body pattern

Finished angel house guardian

Angels of Leo (July 22/23 through August 22/23)

Colors: Orange and yellow

Ruling planet: Sun

Angelic hour: Michael

Herbal associations: Bay, basil, cinnamon, frankincense, ginger, juniper, lime, nasturtium, neroli, orange, petitgrain, rosemary

Sigil: ♌

The primary angel of Leo in ceremonial magick is Verchiel. Angels governing this sign are Sagham and Seratiel. Angels of Leo are flamboyant, optimistic, enthusiastic, and incredibly loyal. They are quick to help with matters of the heart, from starving children to couples in love. Flowers and candlelight attract Leo angels. They like to help individuals who have a strong love for life and understand the need for being charitable.

The best way to thank the Leo angels is to do something special for someone. A random act of kindness makes them extremely proud. Those who wish to achieve great accomplishments, whether in the home or in a stadium full of cheering fans, should look to the Leo angels for assistance. Comfort, imagination, ease, and pleasure are in the realms of the Leo angels.

There is no project or tangible article for asking the aid of Leo angels; acts of charity, from the heart, are all that is required.

Angels of Virgo (August 23/24 through September 22/23)

Colors: Silver and deep blue

Ruling planet: Mercury

Angelic hour: Raphael

Herbal associations: Caraway, clary sage, costmary, cypress, dill, fennel, lemon balm, honeysuckle, oakmoss, patchouli

Sigil: ♍

Ceremonial magicians call upon Voil or Voel and Hamaliel. The governing angels are Iadara and Schaltiel. Virgo angels are interested in the perfection of a thing, thought, action, duty, or person. Projects involving research, investigation, elegance, and artistic creativity all fall under the realm of Virgo angels. If you need to look at every detail, call the Virgo angels. These angels are also concerned with the principle of harvest, and will assist you in working toward your goals. Virgo angels are interested in your coworkers, subordinates, pets, and beauty. They will enhance these situations as well as work to smooth out difficulties if you ask them.

If you need intellectual communication in a partnership of the heart, Virgo angels will be more than happy to help you. If you need a clever solution to a problem, look to the Virgo angels. At first, Virgo was represented by the Sumerian Corn Goddess. Later in history, she was equated with Mary. Virgo is often depicted holding flowers, sheaves of wheat, or stalks of corn. She is the ultimate harvester, collector, and librarian of facts. The collective unconscious of Virgo is definitely feminine in nature, and to that end, health problems involving female organs and childbirth are under the control of the Virgo angels.

If a female friend wishes assistance in conceiving or is having medical difficulties, place a corn dolly on your altar. Pin your friend's name to the dolly and ask the Virgo angels for assistance in healing and a safe, healthy conclusion, whether it be through an operation she must face or the successful birth of a child. I often give expectant mothers "birthing dollies" fashioned with baby-type things (such as rattles and stork pins) to hang in the delivery room. Later, the dolly is to be placed in the child's nursery so that it can watch over the babe while it sleeps.

Angels of Libra (September 23/24 through October 22/23)

Colors: Pink and light blue

Ruling planet: Venus

Angelic hour: Uriel

Herbal associations: Chamomile, daffodil, dill, eucalyptus, fennel, geranium, peppermint, pine, spearmint, palmarosa, vanilla

Sigil: ♎

Ceremonial magicians employ Zuriel and Jael. Angels governing Libra are Grasgarben and Hadakiel. The prime concern of the angels of Libra are the energies of harmony and balance. What's fair, is fair. They dislike mess, dirt, disorder, noise, confusion, or chaos. Libra angels are drawn to legal incidents, the counsel of others, or when cooperation and interaction are needed among individuals. They are also concerned with the affairs of both the living and the dead, and the interaction between them.

Angels of Libra are interested in the equal give-and-take in any partnership, including marriage. An old custom to bring harmony into a marriage is to take an orange and stick it with holes. Place a clove in each hole, then tie a ribbon of white around the orange. Hang the fruit in the bedroom to bring forth the harmony of the Libra angels.

Libra angels will shine light on your enemies so that you can see who they are. Go to your angelic altar and explain the problem to the Libra angels. Meditate if you like. Tell them your need to have a solution or some assistance. In a few hours or days, your request will be answered.

Angels of Scorpio (October 23/24 through November 21/22)

Colors: Maroon and black

Ruling planet: Pluto

Angelic hour: Cassiel

Herbal associations: Black pepper, cardamom, coffee, galangal, hyacinth, hops, pennyroyal, pine, thyme, tuberose, woodruff

Sigil: ♏

Ceremonial magicians referred to Barchiel and Sosol. The governing angels of Scorpio are Riehol and Saissaeiel. Scorpio angels are primarily concerned with devotion and intellectual pursuits. The angels of Scorpio are very interested in dreams and their interpretation. If a dream confuses you, the angels of Scorpio may give you the answers you seek. These angels are also interested in any type of detective or investigative work. Where the Virgo angels look for minute clues and correspondences, the Scorpio angels are very good at ferreting out the truth and working with large amounts of information to bring a conclusion.

Angels of Scorpio are extraordinarily mystical. Like Libra angels, they are interested in secrets, but in this case, they deal with the secrets of the dead. They are interested in the transformation of the human, whether it be in birth, death, or afterlife. These angels also govern psychic powers and occult studies and knowledge. Request the presence of the angels of Scorpio when learning any divination tool, such as the Tarot, I-Ching, pendulum, etc. Ask them for their blessings on any type of divination. Scorpio angels are excellent when working on criminal cases that involve homicide or an unresolved death.

Scorpio angels massage intense emotions that focus on a specific conclusion or transformation of a matter. These angels will bring power into your life if you specifically request it. They are swift to assist you, should you be attacked for your ideas or beliefs.

Angels of Sagittarius (November 22/23 through December 20/21)

Colors: Purple and deep blue

Ruling planet: Jupiter

Angelic hour: Sachiel

Herbal associations: Bergamot, clove, hyssop, lemon balm, nutmeg, rosemary, saffron

Sigil: ♐

Ceremonial magicians call upon Advachiel or Adnachiel, Ayil or Sizajasel. The two governing angels of the sign of Sagittarius are Vhnori and Saritaiel. The angels of Sagittarius are most interested in dynamic force—the bigger the better, the bolder the more magnificent. They love individuals who seek to extend their energies beyond their own environments. Whenever someone is seeking "status" in life, the angels of Sagittarius are there to assist. These angels enjoy humans who like to travel, teach, lecture, write, and publish, and those who enjoy having clear, concise facts to work with. They also enjoy freedom and laughter and will help you find your unexplored potential.

Pageantry and ritual fall under the auspices of the Sagittarius angels. Be sure to ask these angels for assistance with anything that is of international concern. They also like to involve themselves in universities, religious groups, spiritual growth, and cultural pursuits.

Use the sigil of the Sagittarius angels on school books and papers. If you need freedom from something constrictive, ask these angels for help and carry their sigil with you. Look for help from the Sagittarius angels in any matter in which you need to be profound. They also govern long-distance travel, especially to foreign countries.

If you dream of publishing the "Great American Novel," it is to the angels of Sagittarius you should turn when the manuscript is ready to be sent to a publishing company. Lay the manuscript on your altar with the sigil of the Sagittarius angels on top. Ask that your manuscript be treated fairly, and that it finds the publisher that is right for the work.

Angels of Capricorn (December 21 / 22 through January 19 / 20)

Colors: Brown and black

Ruling planet: Saturn

Angelic hour: Cassiel

Herbal associations: Cypress, honeysuckle, lilac, mimosa, myrrh, patchouli, tulip

Sigil: ♑

Ceremonial magicians incorporate Hamael and Casujoiah. The governing angels of Capricorn are Sagdalon and Semakiel. The angels of Capricorn are primarily concerned with issues of time and space. They focus on the big picture, authority, and regulations. These angels deal with formalities, and you will find them in environments of total seriousness. They are the angels of maturity, self-discipline, responsibility, frugality, business, and honors. The Capricorn angels can help you "make do" when you think you have nothing to work with.

Banking, insurance, health, investigation, medical laboratories, detective agencies, government investigative organizations, and all areas where a level head and great dedication are required belong to the Capricorn angels. If you have worked very hard at achieving a goal, the Capricorn angels will be there to help you. They will carry messages to those of influence who can help you, as they are familiar with raw power and understand it.

Angels of Aquarius (January 20/21 through February 19/20)

Color: Iridescent blue

Ruling planet: Uranus

Angelic hour: Raphael

Herbal associations: Costmary, hops, lavender, lemon verbena, parsley, patchouli, pine, star anise, sweet pea

Sigil: ≈

Ceremonial magicians use Cambiel and Ausiel. The governing angels of Aquarius are Archer and Ssakmakiel. The primary focus of the Aquarius angels is universal communication. These are the angels that spread universal thoughtforms to create harmony. It is the unbiased sharing of information that sometimes causes chaos for the greater good. Angels of Aquarius tend to gravitate toward inventors and explorers. They are not the angels of the long haul, but of the brilliance that begins a mission. If you need the impetus to do or lead something or someone, the Aquarian angels will help you get off your duff.

Aquarian angels deal with friends, hopes, wishes, long-term dreams, goals, intellectual pleasures, clubs, societies, political associations, and harmonious interaction with large groups of people. They may also be entreated for help in the care of children who are not yours by birth, rewards derived from a profession, and the individual gains you can achieve by projecting your energy and talent outward through other people.

Angels of Pisces (February 18/19 through March 19/20)

Colors: Sea greens

Ruling planet: Neptune

Angelic hour: Gabriel

Herbal associations: Apple, camphor, cardamom, gardenia, hyacinth, jasmine, lily, mugwort, myrrh, palmarosa, sandalwood, vanilla, ylang-ylang

Sigil: ♓

Ceremonial magicians entreat the assistance of Barchiel and Pasiel. The two governing angels of Pisces are Rasamasa and Vocabiel. The angels of Pisces concentrate on the energies of inner strength and unseen power. Piscean angels are interested in the healing arts, especially those involving healing with energy. Wherever there is a good Samaritan, there are Pisces angels, whether help is given to humans, plants, or animals. When the wellspring of creativity needs to be tapped, ask for the Pisces angels to help you. Hidden power and psychic talents are tools of the Piscean angels.

Angelic Zodiac Wheel of the Houses

To make your angel workings easier, I have created a chart for your convenience (see below). The chart follows the astrological houses of the zodiac and the corresponding Sun signs, sigil, ruling angels, correspondences, element, color, and angelic hour.

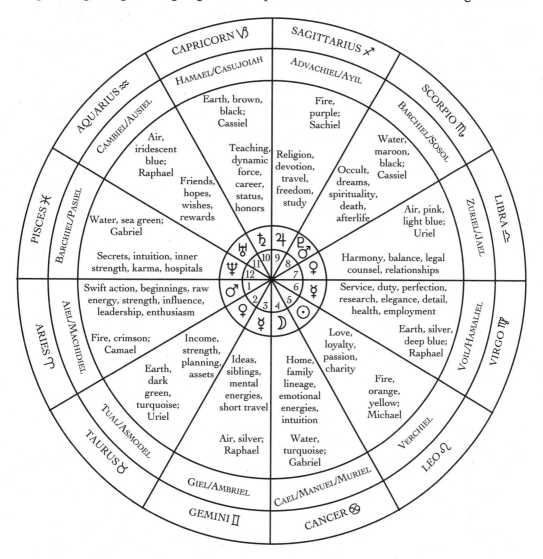

Summary

So far, we've covered a great deal about angels, magickal projects, and correspondences for your workings. I've got a lot more to share. Take your time and go over the information in this chapter again, and just for fun, why not match your goals with the zodiac angels? Which angels do you need to work with to ensure a bright and exciting future?

Affirmations:

I am one with the universe.

I am one with the riches of my conscious and subconscious mind. It is my right to be prosperous, happy and successful. Money flows to me freely, in profusion and endlessly. I am truly worthy of universal riches. The angels bless me with financial wealth and security, and in turn I bless others with my talents and love.

Thirteen

Angels and the Planets

In the last chapter we talked about the angels of the zodiac and how you can use them in your magickal work. You can also call upon the angels of the planets for assistance.

Just as zodiac angels have specific influences in timing and energies, so too do the planetary angels. The angel (or angels) of each planet has specific powers, fields of expertise, and times of power. Must you use zodiac and planetary angels in your magickal workings for a successful outcome? No; you can work angelic magick without using the planetary energies or angelic forms. So why would you want to use either zodiac or planetary angels in the first place? Well, it's sort of like … tomatoes.

I have a friend, Cally, who works at a grocery store as a cashier. When a customer drops code 4802 tomatoes on Cally's scale, Cally looks at the customer with a pleasant smile and says, "Do you know these are the Cadillac tomatoes?"

The customer usually looks baffled and replies, "I beg your pardon?"

Cally cocks her head and points her manicured index finger at the small net bag of tomatoes. "We have Cadillac tomatoes and we have Toyota tomatoes. These," she prods the bag, "are the Cadillac tomatoes. They'll cost you about five bucks."

Most customer's eyes round in shock. "For four tomatoes?"

Cally nods. "These four tomatoes will cost four to five dollars. The Toyota tomatoes will cost you two dollars. Do you really want the Cadillac tomatoes?"

Cally has a practical reason for asking this question. First, she's found that most customers don't pay attention to the sign over the Cadillac tomatoes. Those tomatoes look so good, the customer picks them up on impulse. Cally knows that nine times out of ten, when the customer realizes how much the tomatoes will cost, he or she asks Cally to take them off the order. If the tomatoes have already been rung in, this means a delay of up to five minutes for everyone else in line while the order is changed.

Zodiac and planetary angels are like those beautiful, appealing tomatoes. Working with these two types of angels will require a higher price from you—more time in planning and executing your ritual or magickal act. As the Cadillac tomatoes are a better product, so too will your magick be better if you use the zodiac and planetary angels in your workings. These angels and their correspondences allow you to focus your mind and direct your energies toward a specific desire.

Sun Angels

Sign: Leo

Day: Sunday

Occupations: Advertiser, all positions of authority, actor, park attendant, playground director, managerial and executive, all positions related to organizational ability, biologist, banker, financial planner, stockbroker, government offical, jeweler, lawyer, publicist

Hobbies: Community work, civic action, volunteer services, exercise, outdoor sports

Activities: Advertising, buying, selling, speculating, short trips, meeting people, anything involving groups or showmanship, putting up exhibits, running fairs and raffles, growing crops, taking care of health matters

Associations: Authority figures, favors, advancement, health, success, display, drama, promotion, fun, matters related to pleasures of the body and mind

Gifts: Ambition, confidence, strength, leadership, recognition, individuality, generosity, willpower, loyalty, fairness, honor

Herbal associations: Bay, bergamot, calendula, carnation, cedar, cinnamon, copal, frankincense, juniper, lime, neroli, orange, petitgrain, rosemary, saffron

Sigil: ☉

Many angels—including Arithiel, Galgaliel, Gazardia, Korshid-Metatron, Michael, Och, Raphael, Uriel, and Zerachiel—have been associated with this golden orb that is so important to our survival. In ancient Persian lore, the angel of the Sun was Chur. Sun angels represent power of will, the main direction and focus of any issue. Angels of the Sun will help you command respect and authority and impress and influence other individuals when you are in the right. These angels will assist you with your greatest ambitions.

Sun angels function well with the zodiac angels of Leo, Aries, and Sagittarius. Sun angels are not so compatible with the zodiac angels of Aquarius, Libra, and Gemini. Sun angels function fairly well with the zodiac angels of Taurus, Cancer, Virgo, Scorpio, Capricorn, and Pisces.

Moon Angels

Sign: Cancer

Day: Monday

Occupations: Caterer, domestic scientist, home economist, janitor, nurse, obstetrician, fisherperson, navigator, sailor, astrologer, security guard, diviner, any night work

Hobbies: Community and volunteer work, civic action, exercise, outdoor sports

Activities: Advertising, buying, selling, speculating, short trips, meeting people, anything involving groups or showmanship, putting up exhibits, running fairs and raffles, growing crops, taking care of health matters

Associations: Short trips, women, children, the public, domestic concerns, emotions, fluids

Gifts: Inspiration, magnetism, visionary and positive psychic powers, flexibility, love, creativity, imagination, domestic bliss, sensitivity to others

Herbal associations: Camphor, jasmine, lemon, lily, melon, night-blooming cereus, sandalwood, stephanotis, water lily

Sigil: ☽

It is perhaps the Moon that influences the practice of magick more than any other orb in the heavens. Without her energies, we could not experience the flow and nurturing of life. Angels of the Moon are Yahriel, Iachadiel, Elimiel, Gabriel, Tsaphiel, Zachariel, Iaqwiel, and most often associated, Ofaniel.

Moon angels concentrate on feelings, emotions, and sensitivities. They will help you get rid of habits and fulfill needs and desires that satisfy emotional cravings. Angels of the Moon are most interested in the human subconscious mind, memory, intuition, and instincts. They are highly concerned with the atmosphere of our homes.

Moon angels summoned during an eclipse of the Moon will bring extraordinary insight. If you are blessed with an "eclipse vision," consider yourself both gifted and lucky. These visions are moments of extreme clarity and understanding, an intrinsic truth. Sometimes the vision is for personal matters; at other times it is more global in nature. This message will tend to dominate our subconscious mind for several months. If two eclipses happen close together (for example, within two weeks of each other), then the period in between is excellent for calling on the Moon angels.

Moon angels called on the tenth day after the New Moon (counting the New Moon as day one) and the twenty-fifth day after the New Moon will also bring visions and special insights. For centuries, magickal individuals have set aside these two days for meditation, introspection, and harmonious workings. The tenth day is considered masculine in energy, and the twenty-fifth is thought of as feminine.

Other days in the Moon's cycle that are of interest to people who work angel magick include:

Days 28, 29, 30 (after the New Moon): Protection angels

Days 13 and 14: Purification angels

Days 8 (masculine) and 23 (feminine): Healing angels

Days 1 (New Moon, masculine) and 15 (Full Moon, feminine): Alignment angels

Moon angels function well with the zodiac angels of Cancer, Taurus, and Pisces. Moon angels do not function very well with the zodiac angels of Capricorn, Scorpio, and Virgo. Moon angels function fairly well with the zodiac angels of Aries, Gemini, Leo, Libra, Sagittarius, and Aquarius. As with anything, there are exceptions to every rule, especially when the Moon is involved.

For recovering stolen property, special invocations, and working with the dead, combine the angels of the Moon with the zodiac angels of Taurus, Virgo, or Capricorn. The working is best done when the Moon is in one of these signs, in its own hour, on its own day.

For love, grace, and invisibility, combine the angels of the Moon with the zodiac angels of Aries, Leo, or Sagittarius. The working is best done when the Moon is in one of these signs, in its own hour, on its own day.

For stopping criminals and banishing, combine the angels of the Moon with the zodiac angels of Cancer, Scorpio, or Pisces. The working is best done when the Moon is in one of these signs, in its own hour, on its own day.

Historically there are twenty-eight angels that rule the twenty-eight mansions of the Moon. They are:

1. Geniel	8. Amnediel	15. Atliel	22. Geliel
2. Enediel	9. Barbiel	16. Azeruel	23. Requiel
3. Anixiel	10. Ardifiel	17. Adriel	24. Abrinael
4. Azariel	11. Neciel	18. Egibiel	25. Aziel
5. Gabriel	12. Abdizuel	19. Amutiel	26. Tagriel
6. Dirachiel	13. Jazeriel	20. Kyriel	27. Atheniel
7. Schliel	14. Ergediel	21. Bethnael	28. Amnixiel

Angels of the Phases of the Moon

Lunar tides gleam with solar orb
Moon phase angels I adore.
Weave the magick of heaven's ways
Guide the pattern of night and day.
By Waxing Moon and Goddess might
Circle 'round each day and night.
When Moon be full draw down the power
Lending potency with every hour.
By waning tide and darkening light
Work my will by angel might.
Banish troubles from my gate
Help me build my positive fate.
Lunar ebb and lunar flows
Beating wings and bright halos.
To guide, to help, to guard my door
Bring forth the angels, ever more.

Each phase of the Moon also has its corresponding angelic forces. Moon phase angels can be used in any magickal practice, regardless of what other energies you plan to use.

You may wish to spend some time in meditation meeting each of the angelic forces. Rather than doing it all in one month, I suggest choosing one Moon angel a month to study. Look for messages from these angels after your meditation sequences. We will work more with these angels of the Moon in the divination chapter (see Chapter 16). Keep a journal about your experiences with these angels. I am sure there are other correspondences, including herbs and incense, that you feel work better with these forces. Be sure to keep good records. If you have difficulty with record-keeping, try an index card system for quick reference.

Angels of the New Moon

Workings should be done from the day of the New Moon to three and a half days after. Envision these angels with glittering silver wings, dark hair, skin of dusky caramel, and sparkling dark gray robes. The closer to the New Moon, the better the energies. Issues of beauty and health, farms and gardens, job-hunting, love and romance, networking, and self-improvement all come under the auspices of the New Moon angels. The best time for working with them is at dawn or dusk.

I summon the angels New of Moon
To weave their magick on enchanted loom.
Silver wings and caramel skin
I slowly gather your energy in.
Begin the matter, bring to form
Lend your power—the thing is born!

Angels of the Crescent Moon

This crescent faces west, and the phase lasts from three and a half days after the New Moon through the seventh day. Because this moon rises at mid-morning and sets after sunset, check your astrological almanac for precise midpoint timing. Issues of animals, business, change, emotions, and matriarchal strength come under the reign of the Crescent Moon angels. Envision these angels with aquamarine robes, fiery red hair, peaches-and-cream skin, necklaces of seashells and peacock feather wings, with a glowing, milky Crescent Moon upon their brow.

I summon the angels of the Crescent Moon
Minions of the Goddess, come to me soon.
Mother essence I now draw nigh
Please send your energy from the sky.
Strength of the matter please take form
Powerful magick I perform.
Hair of fire, wings with eyes
The thought is born, it will not die.
Deosil energy circle up and 'round
I reach above and draw it down!

Angels of the Waxing Moon

This phase is from seven to ten and a half days after the New Moon. Here the Moon rises at noon and sets at midnight. Sunset is the prime period for magick involving the angels of the Waxing Moon. Those issues of interest to the angels of this Moon phase are courage, elemental magick, friends, luck, and motivation. These angels work extraordinarily well with fairies and devas. Picture these angels with robes colored like the vibrant sunset, fairy wings, olive skin, and auburn hair.

Waxing angels, sunset bold
I call your essence, energy mold.
Fairy friends with deva wings
Power of the heavens bring.
Potent elements and mystic art
I conjure these angels from my heart.
Olive skin and auburn hair
Build the thing from midnight air.
Autumn breeze and spring's bright kiss
Lend me, please, your heavenly bliss.
All good fortune spiral 'round
Increase each turn, love abounds.
Angel force and energy
The thing is set in eternity.
As I will, so mote it be.

Angels of the Gibbous Moon

This phase begins the tenth day after the New Moon and lasts to the fourteenth day after the New Moon. The Gibbous Moon rises at ten or eleven in the evening (check your astrological almanac) and sets at approximately three in the morning. Work with them at the midpoint between the rising and setting of the Moon. Angels of the Gibbous Moon are concerned with issues of patience and star magicks. Visualize these angels with midnight robes sprinkled with thousands of stars, white hair, fair skin, and wings of gossamer.

Gibbous Moon angels, patience divine
I call you into this circle of mine.
Starry essence with gossamer wings
Build the magick, vibrations sing.
I draw the energy of angelic love
And pull your power from planes above.
Circle 'round as the moon doth swell
Faster and faster, then seal it well.
As the moon turns from dark to light
I release the power of angelic might.
Natural force and energy
That moves the world I cannot see
I bring to form my ardent choice
And touch the strength of angel's voice.

Angels of the Full Moon

The Full Moon phase begins at dusk and ends at dawn, therefore midnight is the most propitious time to call the angels of the Full Moon. This Moon phase occurs from fourteen to seventeen-and-a-half days after the New Moon. The issues of prime concern to the angels of the Full Moon are artistic endeavors, beauty, health, fitness, change, protection, competition, decisions, dreams, families, knowledge, legal undertakings, love and romance, money, motivation, protection, psychism, and self-improvement. Envision these angels with robes of white silk, blonde hair, peaches-and-cream skin, and iridescent wings.

> *When the moon is full and filled with light*
> *I summon forth angelic might.*
> *Beams of love from glittering orb*
> *The Goddess reigns at heaven's door.*
> *Angel essence and I are one*
> *Fortune's touch blessed by the Sun.*
> *I cast the circle and seal it fast*
> *With equal force the magick lasts.*
> *As above and so below*
> *I form the power, then let it go.*
> *She rules the realm I cannot see*
> *And brings to form my reality.*

Angels of the Disseminating Moon

This phase begins three and a half days after the Full Moon and lasts until seven days after the Full Moon. The moon rises at mid-evening and sets at mid-morning, making the hour of souls (3:00 A.M.) the best time for calling these angels. The angels of the Disseminating Moon are concerned with issues of banishment, and therefore you may see them with swords, knives, or scythes. Don't fear them; they only wish to cut away the negative energies surrounding you and do not wish to harm the human essence. These angels deal with addictions, decisions, divorce, stress, protection, and negative emotions in general. They can be envisioned wearing robes of black and white animal skins and heavy silver jewelry, with milky skin, dark hair, and falcon wings.

> *Angels of dissemination*
> *Help me with this conflagration.*
> *Falcon wings banish evil*
> *From myself and all my people.*
> *Addictions vanish with the wind*
> *Bring only positive energy in.*
> *Cut the evil quick and fast*
> *Goddess love be made to last.*

Break this tired and weary affair
Replace the space with fortune's air.

Angels of the Waning Moon

The Waning Moon occurs seven to ten and a half days after the Full Moon. These angels work to release negativity and banish difficulties, though they also deal with problems that extend over several lifetimes. The angels of the Waning Moon work with addictions, divorce, health and healing (banishment; therefore work in a counterclockwise manner), stress, protection, and karmic issues. These angels wear robes of violet, and have slanted eyes and Oriental skin tones. Their hair is as blue-black as a raven's wing, their eyes bright and piercing. They wear a headband of sparkling silver, its focal point a blazing pentacle of banishment. Their wings are gray with plumes of gold.

Angels of the Waning Moon
I summon thee to grant my boon
Widdershins energy in the night
Bind the evil, knot it tight.
Cast it out, heal the pain
End the wretched tyrant's reign.
Wings of grey shot with gold
Beat away the negative hold.
I make the sign of banishment
And leave behind bright content.

Angels of the Dark Moon

Timing here is ten and a half to fourteen days after the Full Moon. This Moon rises at three in the morning and sets at mid-afternoon. Angels of the Dark Moon are known for their acts of justice. They deal with addictions, change, divorce, enemies, justice, obstacles, quarrels, removal, separation, criminals and their acts, and death by unjust means. Oddly enough, their strongest hour occurs around ten in the morning. Visualize these angels with no irises to their eyes, only large, moist pupils that see everything in all realms. Their ebony wings are powerful, their hair a froth of gleaming jet. When they smile, you will see canine incisors. The skin is void of color and they prefer black cloaks edged in crimson over robes of shimmering gray-black gauze. Indeed, sometimes these angels are mistaken for vampires.

Dark Moon angels hear my plight
Come to me, bring second sight.
Wings of ebony, hair of jet
Froth the skies with justice met.
Circle 'round in shimmering gauze

Add your power to my cause.
Banish evil here and now
Bury it with heaven's plow.
Dark Moon angels strong and wise
Rip from evil its disguise.
Cast it out, split asunder
Disseminate and bury under.
Smile of Crone and strength of Sage
I clean the slate, I wipe the page.
As above and so below
Break the hex and overthrow.
Summon, please, the heavenly host
To spook this criminal from pillar to post.
Bring to end evil and strife
Replace with harmony, love, and light.

Mercury Angels

Signs: Gemini and Virgo

Day: Wednesday

Occupations: Accountant, administrative assistant, diplomat, bookkeeper, clerical worker, critic, craftsperson, debtor, disc jockey, physician, editor, journalist, graphologist, interviewer, postal worker, secretary, distributor, inspector, lecturer, librarian, linguist, medical technician, scientist, secretary, student, teacher, writer

Hobbies: Writing stories, watching television, on-line system communication, machines that involve such communication

Activities: Bargaining, dealing with lawyers or literary agents, publishing, filing, hiring employees, learning languages, literary work, placing ads, preparing accounts, studying, using the telephone, visiting friends

Associations: Communications, correspondence, phone calls, fax messages, computers, e-mail, education, students, travel, merchants, editing, writing, advertising, signing contracts, siblings, neighbors, ancestors, kin

Gifts: Adaptability, mental activity, expressiveness, simultaneous activity, quick study, resourcefulness, brilliance, eloquence, dexterity, awareness

Herbal associations: Benzoin, bergamot mint, caraway, celery, clary sage, costmary, dill, eucalyptus, fennel, lavender, lemon verbena, lily of the valley, marjoram, parsley, peppermint, spearmint, sweet pea

Sigil: ☿

The swift angels who govern communicative Mercury are Tiriel, Raphael, Hasdiel, Michael, Barkiel, Zadkiel, and the Bene Seraphim. The Mercury angels are most concerned with communicative perceptions. They are interested in the way information is given and understood, and assist in the formation of ideas and opinions. Mercury angels are concerned with dexterity and manual skills, responses to stimuli, travel, and transportation.

Mercury angels function very well with the zodiac angels of Gemini, Virgo, Aquarius, and Scorpio. Mercury angels do not function well with the zodiac angels of Sagittarius, Pisces, Leo, and Taurus. Mercury angels function fairly well with the zodiac angels of Aries, Cancer, Libra, and Capricorn.

Venus Angels

Signs: Taurus and Libra

Day: Friday

Occupations: Architect, artist, beautician, chiropractor, dancer, designer, domestic worker, engineer, entertainer, fashion marketer, florist, gardener, hotel worker, horticulturist, opera singer, vocalist, musician, painter, poet

Hobbies: Embroidery, making clothes, music, painting, sculpture, handicrafts, sewing, landscaping, gardening

Activities: Amusement, beauty care, courtship, dating, decorating homes, designing, getting together with friends, household improvements, planning parties, shopping

Associations: Affection, partnerships, alliances, grace, beauty, harmony, luxury, love, art, music, social activity, marriage, decorating, cosmetics, gifts, income

Gifts: Love, gentleness, beauty, sociability, charm, refinement, consideration, creativity, inspiration, graceful movement

Herbal associations: Apple, chamomile, cardamom, catnip, daffodil, gardenia, geranium, hyacinth, iris, lilac, magnolia, mugwort, narcissus, palmarosa, plumeria, rose, thyme, tuberose, tulip, vanilla, vetivert, white ginger, wood aloe, yarrow, ylang-ylang

Sigil: ♀

These angels are concerned with matters of the heart and beauty (of course). Angels of Venus are Anael, Hasdiel, Eurabatres, Raphael, Hagiel, and Noguel. The primary concerns of Venus angels are social attitudes and human behavior. Beauty, grace, and artistic talent all fall under the guidance of the Venus angels. They adore cooperation and romantic love, as well as marriage and partnerships of all kinds. Venus angels will help you improve the atmosphere around you, pull in harmonious energies, and achieve the level of attractiveness you desire.

Venus angels work very well with the zodiac angels of Taurus, Pisces, and Aquarius. Venus angels do not work well with the zodiac angels of Aries, Scorpio, Virgo, and Leo. Venus angels work fairly well with the zodiac angels of Gemini, Cancer, Sagittarius, and Capricorn.

Mars Angels

Sign: Aries

Day: Tuesday

Occupations: Athlete, barber, butcher, carpenter, chemist, construction worker, dentist, firefighter, foundry worker, garbage collector, guard, jailer, locksmith, boxer, martial artist, wrestler, football player, metal worker, surgeon, soldier, police officer

Hobbies: Repairing vehicles, gardening, grafting, household improvements and woodworking, marksmanship, collecting weaponry

Activities: Business, mechanical affairs, buying or selling animals, dealing with contractors, hunting, undertaking any type of study

Associations: Strife, aggression, sex, physical energy, muscular activity, guns, tools, metals, cutting, surgery, police, soldiers, combat, confrontation

Gifts: Independence, strength, desire, courage, energy, determination, self-reliance, boldness where needed, devotion

Herbal associations: Basil, black pepper, broom, coffee, coriander, cumin, galangal, garlic, ginger, hops, nasturtium, onion, pennyroyal, pine, rue, woodruff

Sigil: ♂

Rough and ready, these angels can rebound with a virulent punch—they are aggressive, to say the least. The angels of Mars are Uriel, Sammael, Gabriel, and Chamael. Mars angels are most interested in physical energy, action, and power. They fire the emotions and push us into mental endeavors where we will achieve victory. Indeed, no other angels are associated with winning more than the angels of Mars. They help us take risks and encourage physical challenges.

Mars angels work well with the zodiac angels of Aries, Capricorn, and Leo. Mars angels do not work well with the zodiac angels of Libra, Cancer, and Aquarius. Mars angels work fairly well with the zodiac angels of Taurus, Gemini, Virgo, Scorpio, Sagittarius, and Pisces.

Jupiter Angels

Sign: Sagittarius

Day: Thursday

Occupations: Ambassador, appraiser, archer, banker, cashier, counselor, doctor, educator, guardian, horse trainer, hunter, jockey, judge, lawyer, legislator, merchant, minister, pharmacist, psychologist, public analyst, hypnotherapist

Hobbies: Social clubs, travel, collecting coins or rare artifacts

Activities: Charity work, education, science, correspondence courses, self-improvement, reading, research, study

Associations: Publishing, college, education, long-distance travel, foreign interests, religion, philosophy, forecasting, broadcasting, publicity, expansion, luck, growth, sports, horses, law

Gifts: Success, ambition, dignity, wealth, inspiration, reverence, optimism, confidence, honorability

Herbal assocations: Clove, honeysuckle, hyssop, lemon balm, mace, meadowsweet, nutmeg, oakmoss, sage, star anise, tonka

Sigil: ♃

When prosperity and fruition are on the horizon, look for the Jupiter angels. They are Zachariel, Zadkiel, Sachiel, Adabiel, Barchiel, and Zadykiel. Jupiter angels are most interested in growth potential and expansion on a variety of levels. Whether you are talking about physical, intellectual, spiritual, or cultural growth, Jupiter angels are ready to assist you. These angels have the ability to exaggerate and enlarge anything you desire. They govern the accumulation of material assets, power, and status and bolster your optimism, bringing joyful events toward you and helping you develop your aspirations.

Jupiter angels work well with the zodiac angels of Sagittarius, Cancer, Taurus, and Pisces. Jupiter angels do not work well with the zodiac angels of Gemini, Capricorn, Virgo, and Scorpio. Jupiter angels work fairly well with the zodiac angels of Aries, Leo, Libra, and Aquarius.

Saturn Angels

Sign: Capricorn

Day: Saturday

Occupations: Builder, civil servant, excavator, farm worker, mortician, mason, prison worker, refrigeration worker, tanner, magistrate/justice, mathematician, osteopath, plumber, politician, real estate agent, repair person, shoemaker, printer

Hobbies: Gardening, forestry, farming, papermaking

Activities: Taking care of debts, dealing with lawyers, financing, money matters, real estate, relations with older people, anything involving family ties or legal matters such as wills and estates

Associations: Structure, reality, the laws of society, limits, obstacles, tests, catching criminals, hard work, endurance, real estate, dentists, bones, teeth, matters relating to archaeological study

Gifts: Stability, self-discipline, wisdom, thriftiness, patience, endurance, humility, sincerity, conventionality, judiciousness, seriousness

Herbal associations: Cypress, mimosa, myrrh, patchouli

Sigil: ♄

These angels deal with responsibility and change. They are Orifiel, Kafziel, Michael, Maion, Mael, Zaphiel, Schebtaiel, and Zapkiel. The Saturn angels are primarily concerned with authority, karmic lessons, and boundaries. If you need endurance and practicality, call on these angels. If you would like to have an austere presence, the angels of Saturn are the energies you need. They are also concerned with the affairs of the elderly.

Saturn angels work well with the zodiac angels of Capricorn, Libra, and Virgo. Saturn angels do not work well with the zodiac angels of Cancer, Aries, and Pisces. Saturn angels work fairly well with the zodiac angels of Taurus, Gemini, Leo, Scorpio, Sagittarius, and Aquarius.

*T*hese are the seven planets dealt with in historical texts. The following planets and celestial bodies do not have a history of specified angelic hosts. However, the angelic energies can still be called upon in times of need or for magickal endeavors.

Uranus Angels

Sign: Aquarius

Occupations: Aerospace engineer, astrologer, broadcaster, electrician, humanitarian, government officials, inventor, lecturer, metaphysician, tractor driver, x-ray technician, radiologist, computer scientist, zoologist

Hobbies: Air and space travel, electronics, experimenting with extrasensory perception, new ideas (especially science fiction and virtual reality), the occult, studying, computer programming

Activities: Air travel, partnerships, changes, adjustments, civil rights, new contracts, new ideas, new rules, patenting inventions, copyrighting information, progress, social action, starting journeys (inner and outer)

Associations: Astrology, the new age, technology, computers, modern gadgets, divination, lecturing, advising, counseling, inventions, reforms, electricity, new methods, originality, sudden events

Gifts: Strength, unconventionality, originality, intuitive gifts, individualism, clairvoyance, strength of will, humanitarian assistance, personal magnetism, resourcefulness

Sigil: ♅

Freedom and independence are the key words of the angels of Uranus. These angels are concerned with anything "original," whether it be thought or expression. They are revolutionary angels who will upset the status quo if necessary (for a good reason, of course). They will help you understand an unpredicted change or help you make an unpredicted thrust into the world. Angels of Uranus are interested in thoughts that will change the atmosphere and minds of many people. To that end, they adore mass media and communication on a grand scale.

Uranus angels work well with the zodiac angels of Aquarius, Scorpio, Gemini, and Libra. Uranus angels do not work well with the zodiac angels of Leo, Taurus, Sagittarius, and Aries. Uranus angels work fairly well with the zodiac angels of Cancer, Virgo, Capricorn, and Pisces.

Neptune Angels

Sign: Pisces

Occupations: Alchemist, limousine driver, medium, oil field worker, poet, chain store manager, character actor, chemist, diplomat, photographer, psychiatrist, secret agent, wine merchant, religious leader, shipper, anything having to do with the sea

Hobbies: Acting, photography, music, movies, boat racing, water skiing, swimming

Activities: Advertising, dealing with psychological upsets, health foods, health resorts, large social affairs, nightclubs, psychic healing, travel by water, restaurants, visits, welfare, working with institutions

Associations: Mysticism, music, creative imagination, dance, illusion, sacrifice, service, oil, chemicals, paint, drugs, anesthesia, sleep, religious experiences, matters related to dreams

Gifts: Mystic experiences, clairvoyance, inspiration, genius, devotion, reverence

Sigil: ♆

These angels deal with legacies and historical discoveries. They are the caretakers of the oppressed and the misfits of society. They are interested in people who are considered visionaries, who enjoy being glamorous and charismatic. Angels of Neptune love mysticism, psychic awareness, and compassion. They will help in experiences related to confinement, abandonment, addiction, or physical intolerance to drugs.

Neptune angels work well with the zodiac angels of Pisces, Sagittarius, and Cancer. Neptune angels do not work well with the zodiac angels of Virgo, Gemini, and Capricorn. Neptune angels work fairly well with the zodiac angels of Aries, Taurus, Leo, Libra, Scorpio, and Aquarius.

Pluto Angels

Sign: Scorpio

Occupations: Acrobat, athlete/athletic manager, atomic energy worker, researcher, speculator, stockbroker

Hobbies: Those purely designed for personal enjoyment; working with children

Activities: Anything requiring energy, enthusiasm, skill, and alertness; personal relationships; original thoughts that will affect many people; pioneering

Associations: Probing, penetration, goods of the dead, investigation, insurance, taxes, other people's money, loans, the masses, the underworld, transformation, death

Gifts: Extrasensory perception, intensity, the ability to restructure anything, spirituality, transformation, revitalization

Sigil: ♇

The primary attribute of these angels is intense energy. Pluto angels are concerned with karmic issues on a grand scale (races, religions, institutions, cultures, etc.). If you need power and control over an issue, the Pluto angels will help you.

Pluto angels work well with the zodiac angels of Scorpio and Aquarius. Pluto angels do not work well with the zodiac angels of Taurus and Leo. Pluto angels work fairly well with the angels of Gemini, Virgo, Sagittarius, Pisces, Aries, Cancer, Libra, and Capricorn.

Angels of the Asteroid Ceres

Occupations: Nurse, homemaker, hypnotherapist, charitable coordinator, child-care facilitator, farmer, psychic hotline worker, chef, animal caregiver

Hobbies: Gardening, volunteer work, counseling friends, divination for the sole purpose of helping others

Activities: Tact, diplomacy, sharing, universal love and acceptance, finding and healing lost pets and children

Sigil: ⚳

The nurturing angels of Ceres are most interested in the principle of unconditional love. They are the angels of the Great Mother. They support the principles of sharing and caregiving and work with Goddess energy and the female divine. Should we wish to make up a name for the Ceres angels (why not; everyone else made up angelic names and they were no better than we are), I would choose "Annaelle"—*Anna* for the first mother and *elle* for shining, meaning shining mother, or mother shining.

Angels of the Asteroid Pallas

Occupations: Artistic endeavors (painting, drawing, cartooning, designing, sculpting, hand-crafts, pottery, jewelry making and design, interior design, architecture, ritual tool construction and design), occupations associated with holistic healing

Hobbies: Handicrafts, sewing, decorating your home, creating divination tools, writing poetry

Activities: Guided imagery, meditation, visualization, mental self-healing, developing new ideas and theories, creating psychic breakthroughs

Sigil: ⚴

The angels of Pallas are the feminine energy involved in intuition, flashes of genius, keen insights, and our ability to formulate new and original thoughts that are auspicious to the feminine collective unconscious, and the planet in general. The key phrase here is "creative intelligence." They are a part of any psychic pursuit that will uplift self-esteem and spirituality. Pallas angels are very interested in helping us plan strategies that lead to tangible results. They enjoy artistic ability and will help draw the creative energies out in you.

Angels of the Asteroid Juno

Occupations: Marriage counselor, female religious leader

Associations: Passion, balance, comfort, stability, consistency, shared visions, independence in love, emotional rapport, support, true understanding

Sigil: ✳

The prime concern of Juno angels is the balance of power and our individual freedoms. Juno angels are interested in the feminine surge for harmony and happiness in relationships.

Angels of the Asteroid Vesta

Occupations/hobbies: Any

Associations: Developing physical discipline and the inspiration to create, the learning and sharing of ideas, mental and spiritual merging and bonding

Sigil: ⩔

Vesta angels represent the feminine aspirations to particular paths or goals. The are interested in those who work hard for the sake of the thing. The angels of Vesta are the Guardians of the Witches, those individuals who have taken an oath to serve humankind with dedication and positive endeavors. Vesta angels help us focus and integrate ourselves into the bigger picture or into a lofty goal.

Angels of the Asteroid Chiron

Occupations: Healer, counselor, teacher

Sigil: ⚷

These are the angels who hold the keys to the universe. Chiron angels are thought to be the male aspect of the wounded priest or wounded healer, and in modern artwork appear as half-horse, half-man (centaurs). They can unlock any door, plumb any depths for an answer, and heal anything that is broken, hurt, diseased, or unwhole. Chiron angels are willing to help anyone who is self-sufficient or working toward that goal. They do not encourage us to sit back and take it easy, but push us toward action and controlling our lives and destinies. You will find Chiron angels whenever there is a shift in group consciousness.

Planetary Hours

Remember the angelic hours in Chapter 4? The planetary hours work precisely the same way (see the chart on the next page). Each hour of the day has an assigned angel that can assist you in your workings. When a project begins, its hour of origin will carry the energies of that hour throughout the working. You can also judge a matter from the hour in which you were first notified about it. Each of the days and hours are excellent for certain purposes.

The Sun: Business, possessions, goods, seeds, fruits, learning to use tools, good fortune, contacting the dead, protection during sleep

The Moon: Trips, messages, reconciliation, love, the buying and selling of goods, treating feminine illnesses, psychism

Mars: Military honors, acquiring courage, overthrowing enemies

Mercury: Communications of all types, eloquence, intelligence, science, divination, ghosts, writing, and buying (the first hour of Mercury after the sun rises is always a good time to begin a project or endeavor)

Jupiter: Obtaining honors, acquiring riches, contracting friendships, preserving health, planning goals and aspirations

Venus: Love, forming partnerships, recreation, traveling

Saturn: Banishing unwanted items, criminal magick, communicating with the dead, recovering lost items

Summary

As we start making talismans and performing some of the rituals in the following chapters, you will see how these correspondences can be used. Do these correspondences work? Yes, indeed.

In the hour of Saturn on the eve of a New Moon, I called the Dark Moon angels to help me with a little problem. One of my clients had had child services called on her five times. The caller, of course, was anonymous. Each time my client was vindicated; however, the issue was out of control. Child services' last visit was at two in the morning. They woke up her oldest daughter and thoroughly checked her body for bruises. They found none. Did they apologize? No way. Was the child traumatized? Yes!

After a little investigative work, we found that the caller was a male acquaintance of my client who had some unpleasant habits. I called the Dark Moon angels, as well as "Mother" (the Crone aspect of the Goddess). Needless to say, justice was served.

Planetary Hours Chart

Day

Hour	Sunday	Monday	Tuesday	Wednesday	Thursday	Friday	Saturday
1	Sun	Moon	Mars	Mercury	Jupiter	Venus	Saturn
2	Venus	Saturn	Sun	Moon	Mars	Mercury	Jupiter
3	Mercury	Jupiter	Venus	Saturn	Sun	Moon	Mars
4	Moon	Mars	Mercury	Jupiter	Venus	Saturn	Sun
5	Saturn	Sun	Moon	Mars	Mercury	Jupiter	Venus
6	Jupiter	Venus	Saturn	Sun	Moon	Mars	Mercury
7	Mars	Mercury	Jupiter	Venus	Saturn	Sun	Moon
8	Sun	Moon	Mars	Mercury	Jupiter	Venus	Saturn
9	Venus	Saturn	Sun	Moon	Mars	Mercury	Jupiter
10	Mercury	Jupiter	Venus	Saturn	Sun	Moon	Mars
11	Moon	Mars	Mercury	Jupiter	Venus	Saturn	Sun
12	Saturn	Sun	Moon	Mars	Mercury	Jupiter	Venus

Night

Hour	Sunday	Monday	Tuesday	Wednesday	Thursday	Friday	Saturday
1	Jupiter	Venus	Saturn	Sun	Moon	Mars	Mercury
2	Mars	Mercury	Jupiter	Venus	Saturn	Sun	Moon
3	Sun	Moon	Mars	Mercury	Jupiter	Venus	Saturn
4	Venus	Saturn	Sun	Moon	Mars	Mercury	Jupiter
5	Mercury	Jupiter	Venus	Saturn	Sun	Moon	Mars
6	Moon	Mars	Mercury	Jupiter	Venus	Saturn	Sun
7	Saturn	Sun	Moon	Mars	Mercury	Jupiter	Venus
8	Jupiter	Venus	Saturn	Sun	Moon	Mars	Mercury
9	Mars	Mercury	Jupiter	Venus	Saturn	Sun	Moon
10	Sun	Moon	Mars	Mercury	Jupiter	Venus	Saturn
11	Venus	Saturn	Sun	Moon	Mars	Mercury	Jupiter
12	Mercury	Jupiter	Venus	Saturn	Sun	Moon	Mars

Fourteen

Angels, Sigils, and Symbols

*S*igils are economical, efficient, and fun to use in the pursuit of angel magick. I love this type of enchantment because you don't use complicated mumbo-jumbo or burn a hole in your pocketbook. You don't need a bunch of supplies—if necessary, a crayon will do. Sigils are virtually mistake-proof. You draw it, you empower it, and that's all there is. No complicated ritual, no worry that you've done something wrong. They are straightforward, simple, and non-threatening. Since you've drawn the symbol, you know exactly what it stands for—no mystery to contemplate.

There are all sorts of magickal sigils, including pictograms, alphabets, words, and numbers. You'll find this chapter stuffed with enough sigil information to keep you working for quite a while. Don't worry about learning it all at one time.

Personalized Sigils

Sigils are developed by fusion and stylization of letters.[1] Let's start by making your first sigil connection with the angelic realm.

Write your name in capital letters. Here's mine as an example:

SILVERRAVENWOLF

Now, beside your name, write ANGELS CONNECT, like this:

SILVERRAVENWOLFANGELSCONNECT

All the letters that appear more than once need to be deleted. Only one of each letter will remain. The letters I have left are:

SILVERANWOFGCT

With these letters I will design my own angel sigil by concentrating on the essence of what I want to do, which is connect me and the angels. Don't worry about how artistic your representation is.

I will also use as few lines as possible. This means I can use block letters, thereby eliminating the curves for letters like "S" "C" "G", etc. Only you need to know what this sigil means.

It may take you several tries until you get the sigil you like factored down to its simplest design. Don't give up. This sigil is worth it. Here is mine:

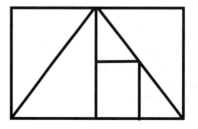

---

1. *Practical Sigil Magic* by Frater U.D., page 7.

When you are finished, you need to activate it. Most sigil magick is designed, activated, then destroyed, but we want this angel connection to hang around, so we aren't going to do that. Take your sigil to your angelic altar and light a candle. Spend a few minutes concentrating on your sigil and what it will now mean to you. Close your eyes if you like and relax, feeling your energy flow into the sigil. Imagine the angels touching the sigil and smiling. This is a personal connection with them. When you are finished, thank the angels and put the sigil where you won't lose it.

This sigil will come in handy for all sorts of things. You can use it in magick when you want to feel the angels around you. It can help make your connection with the angels firm in your mind during meditation. Wearing it on your person, or engraved on a ring or embroidered on a piece of clothing, will help you stay connected to the angels. Setting the design on your altar can also remind you of your angel connection and keep you focused.

Another project for you to work on is creating your own sigils for the angels you work with the most. For example, try one for your guardian angel. Here are two using the same letters:

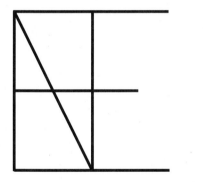 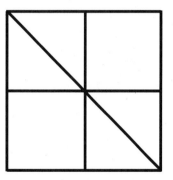

How about some for the Archangels? This time I've used some curves. Here are some of my interpretations:

Raphael   *Gabriel*   *Michael*   *Uriel*

Now, let's try some angel sigils in magickal applications. We will still use the same basic format. This time let's write out a sentence:

R A P H A E L H E A L I N G F O R F A L Y N N

First, we will factor it down:

R A P H E L N F G O Y

Now, we design the sigil. Here is what I came up with:

The next step is to activate the sigil. This can be done in a healing ritual, or I could simply activate the sigil at my altar. If the person you are requesting healing for is close by, you can give it to the person to carry. If not, you can put it in an envelope on your altar. Adding a picture of the individual in the envelope would be helpful. At the completion of the healing, deactivate the sigil by drawing a banishing pentagram over it, then burn the sigil. Scatter the ashes to the winds. Be sure to thank the angelic forces for their help.

In this type of sigil magick, try to remember the following points:

Always word your desire in a positive manner. Avoid negative words such as "not," "won't," "can't," etc.

Be specific. "Well, I think I want to go to Hawaii...." Nix on that. Either you do, or you don't.

Keep it simple. "Healing for Falynn" is specific and short. "Healing for Falynn because she is suffering from a temperature of 108..." is too long and she'll either be dead or well by the time you get the sigil made. Of course, you've already taken care of the mundane things like a trip to the doctor, aspirin, cold compresses, etc., whatever you would normally do. Magick cannot replace good medical care, but it certainly helps it along much faster than if you didn't use magick at all.

You can add a time factor to your sigil sentences. This month, this week, today, etc.

Try adding a border around your sigil. This helps you focus on the sigil itself and helps awaken archetypal material in your subconscious.

Keep your sigils as uncomplicated as possible—factor, factor, factor. The idea is to be able to possibly rediscover all the basic letters in the sigil. As long as you feel comfortable with the sigil, it will work. In actuality, the process of constructing the sigil itself is more important than your artistic rendition of it.

You can add little magick touches to your sigils. For example little triangles on the ends of straight lines, a few circles (not too many), perhaps a star, a symbol for angel wings (that you design yourself). Use your imagination.

Consider the magickal correspondences in Chapter 4. How can they be used? Draw the sigil at the right angelic hour, for instance. Or in this example, use a green colored pencil to draw the design (green denotes healing). I may wish to draw the design in two or three colors. It is my choice.

You do not have to use a specific angelic name. You can make sigils to stand for "angel of healing," "angel of love," etc.

Sigils that require action, like "Healing for Falynn," require deactivation and destruction after the magick completes the planned action. However, some magickal people destroy their sigils immediately, feeling that once the sigil is encoded in your brain and the message is sent out into the universe, the physical form is no longer necessary. Again, this is your choice. I have worked this magick both ways with great success, so I'm a poor person to tell you which way is right and which is wrong.

Pictorial Sigils

Pictorial sigils do not use words as their base, but ideas and symbols. This type of magick needs only desire, not letters, and allows you to access your unconscious mind without the translation process. Let's go back to healing Falynn. First, I'm going to draw a stick figure, add her initials and a pair of wings to pull in angelic energy, then stylize it. This is what I came up with:

The rules mentioned earlier still apply. You can use your correspondences during the development process, and remember to deactivate the sigil when the need has passed.

As you become familiar with magickal pictures, you may want to add some common symbols to your own pictorials:

| *Fire* | *Water* | *Air* | *Earth* | *Spirit* |

You can also add astrological symbols (see Chapter 12, Chapter 13, and elsewhere). There is no end to your creativity.

Let's look at some other universal symbols:

Serpentine: Undulating motion, waves, current, potential, movement of time, free thought.

Circle: A balance between two opposites, the universe, creation of a world.

Point: The symbol of the self. Each universe begins with the perception of its creator.

Ray: Joins the individual with the object of the desire. This is will in action.

Equal-armed cross: Balance, interlocking between divinity and human or angel and human as well as the four Archangels, four elements, and four compass points all joined at the center by divinity.

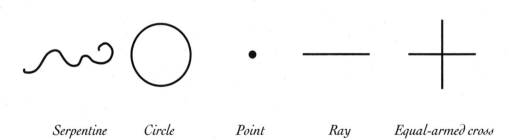

| *Serpentine* | *Circle* | *Point* | *Ray* | *Equal-armed cross* |

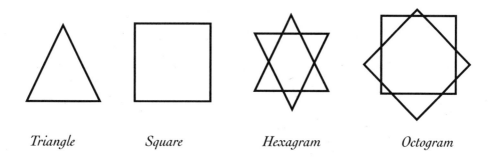

| *Triangle* | *Square* | *Hexagram* | *Octogram* |

Triangle: Made from three rays; it is fixed. One part cannot be moved without destroying the whole. Upright it stands for the male aspect; reversed, it represents the feminine. Point up indicates fire; point down is water. The number three symbolizes the Trinity, the three faces of the God/dess.

The square: Represents the manifestation of perfect forces. The square is associated with the four elements, the four winds, the four corners of the Earth, the four beasts, the four rivers, the four Archangels, the four seasons, the four instruments used in ritual (wand, cup, athame, and sword), and the four letters of Tetragrammaton (the unspeakable name of God).

The hexagram: Expression of opposites, but with perfect balance. This symbol represents the will of divinity manifested with humanity in complete harmony with cosmic law.

The octogram: The angelic star. The octogram shows the duality of fours—material reflecting non-material.

Spiral: Mind connected to divinity, balance, cone of power. There are four kinds of spiral motion:

Inward clockwise (light)   Inward counterclockwise (dark)

Outward clockwise (dark)   Outward counterclockwise (light)

| *Inward clockwise* | *Outward clockwise* | *Inward counterclockwise* | *Outward counterclockwise* |

The inward spiral in either direction shows focus and projection of intent. Prayer involves the inward spiral. This is a symbol that moves toward divinity.

The outward spiral shows something coming into being—the process of manifestation. This is the answer from divinity and considered an instrument of God/Goddess. Clockwise motion is in harmony with divinity and shows construction, evolution, law, and order. Counterclockwise motion turns to create destruction and confusion.[2]

The Hermetic Rose

Another sigil method you can use with ease is called the Hermetic Rose, designed by followers of the Golden Dawn. There are three circles of symbols, divided to look like a flower. Originally, these symbols were Hebrew letters. They are arranged according to a description of letters in the Sepher Yetziarah.

---

2. *New Millennium Magic* by Donald Tyson, page 69.

Here is the English translation:

To create your sigil, follow these simple instructions:

Lay a piece of tracing paper over the English translation of the Hermetic Rose.[3]

Find the first letter of the word you wish to symbolize. Draw a circle in that section.

Find the second letter in your word. Draw a line from the first letter to the second letter.

Find the third letter in the word. Draw a line from the second letter to the third letter.

Continue this pattern until you have finished the word.

Draw a short line horizontally across the bottom of the last line.

If you have double letters in the same word, draw a loop back to the same letter. If you have duplicate letters in a word (as in the personal sigil examples at the beginning of the chapter) you can use the letter only once, if you wish.

It is okay if lines cross each other.

---

3. Some occult practitioners say that sigils based on Hebrew names must be created using the Hebrew Hermetic Rose. I disagree. The angels understand every human language, and will work with us no matter what language we choose to use.

Once you have made your sigil, you need to activate it, following the instructions at the beginning of this chapter.

What do the Archangel names look like if you use this type of sigil? Here are some examples (using Hebrew letters):

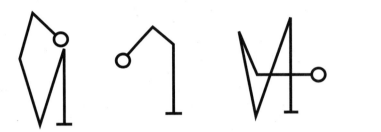

| *Ariel* | *Raphael* | *Gabriel* | *Michael* |

The Angelic Alphabet

From sigils and symbols we move into the angelic alphabet, designed by Dr. John Dee. By transferring your desires into angelic writing, you are focusing on the matter in a positive way by wording your desire in a positive fashion. The fact that you are choosing to take action can help remove fears and uncertainties related to the situation. You are also connecting with the angels in a physical way (the piece of paper on which you recorded your desire).

As with other symbols and sigils, you do not need an elaborate set of tools. Basically, pen and paper will suffice. You can use colored pencils if you like. The choice, again, is yours. Follow these simple steps:

Check your magickal correspondences, such as angelic hour, day, etc.

Formulate your desire specifically in your mind.

Ground and center.

Write your desire on a piece of paper. Keep it positive and specific.

Using the chart on the next page, record the translation on another sheet of paper.

Activate the desire.

That's all there is to it. When the desired outcome is reached, deactivate the paper and burn it. You can use the angelic alphabet for a variety of purposes, including writing it on candles, embroidering it on clothing, inscribing it on jewelry, etc. You can encompass the script with a circle or square, add it to a pictogram, etc. There is no end to its uses.

The Angelic Alphabet

X	Ʒ	∏	˥	ʒ	U	ᶘ
A	B	C	D	E	F	G

∏	△	C	⸾	⅄	⅄	⅄
H	I/J	K	L	M	N	O/Q

ⱷ	˥	U	⸾	ᴜ	⅂	⊤
P	R	S	U/V	X	Y	Z

Let's go back to my example, "Healing for Falynn." Transferred into the angelic alphabet, it would look like this:

∏ʒX⸾△⅄ᶘ U⅄˥ UX⸾˥⅄⅄

On the other side, I would write the name "Raphael," because he is the angel of healing and this is a message for him. Raphael would look like this:

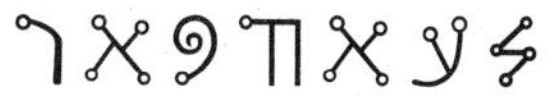

˥Xⱷ∏Xʒ⸾

After I activate the paper, I would either give it to Falynn or I could place it on my altar. Of course, I won't know what works best until I try it out. And that goes for all the things I've shown you in the chapter. The more your practice the magicks given, the better your connection with the angels and the more open your subconscious becomes to divine and angelic forces. By working positive magick for others with the help of the angels, you will see an increased stability and peace in your own life.

Practical Magick Symbols

Not all symbols have to be decorative or take lots of time to compose. Think of an item and the angel of that item, then draw a symbol to represent them. If you aren't satisfied, work on it a bit until you like what you have drawn. I like to save my symbols on index cards and put them in a box with index tabs so that when I need one quickly, I have the symbol and the name of the appropriate angel. That way, when I'm in a hurry, I don't have to go leafing through my journal or a ton of books to find exactly what I need. On the back of the index card you can write other correspondences as you think of them, such as timing, colors, etc. Here are a few simple symbols to add to your collection:[3]

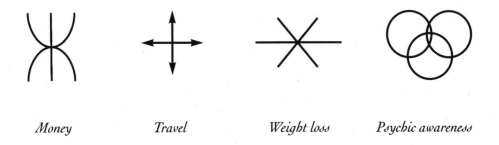

Money   *Travel*   *Weight loss*   *Psychic awareness*

In this chapter we covered a great deal of information, but it will only be useful if you practice it. Angels love to work with people who are determined and willing to help themselves. The more creative you are, the better they like it because it shows you are directing positive energy toward a specific goal.

---

3. Some of these symbols are from *Living Wicca* by Scott Cunningham, Chapter 20.

Fifteen

Angel
Talismans

Magickal people create talismans
to draw things toward them, whether
it be protection or a talent, such as
speaking eloquently. Most magickal
talismans work with angelic and
astrological forces as well as divinity.
Up to this point, I've given you plenty
of correspondences that you can use
in making your own talismans. This
chapter is designed to give you lots of
ideas for angel talismans.

Materials

You can make talismans from wood, metal, or paper. You can make your own, or buy wood or metal disks at a craft store in a variety of sizes. You can also purchase wooden shapes, such as angels, houses, animals, people, etc. Although the round disk is standard, I've found that using the shape of whom or what you are working for brings sympathy to the project. The week after I made a talisman out of a wooden book, one of my books was chosen as a Book of the Month Club selection.

Some people like to use posterboard or oaktag for their talismans. Many individuals laminate their paper talismans to keep them from getting soiled. A few years ago a friend of mine bought a button-making machine. She makes her talismans from computer graphics she designed herself. She colors and empowers them, then cuts the graphics to the size of the button. Then she puts them through the machine so she can wear them pinned to her clothing. You might prefer to make talisman pins in a simpler way. Office supply stores sell boxes of plastic tags with plain inserts that will work in a laser printer, or you can draw them freehand. Finally, I've made talismans on circles of bisque with ceramic paint, then coated them with clear gloss. Fire them during the correct planetary hour on the corresponding day of the talisman.

If you choose to work with wood, you will need a woodburning tool, tracing paper, acrylic paints, and a drill (should you want to put a hole in it to wear around your neck). For paper talismans, you will need tracing paper, magic markers or colored pencils, and the type of paper you wish to use. You may use colored pencils to shade the entire paper, or you may wish to purchase papers of assorted colors.

The talismans in this chapter use angelic correspondences and forces listed throughout the book. Feel free to write your own rituals and use your creative talents when interacting with angelic beings. Experiment with candle colors and sympathetic associations. Keep your magick positive and your mind spirit-filled, and you will do well.

Talisman for Eloquence

If you are involved with any type of public speaking or in a situation where your words will count and saying the right thing at the right time is of utmost importance, then the talisman for eloquence is for you.

Construct this talisman on a Wednesday, a Mercury day, and cleanse, consecrate, and empower during the angelic hour of Raphael. Wednesday's colors are orange, light blue, violet, and gray. You may wish to choose your illuminator candles from these colors. The angels for Wednesday are Raphael, Miel, and Seraphiel. You may choose to invoke them together or separately, or you can simply call upon the angels of eloquence. I suggest making the talisman out of light blue paper and dark blue or silver ink.

Keep these other correspondences in mind:
Best done when the Moon is in Gemini, Virgo, Aquarius, or Scorpio.
Best done when the Moon is full or waxing.
Do not perform when the Moon is void of course
(check your daily astrological planner).
Weakest when the Moon is in Sagittarius, Pisces, Leo, or Taurus.

Talisman for eloquence

Guardian of Health Talisman

This talisman belongs to the angel Raphael, and is to be given to those who wish to improve their health, maintain good health, or who practice non-invasive holistic healing procedures. Best constructed on a Sunday and cleansed, consecrated, and empowered in the hour of Raphael. Construct this talisman on Tuesday for surgeons, soldiers, and those who face invasive medical procedures.

Corresponding colors are gold and yellow for Sunday, and yellow, gold, or blue for Raphael. You may wish to burn illuminator candles in these colors. With this talisman you should also burn a separate candle for Raphael, and speak the invocation given in Chapter 2 for that angel. Choose yellow paper for the talisman and write with blue ink. Store the talisman in silver, blue, or violet cloth.

If you are constructing the talisman on Tuesday, keep in mind the additional colors of red and scarlet. Use yellow paper and red ink. Construct/perform during the hour of Raphael.

Raphael flows well with the element of air. You may wish to place a symbol of air on your altar as well, along with the picture of the individual for whom the talisman is designed. Cultivate added energies through construction when the Moon is full (for healing and continued good health), dark (for banishing illness), or when it is in the signs of Gemini, Libra, or Aquarius (as these are the zodiacal signs linked to Raphael). Raphael loves the dawn, so you may wish to rise early on Wednesday to catch the double energies of healing during the first hour of Raphael. Store the talisman in gold or yellow cloth.

Remember, if you do not wish to call a specific angel by name, you can call on the angelic forces of healing.

Weakest times of performance would be when the Moon is void of course (check your astrological almanac) or when the Moon is in the signs of Sagittarius, Pisces, Leo, or Taurus.

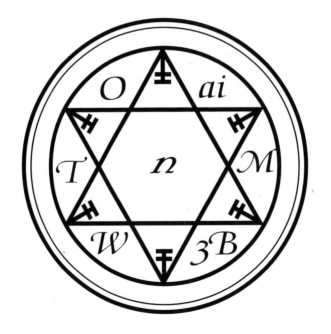

Guardian of health talisman

Planetary Talismans

Use planetary talismans (seals) to invoke the powers of the angels and energies of the planets for a particular purpose. In Chapter 13 we covered the correspondences of the planetary angels, and you will need to refer to that information when choosing the correct seal for the working.

Make these talismans from a single sheet of paper with a tag that connects the circles. This tag, or stem, is used to fold the talisman and connect the energies. If you like the idea of the button-making machine, you will need to seal the two sides (as the tag will not be practical) with a little wax in the color of the corresponding angel.

It is wise to store all talismans in a piece of cloth (preferably silk) that corresponds with the color of the planet. Each talisman should be constructed on that planet's day and in that planet's angelic hour. On one side of the paper will be the magick square of the planet, its astrological sigil, and the highest planetary number. On the reverse side of the talisman are the seal of the planet, the sigil of the angel, and again, the astrological sigil. You may also wish to add your personal sigil as well. Most important with these planetary talismans is the color of paper you use, so be sure to match the colors perfectly.

General Rules to Follow with the Planetary Seals (Talismans)

Construct on the appropriate day in the appropriate hour for best results. Empower in the same fashion.

Use the appropriate color(s) for best results. Take your time in the construction. Play soft music if you like, and work by candlelight or low lighting to give the atmosphere of safe, comfortable magick. Be sure to call on your guardian angel before you begin constructing any talisman.

Perform a short meditation and/or cleansing procedure before constructing any talisman. Always activate the talisman in a magick circle.

Keep a photograph or something "in sympathy" (an object that belongs to the individual) of the person for whom the talisman is fashioned.

Never construct a talisman when you are angry, sick, or tired.

Although each planetary talisman has its own hour of construction (for example, construct a Moon talisman on Monday in the hour of Gabriel), you may wish to pull in other energies to enhance the power of the talisman.

If something doesn't feel right while you are constructing the talisman, stop. Try again at another time. If it still doesn't feel right, drop the project and consider another type of magick. When the talisman has done its work and you no longer need it, be sure to deactivate the magick, then destroy the talisman.

Talisman of the Sun

Angels of the Sun deal with the power of will, authority, and recognition. Issues of concern to them are advancement, health, fun and pleasures, loyalty, and generosity. Talismans of the Sun should be constructed on Sunday in the hour of Michael. Colors associated with both Michael and the Angels of the Sun are red and crimson, and gold and yellow, respectively. Use yellow paper and gold ink.

Other correspondences to keep in mind:

Energies are highest when the Moon is in Leo, Aries, or Sagittarius.

Energies are weakest when the Moon is in Aquarius, Libra, or Gemini.

Use the angels of the phases of the Moon to add subtle energies to the talisman.

Never construct this talisman when the Moon is void of course.

Use the energies of a solar eclipse wisely.

You may wish to use the invocation to Michael found in Chapter 2.

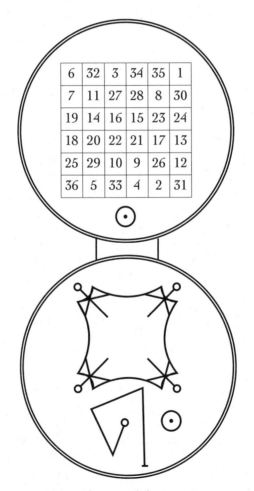

Talisman of the Sun

Talisman of the Moon

Moon angels concentrate on our emotions or the emotions of others; however, as mentioned in the last chapter, they will also assist us in special services of honor and matters involving contacting the deceased, recovering stolen property, taking care of criminals, psychism, short trips, feminine energies, and the welfare of children. Angels of the Moon correspond to Monday, therefore construct this talisman on a Monday, in the hour of Gabriel. Colors associated with this planetary seal are silver and white, therefore use white paper and silver ink. Gabriel's colors are blue or aquamarine, so you may wish to burn illuminator candles of those hues.

Other correspondences to keep in mind:

Best if fashioned when the moon is in Cancer, Taurus, or Pisces.

Since Moon energy covers such a vast array of situations and circumstances, you will need to consider the issue and the phase of the Moon that will best serve your working. Refer to the information covered in Chapter 13 under the topic of angels of

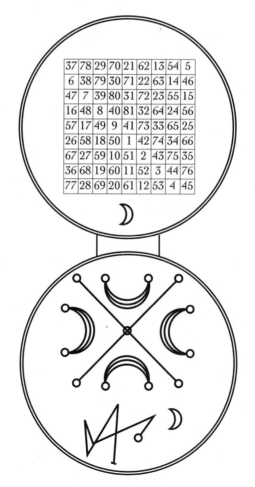

Talisman of the Moon

the Moon. You may also wish to use the invocation of Gabriel found in Chapter 2. Sympathetic correspondences can include flowers of all fragrances and hues. Remember that Goddess energy reigns over all the angels of the Moon.

The weakest energies for this talisman occur when the moon is in Capricorn, Scorpio, or Virgo. Do not even attempt to make this talisman when the Moon is void of course.

Talisman of Mercury

Mercury angels deal with speed and communication. They assist in areas of bargaining, dealing with lawyers, publishing, filing, hiring employees, learning languages, literary work, preparing accounts, studying, using the media, and visiting friends. The talisman of Mercury should be constructed/empowered on a Wednesday, in the angelic hour of Raphael. Associated colors are orange, light blue, violet, and gray. Paper color should be violet with silver or blue ink.

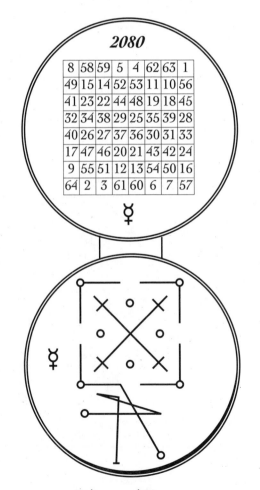

Talisman of Mercury

Other correspondences to keep in mind:
Best fashioned when the moon is in Gemini, Virgo, Aquarius, or Scorpio.
Energies are weakest when the moon is in Sagittarius, Pisces, Leo, or Taurus.
Keep the angels of the phases in mind when adding subtleties to your work.
Never construct when the Moon is void of course.

Talisman of Venus

Matters of the heart and beauty are of primary focus here. The day of Venus is Friday, and the angelic hour for this talisman is Uriel. At first I found this rather surprising, as Uriel is often seen as one of those fighting forces in the angelic community; however, consider also that Uriel is associated with deep mystery, and what is more mystifying than love? Of course, there are times when we have to fight for what we love most, whether it be in words or hand-to-hand combat. To say that physical force is unnecessary would not be looking at the world realistically, would it?

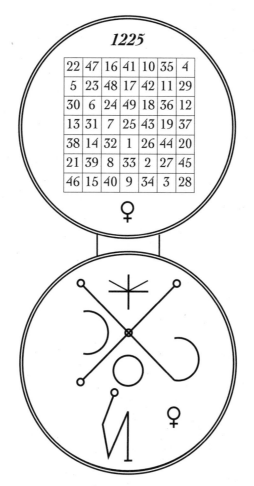

Talisman of Venus

Colors associated with these planetary angels are emerald green and pink. Uriel's color associations are brown and forest green. Use light green paper and green ink, or pink paper and green ink.

Other correspondences to keep in mind:

Best time of construction is when the moon is in Taurus, Pisces, or Aquarius.

Lowest energy level occurs when the moon is in Aries, Scorpio, Virgo, or Leo.

Use the angels of the phases of the Moon to add further nuances.

Never construct during Moon void of course.

Talisman of Mars

Construct this talisman on a Tuesday, in the hour of Camael. Remember that Mars angels are aggressive in nature. (Camael is a terminator angel, after all.) Think carefully when you employ their energies, so that you will not turn a distasteful situation into a horrid one. The angels of Mars primarily deal with issues of business,

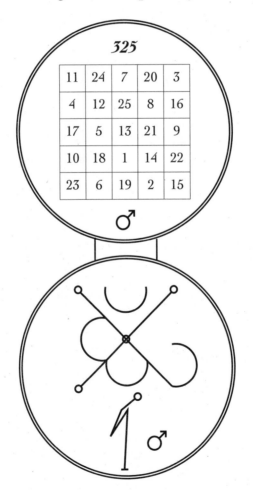

Talisman of Mars

mechanical things, buying and selling animals, hunting, beginning studies, gardening, sexual activities, and confrontation. Colors associated with these angels are red, rose, and scarlet. Use rose-colored paper and red ink.

Other correspondences to keep in mind:
Best constructed when the Moon is in the sign of Aries, Capricorn, or Leo.
The energies are weakest when the Moon is in Libra, Cancer, or Aquarius.
Match the Moon phase to add subtle energies to the talisman.
Never construct this talisman when the Moon is void of course.

Talisman of Jupiter

Jupiter angels pull in the essence of prosperity, growth, and fruition. Jupiter's day is Thursday, and all talismans made calling these planetary angels should be made on Thursday, in the angelic hour of Sachiel. Colors are purple and royal blue. Use azure blue paper and dark ink.

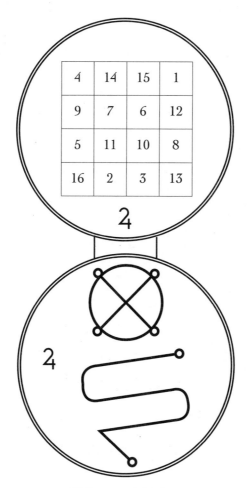

Talisman of Jupiter

Other correspondences to keep in mind:

For growth, choose the Waxing Moon.

For prosperity, choose the New Moon.

For fruition, choose the Full Moon.

Best if fashioned when the Moon is in Sagittarius, Cancer, Taurus, or Pisces.

Weakest if created when the Moon is in Gemini, Capricorn, Virgo, or Scorpio.

Do not construct when the Moon is void of course.

Talisman of Saturn

Saturn angels focus on karmic lessons and boundaries, longevity, and authority. They are around when a great change is instituted. This talisman should be constructed on Saturday in the hour of Cassiel. Remember that Cassiel is the angel of patience. Corresponding colors are black, gray, and sometimes silver. Use gray paper with black ink, or black paper with silver ink.

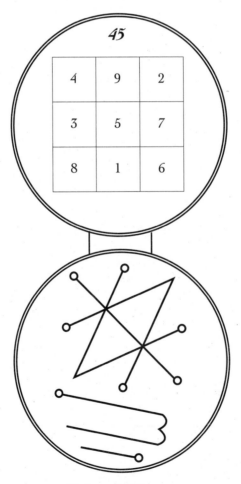

Talisman of Saturn

Other correspondences to keep in mind:

Energies are best for the construction of this talisman when the moon is in Capricorn, Libra, or Virgo.

Energies are weakest when the moon is in Cancer, Aries, or Pisces.

Use the Moon phase angels (especially Disseminating, Waning, and Dark Moon angels) for added subtle energies.

Never construct when the Moon is void of course.

Consider using the eclipse angels for extra assistance.

Color Wheel of the Planetary Angels

Remember the color wheel we did back in Chapter 4? While that one is not necessarily permanent in nature, this one will be. You can use the planetary angelic wheel as a centerpiece for your angelic altar when you are constructing the planetary talismans. Create it from a round piece of heavy paperboard, or you may use wood if you so desire. You will also need colored pencils or acrylic paints and a black marker. Copy the pattern below. You may make your board as large or small as you like.

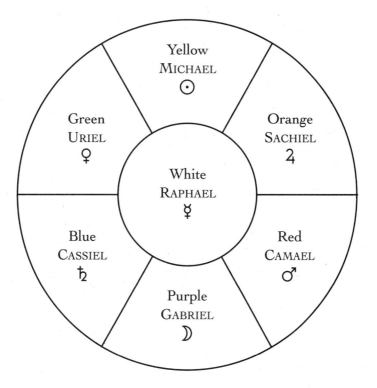

The Angelic Sigil Wheel

In the last chapter I showed you the Hermetic Rose and how one constructs sigils using that design. Here is another way to construct these magickal symbols by using the angelic sigil wheel.

This wheel works in the same manner as that of the Hermetic Rose. It is important to this chapter because it is this wheel that we will use to draw any sigils for the angels of the asteroids (Chiron, Pallas, Vesta, Juno, and Ceres). Remember that the sigil starts with a small circle, and ends with a perpendicular line.

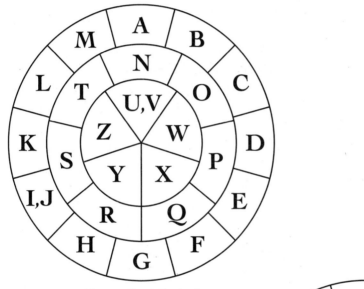

The angelic sigil wheel

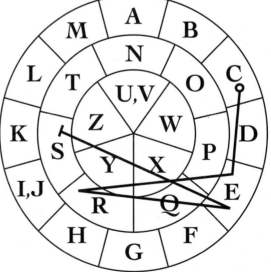

Creating the sigil for Ceres

Ceres Angels

The prime directive of the Ceres angels is nurturing, thus their colors are a rainbow of pastels. Ceres angels have ample forms, brown skin tones, and triple sets of wings, and usually appear as female in form; however, this does not mean they will not take on the form of a male in order to assist a human in need. Notice that the sigil looks a bit like the open arms of a mother. Ceres angels will watch over the cradle of a babe or rock a grieving adult to sleep in their tender arms. This is an excellent sigil to place upon the card of that special someone on Valentine's Day, or draw upon the walls of a child's room. Embroider it on the silks that house your divination tools, as those who are truly diviners feel with great intensity the responsibilities they have toward their clients.

I designed the following talisman for the angels of Ceres, to pull the fruits of the earth toward you in a loving and nurturing manner. It contains the four elements, the sigil of Ceres, the name of Anaelle, and the astrological symbol for Ceres. Use white paper and green ink. Best designed on Friday (a Venus day) in the planetary hour of Venus. Use the Moon phase angels to add nuances. This talisman is weakest when the Moon is in Aries. As with any talisman, do not construct when the Moon is void of course.

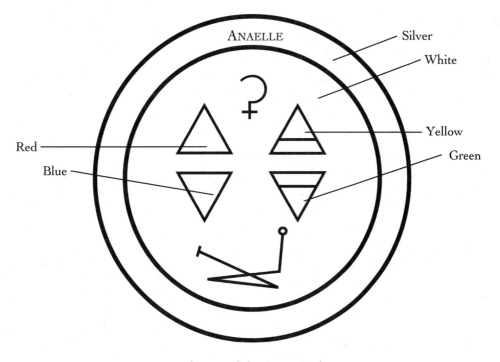

Talisman of the Ceres angels

Pallas Angels

The angels of this asteroid focus on feminine energy involved in intuition, flashes of genius, and keen insights, as well as our ability to formulate new and original thoughts that are auspicious to the feminine collective unconscious and the planet in general. The primary colors of the Pallas angels are violet, blue, white, and silver.

Triple-winged angels, slight of form with straight, dark hair, they aspire to bring creative genius to humans. Their violet eyes see through any lie or deception, searching only for the truth; therein lies pure creativity.

Use the sigil of Pallas over any work area, from the machine shop to the sewing room. Whether you are designing dresses or buildings, the Pallas angels will flutter to your aid. Place the sigil and the astrological sign of the Pallas angels on your altar when you are meditating or working in hypnotherapy. Doodle the symbols on a piece of paper when you are brainstorming, and always carry the sigils into a meeting where it is necessary for you to come up with a creative idea that will have universal appeal.

The asteroid angels are minions of the Goddess, therefore you may wish to add a universal symbol of the Goddess in any talisman you design using the Pallas angels. These angels correspond to the element of air, and those correspondences are usually associated with Mercury. Therefore, fashion your Pallas talisman on Wednesday in

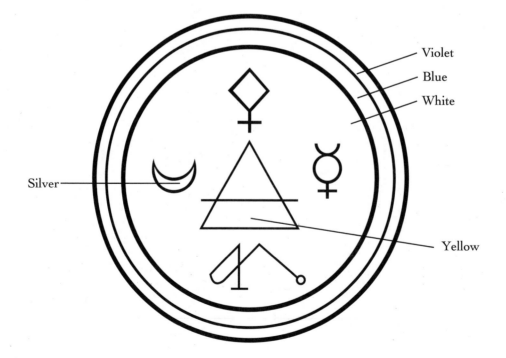

Talisman of genius (talisman of the Pallas angels)

the planetary hour of Mercury. Use the Moon phase angels to add subtle energies. Of course, never construct the talisman when the Moon is void of course. Pallas angels do not work well when the Moon is poorly aspected or if the Moon is in Leo, Sagittarius, or Taurus (the stubborn signs of the zodiac).

The Talisman of Genius (previous page) is a Pallas angel talisman constructed with the astrological signs of Pallas and Mercury and the symbols of the element of air, Pallas, and Goddess energy. The enclosing three circles represent the three planes of spiritual, mental, and physical, respectively, beginning with the outer circle.

Draw your personal sigil or write your name on the back of this talisman.

Juno Angels

These are the relationship angels. They focus on our individual balance as well as the balance in human interaction. Use the sigil and symbol of Juno whenever you need compatibility in your life, as well as the freedom to do what you feel is best for yourself, regardless of the well-meaning advice that friends and family pound into your head. Often, advice may not come from the heart, but from the restrictions of society. I don't mean you should go out and do something stupid that will risk life and limb, but in a case where a spouse or lover is imposing a jealous streak on you and

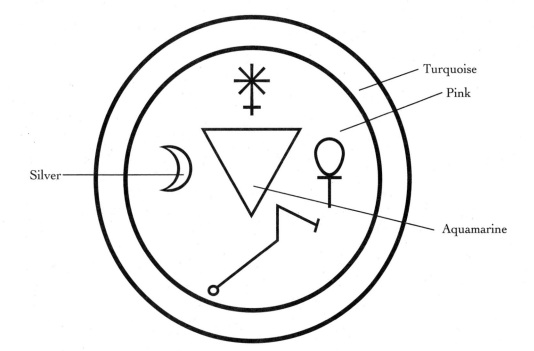

Talisman of the Juno angels

limiting your freedom, you may wish to invoke the angels of Juno to help you get things on a more balanced track. Or, if you are about to enter a partnership of any sort and feel you don't have all the information you need to make a correct decision, ask the angels of Juno for assistance.

The element of water corresponds to the angels of Juno. Their colors are aquamarine, pink, and turquoise. The universal symbol of these triple-winged angels is the dolphin. Juno angels have almond-shaped green eyes and white-blonde hair, and prefer flowing robes of shimmering material. Pearls, gifts of the sea, adorn their necks and wrists and appear in beaded designs on their clothing. You may wish to place sea treasures on your altar when invoking these angels. Inscribe their sigils on small seashells to carry in your pocket or purse.

The angels of Juno are sinewy feminine angels who help us work on our self-esteem. We can't go out fixing the world if our own backyard is in a shambles. Choose Monday (the day of the Moon) to make a Juno talisman, in the hour of the Moon or in the hour of Venus. Both are propitious to these angels. Add the Moon phase angels for additional subtle energies. Energies of this talisman are weakest when constructed when the Moon is in Capricorn, Scorpio, or Virgo. An eclipsed Moon is especially propitious; however, never fashion this talisman when the Moon is void of course. Included in this talisman is the astrological sign of Juno, the symbol of the element of water, the ankh (the univeral symbol of love and the union of male and female), the symbol of the Moon to pull in the energies of communion, and the sigil of the Juno angels.

Vesta Angels

These angels of pure inspiration and dedication seek to pull our feminine aspirations and goals toward us. The angels of Vesta are truly the guardians of the Witches, and therefore their astrological symbol shows power in its purest form. They are the temple guardians, those who light the lamps of truth and knowledge, guarding the secrets of the hidden children. Truly, they are the protectors of the shining ones.

Vesta angels are triple-winged, with strong bodies and burnished skin, fiery hair and tawny eyes, and robes of gold and saffron that flicker like grasping flames in the wind. They wear golden crowns upon their heads; their arms and ankles are encircled by gold.

Vesta angels focus on the element of fire. The day to fashion any talisman for them is Sunday, in the planetary hour of the Sun. Add the angels of the phases of the Moon for additional nuances. Eclipses of the Sun are especially propitious, depending on what energies you wish to add. The weakest timing would be when the Moon is in Aquarius, Gemini, or Libra. Do not fashion this talisman when the Moon is void of course.

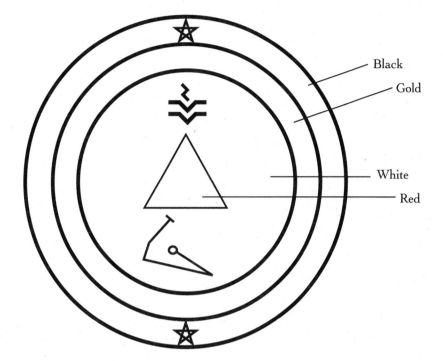

Black
Gold

White
Red

Talisman of the Vesta angels

Use the symbols of Vesta when working on major projects that require an immense amount of creativity during the mechanical process, whether it be writing, drawing, or constructing an office building. Place the symbol of Vesta above your front door and to the inside left of your home, as that corner of the house symbolizes what you hope to accomplish with your life as well as your planned prosperity. To the right inside the front door of your home represents the love and unity that lies therein.

If you are an athlete, embroider the symbols of Vesta on your sportswear and stencil them on your equipment to help you reach your potential. Use the symbols of Vesta when meditating on goals and projects that are designed to change the course of your life. Witches should paint the symbol of Vesta in red on their altar stones to symbolize the service, protection, and laws surrounding the oath they have taken.

The color correspondences of Vesta are red, white, gold, and black. Red symbolizes the blood and courage of our human ancestors, white stands for the purity of the divine, gold represents our highest attainment and the strength of the Sun, and finally, black is for both protection and the fertile environment of the earth. This talisman includes the astrological symbol of Vesta, the symbol of the element of fire, the sigil of the Vesta angels, and the pentacle for protection.

Chiron Angels

These are the Akashic angels. If you want to look into the "universal library," ask these angels for assistance. Chiron angels are the record-keepers, weaving the past, present, and future together in a brilliant tapestry of life. They know every thread, every warp, and every weave. They will help you fix what is broken and explain what you don't understand. A warning in contacting these angels: you must be willing to know the truth rather than be satisfied with the illusion of the situation, and you must be willing to work for your answers—no proverbial silver-platter service here.

The element associated with the Chiron angels is Akasha, the spirit. These angels are formless intelligence, too busy to manifest in a particular form for the benefit of humans. Draw the symbols of Chiron when you seek to tap into universal spirituality, efforts to heighten spirituality, studies of religion, and the use of positive energies to assist humankind. Both teachers and healers will benefit from the assistance of the Chiron angels.

Choose the correspondences for Chiron based on your needs. Chiron angels focus on the colors of white, silver, and gold—those colors that are recognized as near divinity. The color violet can also be added to this list, as it is seen to represent the higher vibrations of the human spirit. Rather then depending on an appropriate day and hour, I suggest leaning more toward the correct Moon phase, as the angels of Chiron are not confined to specific timing, either in their work or their energies. Spirit is omnipresent.

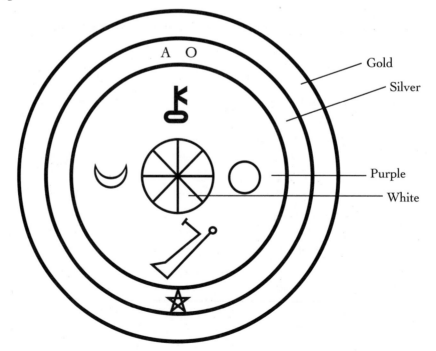

Talisman of the Chiron angels

230

The talisman provided here works from year to year, therefore you may wish to create it on your birthday or other special occasion. It can be given to a child at its christening, wiccaning, or bar mitzvah, or to an adult at the Wiccan initiation, twenty-first birthday, wedding day, or silver or gold anniversary. Use your wisdom to choose when to fashion this talisman and to whom it is given and when. Although you can use paper, you may wish to consider using white doe or elk skin to cause sympathy between the physical world (the world of the human animal) and the angelic realms. (If you are an animal activist, consider using a synthetic substitute.)

This taliman includes the astrological symbol of Chiron and the symbols for Akasha, the Sun and Moon (symbols of the God and Goddess) or equal-armed cross (if you are Christian), the sigil of the Chiron angels, and the letters A and O (symbolizing alpha and omega—all that is, was, and ever shall be).

From this point there is no end to the talismans you can create yourself. Don't be fooled that older is better when it comes to magickal applications. Those talismans you construct with associations only you understand are the most powerful. Get that magickal thinking cap on and review the angels, their energies, and correspondences, and apply your own intuition and creativity. I'm sure your talismans will far exceed any I've shown you.

Sixteen

Angels and Divination

Although I had worked up fairly good readings with divination tools, I can honestly say that when I brought angels into the picture, things turned upside-down. I've been reading the Tarot since I turned fifteen (for over twenty-five years); however, I always held back—feared letting it all go. Readers have a great responsibility to their clients. Your integrity must be impeccable. Your clients depend on you to be absolutely honest. If you don't know an answer, you can't make one up and hope for the best.

In this chapter we will cover the basic rules for divination along with a few specialized forms of the art. No matter what divination tool you use, I am confident your work will be far better with the inclusion of angelic energy.

Ground Rules for Divination

You can make the process of divination as simple or complicated as you desire. For example, I know an excellent Tarot reader who keeps her deck on the kitchen table. If you want a reading, she says, "Shuffle and cut." No fancy silks or divining scarves for her. In fact, her cards are in their original box. I know other readers, equally as good, who wrap their divination tools in black silk, use gems or herbs, light candles, say prayers, etc., etc. Your style in using your divination tools is a part of your being. It should be individual and comfortable. If you feel silly saying something special aloud, then don't. If you find yourself embarrassed to light a candle, why do it? Granted, you won't feel silly once you have established a pattern, but if something does not feel right to you, then don't do it.

The most important rule I can think of is this: **Don't ever frighten the client.** It is cruel to scare someone, no matter the reason.

Other rules that come to mind are:

Ground and center before every reading. Take three deep breaths and relax. Pull your energy in, then let it out. Connect with the universe. A short invocation could be the following:

Angels of prophecy
Touch my heart, my mind, my soul.
Bring the answers sought to form.
Bless me with wisdom and knowledge in this hour of divination.

If you would like to work with a specific angel, try Bath Kol, a female angel who encourages words of truth and aids in prophecy. If asked politely, she will grant insight into the future. Another divination angel is Hahaiah, who will give insight into deep mysteries and hidden knowledge.

Don't divine if you are sick, extremely tired, or angry. Your health or state of mind may affect your readings. When you get very good at your craft you will find that you can influence the results, giving you a twisted reading. For example, if I think of a particular Tarot card too hard, guess what comes up right away? This is why I never associate people with cards when they walk in through my door. Nor do I do Tarot readings for myself anymore. I call my friend Diane instead. When you are sick you may not reach the state of mind you desire for a clean reading. Because your body fills with "dis-ease," your readings may appear more negative in nature. Have a friend read for you, or if someone is asking you to read, decline graciously.

Don't divine for anyone whose guts you absolutely hate. If you can't stand someone, can you be truthful with him or her? Will you be frustrated if you see bright and beautiful things for this person, or will you be thrilled if things look unpleasant? If you intensely dislike someone, your negative feelings may move into your reading, twisting it. Again, decline gracefully.

Don't exaggerate or lie. If you don't know an answer, say plainly, "I don't know." Time and again I've gotten clients who like to grill the reader. They ask one question, which leads to another, then to another, and before long all they are doing is rephrasing the original question. The reader is never on trial. You are not on the witness stand. There is no such thing as "redirection." "Leading the reader" does not exist (or it shouldn't). If you get a client like this, say plainly, "I don't know," or "I'm sorry, there is nothing more here." Occasionally I will say bluntly, "I'm sorry, but I'm not God. The information is not coming through."

Be sure you explain the divination tool thoroughly to a new client. Don't assume the person knows what you are doing. If you are reading the Tarot, take the time to explain the images of the card a bit, so the client knows where you get your inspiration. This goes for any physical tool (Runes, Cartouche, Medicine Cards, etc.). The more you explain to a client (or a friend), the fewer questions they will have, and the more they will understand the mechanics of a divination session.

Don't act like a snot. The worst thing you can do is act like an all-knowing fool. Never be rude or speak distastefully to a client. Don't be a phony. Even if your clients don't spot you right away, others in the area who also work with divinatory tools will. If they speak poorly of you, eventually it will get back to your clients.

Never impose on another's free will. Don't force a divinatory reading on anyone. Don't offer to do magick for money. If someone is interested in angel magick (or other forms of magick), explain how to do it. You can give friends and family simple magicks to do that will raise their self-esteem and bring happiness into their lives. Don't let them depend on you to do it for them all the time. They need to learn, too.

Learn to take your time. When using any divinatory tool, don't rush the process. When my clients come calling we relax and have a cup of tea, catch up on the gossip or goals in their lives, and generally enjoy each other's company. This allows them to move into the proper frame of mind, just like you, and it is easier to form a bridge between yourself and the information you need. If you get stuck during the divination process, don't panic. Sit back, take a deep breath, and change the subject to give yourself time to clear out those mental cobwebs. If you still can't make sense of the reading, don't despair. In truth, ninety percent of the time the client is either outright lying to your face or in denial. If nothing gels for you, gather up the cards and say, "Perhaps another time."

If you aren't in the mood for marathon readings, gently explain to the client approximately how long you plan to spend on the reading. There are ways to control those people you like who hang around forever:

Schedule another divination appointment directly after your present client.

Plan to run an errand and explain to the client that you must leave.

Charge by the hour and make the fee high enough so the person will not wish to stay too long.

Angelic Pendulum Magick

One of the oldest forms of divination uses the pendulum. A pendulum is a weighted object suspended from a chain or string, whose movements provide answers to the questions you ask out loud. Pendulums can be natural (such as a crystal or favorite gem) or manufactured. I prefer the weighted, manufactured type. You will find these in most occult stores.

The most important rule to keep in mind when you are using the pendulum is to relax. Tensing up blocks your receptivity. Remember to use your magickal correspondences when working with the pendulum. For example, you may wish to burn a candle (choose the appropriate color for the occasion), burn some incense (check your herbal associations), or choose a particular time of day or angelic hour.

Cleanse, consecrate, and bless your talisman on your angel altar. Ask the angels of prophecy to assist you and bring wisdom and helpful answers whenever you use the pendulum.

Put your elbow on the table and suspend the chain or string of the pendulum through your thumb and first two fingers. Allow the chain (string) to trail down the back of your hand.

Ground and center. Take a few deep breaths, remembering to relax the muscles around your eyes and mouth. You may wish to recite the angelic divination prayer given earlier.

Wait until the pendulum is still. Then say, "Show me yes." Wait for the pendulum to move. It may move clockwise, counterclockwise, forward, or backward. This will indicate your yes answers for the reading at hand.

Wait until the pendulum stops spinning from your previous movement. Say, "Show me no." Wait for the pendulum to move. It may move clockwise, counterclockwise, forward, or backward, but it cannot be the same movement for your yes answer. If you get the same movement, try again. Once you have settled on the answer, keep in mind that this will indicate the no answer for the reading at hand.

Wait until the pendulum comes to a halt, then say, "Show me I don't know." Wait for the pendulum to move. It must be a different movement from your yes and no answers. Once you have settled on this answer, you are ready to begin asking the questions you've planned for this divination session.

Keep a record of your "hits" and "misses." To practice, predict the weather, or use the stock market pages from your newspaper. Be sure you work with something you couldn't possibly have known beforehand. You will notice that some days you will do exceedingly well, and other days maybe not so hot. This can be attributed to your state of mind, your health, or current astrological correspondences.

Some people prefer to use a chart for pendulum divination. You can cut it out of poster board, or make it out of wood or metal. The choice is yours. If you are artistic, use canvas board and paint the chart, as well as angelic characterizations. Here are a few charts you may like to try:

The Basic Chart

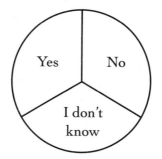

The Archangel Chart

This is a quick way to discover where you need to concentrate your energies or what most concerns a friend or client. You can add other items to the chart in each quarter. This one is designed to give you an idea. For example, Gabriel often predicts births, and Uriel deals with property and acquiring physical items. You could add those traits to your chart.

Planning Chart

This chart helps show the possible outcome of a situation. For example, if Susie wants to find a good relationship, there are places that she knows she could look; some may have drawbacks. The first thing she should do is ask her guardian angel to help her. Then she could draw a chart something like the one below, and try her hand at the pendulum to help her make the best choice of where to look (or where not to look).

Angel Runes

Simply put, runes are sigils. Some of them are very old and will not be covered in this book. (If you are interested in traditional runes, many other books on the topic are available.) The runes provided here are designed specifically for use in angelic divination and magickal practices.

The Angel Runes (see pages 240-244 for illustrations and descriptions) are twenty-six pictographs (universal symbols) of common subjects that we deal with in our everyday lives. They are a tool for you to understand the past, see the present clearly, and consider the future. They can also be used on your altar when working magick to assist in drawing the energies you need to perform a working.

Most runes are made from small circular tiles, round disks, round gemstones, small pebbles, or even round pieces of heavy paper (you can make your own runes out of anything you like). There are many sets of runes on the market today. Some are very old (as mentioned earlier) and some have come about in the last fifty years or so.

Start with the runes on pages 240-244 when making your personal set of Angel Runes, but feel free to tailor your set of runes to your belief system and your lifestyle. I have chosen symbols that represent what each rune means to me. Feel free to add an extra pictograph or two to cover areas and situations that are commonplace in your life. For example, because I work with hypnotherapy, I have designed a rune for that particular study. Not everyone will need that rune in their set. If your work includes healing through the magickal and medical properties of herbs, you may wish to create symbols that indicate some standard plants—such as cinquefoil, rosemary, etc. If you are sports-minded, you may wish to add a rune that represents athletic energies. If you own a business, you may find that designing a rune that represents that business is very helpful. The ideas for runes are endless.

It is traditional that once you receive and learn to use a set of runes, no matter what type they are, that you make a set for two other people, teach them the system orally, and give them each a set as gifts. This ensures the group mind around the tool you designed remains stable and grows. Carefully choose recipients for your Angel Runes.

General Rules

Cleanse, consecrate, and empower your set of runes before you use them. Choose a particular angel to be the guardian of the set. This is the angel you will invoke every time you use the divination tool, so choose wisely. You may wish to find a symbol of that angel and place it in your rune bowl or bag, or draw a sigil representing the guardian on the sides or bottom of the bowl itself.

Cleanse your runes after each working by setting them in the sunlight, the moonlight, or running them through incense.

Read Angel Runes for immediate timing—not six months or a year in the future. They let you know what energies are hanging around you right now, and what is moving toward you within a week or so. Occasionally, a rune will fall way out on the corner of the table. View this as a signal that this issue, though not immediately present, may be affected by your current choices. Likewise, word your questions carefully, as some may be better served by the use of a more elaborate tool, such as the Tarot.

You may wish to make your Angel Runes all one color, or you may choose to assign them specific colors. The choice is yours.

All Angel Runes are tossed, save for the significator rune. This rune represents the querent (the person you are reading for). Because the angels don't care whether you are male or female, the significator rune is a universal symbol.

Casting the Runes

Put all the runes in a small bowl or bag. Shake them around and consider the question. Ground and center, taking several deep breaths and relaxing. Connect with your guardian angel and the angel you have named as the guardian of your runes. Ask for their help. Ask your question, then lightly toss the runes on a flat, stable surface.

Reading the Angel Runes

Ignore runes that are face down. They are not issues or situations that you need to deal with for this particular question. Read from the significator rune outward. Those runes closest to the significator indicate more immediate concerns. Those further away indicate events or states of mind moving toward or away from the querent.

Those runes touching each other deal with the same issue. Those with space or blank runes in between are either separated issues, or issues that have some sort of barrier between them.

After practice you will note that the runes form patterns around issues. The patterns are usually linear or circular.

When you become proficient with your Angel Runes, you may wish to draw a chart much like the ones I showed you for the pendulum tool, or you can try the one below by drawing it on a poster board or embroidering the design on a piece of white linen. You may wish to surround the circle with astrological symbols, phases of the Moon, etc. The choice is yours. Be sure to personalize your chart. Interpretations are best when you have taken the time to meld your energies to the tool.

The Meanings

Guardian Angel: This rune signifies the querent's guardian angel and what he or she is working on right now, whether or not he or she she is blocked, and if so, by what. If the guardian angel rune is upside down, it means that the querent hasn't been taking the guardian seriously or is simply not paying attention.

Religion: This is the sacred spiral. When this rune is nearby, look to future training, petitions to divinity, and your relationship with the universe. Consider conducting a ritual, a rite, or a devotion to help you solve a problem or give you new insight into your life patterns. Perhaps the difficulty lies in how you perceive religion and handle it in your life. If this rune is face down, it basically means you've been too busy with mundane things and have not used your spiritual gifts, or it can simply mean that religious issues are not a focus at this moment.

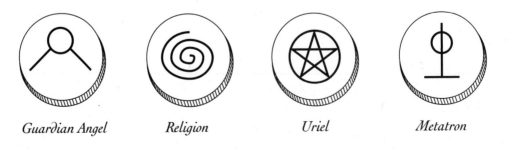

Guardian Angel   *Religion*   *Uriel*   *Metatron*

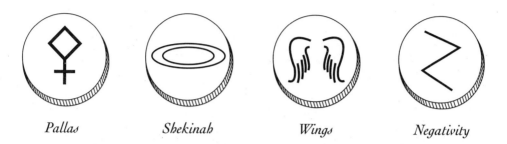

Pallas　　　　*Shekinah*　　　　*Wings*　　　　*Negativity*

Uriel: Magick. If there is good or bad mojo involved, this rune will tell you, especially if it is inverted. If it is near the negativity rune, it means that magick has been cast that isn't necessarily meant to harm you, but isn't going to be any good for you. It means that the best intentions can bring the worst possible results for you. If this rune is inverted, it definitely means you've been targeted with negative thoughts by someone in particular. This could stem from jealousy or mere misinformation.

Metatron: Wisdom. This is the ability to make good decisions (upright) or bad ones (inverted). Check the surrounding runes to see if wisdom is coming your way, or perhaps you may need to seek wisdom from a friend or family member. Inverted, this rune can signify a hasty decision that may lead to problems or a thoughtless act.

Pallas: Meditation. The situation will go better for you if you meditate on it and begin to plan appropriate action. Inverted, the rune may show that you have not put enough positive thoughts into the situation, indicating a need for you to begin affirming a more positive lifestyle.

Shekinah: Halo. This rune represents your higher self and the best that you can accomplish in any given situation. It does not have a specific inverted meaning. It is a rune of spiritual blessings and Goddess energy.

Wings: Messages. Upright means good messages, inverted may mean you won't get the message you want or may not get a message at all.

Negativity: This is negativity projected into the situation, such as gossip, bad intentions, hidden agendas, dirty deeds, or jealousies, either on the part of the querent or on someone else's behalf. Check the surrounding runes. Inverted indicates a possible chance of recovery from the situation. Again, check the surrounding runes to see how the querent can possibly get free of the problem.

Gabriel: Beginnings. This rune represents the beginning of any situation. Near the family rune, it means possible birth or marriage. If it is inverted, the hope for a fresh start is blocked and may not manifest.

Azrael: Endings. This rune represents the ending of a matter. If it is inverted, the situation may end badly should you not move to do something about it, or possibly an ending is not in sight at this time. Again, check the surrounding runes for clarification.

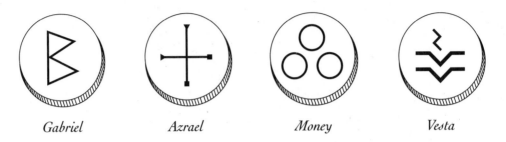

| *Gabriel* | *Azrael* | *Money* | *Vesta* |

Money: This one is fairly straightforward. Check the surrounding runes for the source and amount of money. If it is near family or legacy, there may be a gift from a family member or a death in the family providing an inheritance. If it is near negativity, look out—someone is trying to take you for a ride.

Vesta: Inspiration and protection. Look to something new to help you along. This could be a new hobby, a new job, a new partnership, etc. (check the surrounding runes). Inverted, this rune indicates a lack of inspiration on the part of the querent.

Conflict: This rune means what it says: there is a fight brewing, an open-mouth battle, or perhaps a physical confrontation. Near the family rune means family disputes. Near negativity, an open argument. Near addiction, possible criminal activity or fallout from an addictive or obsessive behavior. The further away this rune is, the most likely the querent can control damage now, or negate the conflict entirely. If inverted, the conflict has already happened and steps to resolution are under way.

Anaelle: Family. Again, a straightforward sigil. Anything linked by blood or spirit. This can be your immediate relatives or extended family. Upright, all is perking along well (though check the surrounding runes). Inverted, possible dysfunction or temporary imbalance.

Raphael: Harmony. Joy, excitement, pleasant events, happiness, love, self-esteem. The blending of harmonious energies. The receiving of gifts. Inverted, exhibits unhappiness, things of pleasure stalled or destroyed, or lack of self-esteem.

Star: Hope for the future, green light, things are fated to be very good for the querent. This rune does not have an inverted meaning. Check the surrounding runes for further clarification.

| *Conflict* | *Anaelle* | *Raphael* | *Star* |

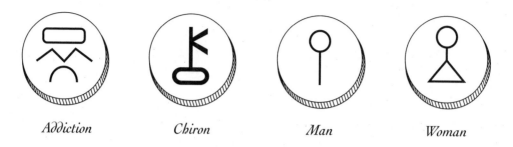

Addiction   *Chiron*   *Man*   *Woman*

Addiction: Means what it says. Addiction to drugs, alcohol, sex, or obsessive habits—even power, such as an egomaniac. Inverted, this rune indicates the addiction is past or the individual in question is making a great effort to overcome the problem.

Chiron: Karma. The situation at hand is karmic in nature—a situation you may have been working on for several lifetimes, or one you have just begun. Inverted indicates the process of denial in the situation and refusal to work on the pattern constructively.

Man: This is a man or male energy that in some way affects the querent. The tiles surrounding this rune indicate his intentions. Upright indicates he is a positive influence or a nice person at heart (the runes around him may indicate he is making good or bad decisions). Inverted shows a gutless swine, and his effects on the querent will be poor.

Woman: This is a female or female energy that in some way affects the querent. The tiles surrounding this rune indicate her intentions. Upright indicates she is a positive influence or a nice person at heart (the runes around her may indicate she is making good or bad decisions). Inverted shows her to be a thoughtless, gossipy viper, and her effects on the querent will be poor.

Juno: Partnership. The union of two people for love or business (check the surrounding runes). Inverted shows the partnership is going down the drain or true feelings are hidden. Again, check the runes closest to this one for more details.

Work: The work that is most important to the querent at the present moment. This could be a full-time job, a part-time venture, community service, even inspirational work. The key here is *that which is most important*. Inverted indicates that the querent is not following the work he or she truly wishes to do, or his or her current work.

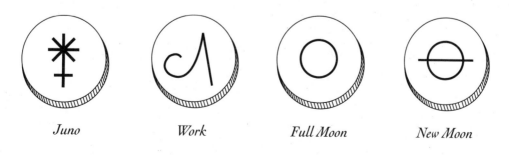

Juno   *Work*   *Full Moon*   *New Moon*

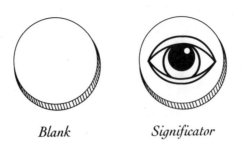

Blank   *Significator*

Full Moon: This is a rune of timing. Runes around this one show what will happen by the next Full Moon.

New Moon: This is another timing rune. Runes around this one show what will happen by the next New Moon.

Blank: The outcome is unknown or there is an unknown influence involved in the situation.

Significator: Stands for the querent. Upright means that the querent has his or her eyes open and is ready to learn the facts and hear spiritual messages. Inverted indicates the querent is in a state of denial, not looking rationally at all the facts, or is so caught up in other ventures that he or she is not paying attention to business.

Angels and the Tarot

For angelic spreads, you will need a deck of cleansed, consecrated, and empowered Tarot cards. Choose a deck that appeals to you. Don't worry if your usual interpretations are a little different than the standard ones I will deal with here. You can work out any disagreements in your own mind.

Since I've been working with the angels, I've found hidden meanings in the Tarot cards, indicating who to contact for help in the angelic realms. I've also found that if I ask my guardian angel for assistance before any reading, my predictions and insights are more accurate. I've included some basic Tarot information for you here in case you, like me, love the Tarot cards and use them often, but I have also included angelic correspondences in assisting you to find solutions to your problems through the Tarot.

Meaning of the Major Arcana

The Fool: The beginning of a new cycle or enterprise; a matter that is unexpected or unplanned; moving in a different direction, heading toward an unknown future; look before you leap; use your hidden talents.

Ask your guardian angel which direction you should travel and how hard you should tread the path. Use your angel eyes in meditation. Aries angels, those who tread where others fear to go, are excellent helpers for the Fool. Angels of Aries are Ariel, Machidiel, Satararan, and Sariel. These angels are courageous, wild, and passionate. Angels of Aquarius give the push to start something new.

The Magician: Having the ability to bring matter into form. Creativity, insight.

Raphael best represents the Magician, with his power over the winds, science, creativity, healing, magickal tools, and the gifts of the pentacle. When the Magician appears in your reading, look for a message from this blessed archangel. Remember that Raphael is also a Seraphim. The Dominions fulfill the role of divine leaders whose efforts involve integrating the material and the spiritual without losing control. The prince of the Dominions is either Hashmal or Zadkiel. Remember, Dominion is also the name of the first recorded angel. Here, Dominion and the Magician are one. Capricorn angels can help you "make do" when you think you can't bring thought into form.

The Priestess: Awareness of planes of existence; hidden forces with new solutions; feminine balance and occult learning; leadership potential; matriarchal thought.

Ask Gabriel for help in the women's mysteries. Ask Uriel to reveal hidden knowledge (he is both Archangel and Seraphim). Shekinah holds the key to all hidden secrets. Raziel is the divine snoop, and can help you ferret out hidden agendas that may be affecting your life. Remiel is the angel of true vision, but his assistance demands that your intentions be honest. Vesta angels represent feminine aspirations toward particular paths or goals. Pallas angels focus on feminine energy involved in intuition, flashes of genius, keen insights, and the formulation of new and original thoughts. The Thrones are interested in divine knowledge and the dispensation of this knowledge to humanity. Ariel is the guardian of visions, dreams, and prophecies. Although Ariel was first recorded as male, many angel believers today associate Ariel with the feminine divine. Angels of Neptune will give the querent mystic experiences, clairvoyance, and inspiration. You may wish to use Gabriel's prayer:

> *Hail, Lady, full of grace—the God is with you. Blessed are you among women and blessed is the fruit of your womb, the Consort and Son. Holy Goddess, Mother of Earth, work your mysteries for your children, now and in the hour of our need. So mote it be.*

The Empress: Financial and emotional security; motherly or womanly love; good fortune and happiness; a female partner; pregnancy; the matriarch of a family.

Ask the Queen of Angels for assistance in matters of fertility or manifestation for the good of yourself or others. The nurturing angels of Ceres, most interested in the principle of unconditional love, and the angels of the Great Mother are also associated with the Empress. Venus angels are concerned with matters of the heart and beauty. Angels of Venus are Anael, Hasdiel, Eurabatres, Raphael, Hagiel, and Noguel. As the Empress can also stand for fertility, any entreaty to Gabriel regarding this condition might be a good idea. Gabriel is the guardian of Goddess energy on earth, and the protector of childbirth and pregnancy.

The Emperor: Reason over emotion; government, politics, system; command and authority; patriarchal thought; the need to be famous; the patriarch of a family.

Michael, chief among the Virtues, chief of the Archangels, a Seraphim, and the guardian of those organizations or groups in need of structure, will always help someone who has questions of business, order, and structure. Angels of the Principalities (guardians of large groups), Dominions (divine leaders), and the Thrones of Earth can all be seen in the Emperor card. The Cherubim also function under the energies of the Emperor card, as they are available when you are seeking divine protection, wisdom, and knowledge to bring order out of chaos. Virgo angels are excellent representations of the Emperor card. Angels of Virgo are Voil, Voel, Hamaliel, Iadra, and Schaltiel. These angels are interested in the perfection of a thing, thought, action, duty, or person. Angels of the Sun (Arithiel, Galgaliel, Gazardia, Korshid-Metatron, Michael, Och, Raphael, Uriel, and Zerachiel) will assist the querent in his or her greatest ambitions. These angels are associated with authority figures, favors, advancement, health, and promotion. Angels of Capricorn are concerned with banking, insurance, and the government.

The Priest: Conformity and tradition; going with the flow because everyone else is; dealing in a facade; karma; marriage or a ceremony of some kind; pomp and glory.

Metatron fits especially well here. Metatron is a super angel, a divine prince, and all sorts of glorious good stuff. He is both creator and librarian of the Akashic records. He holds all secrets and keeps track of what all humans are doing. Truly, no better card represents Metatron than the Priest. Angels of Neptune will provide seriousness, humility, sincerity, and wisdom.

The Lovers: The choice between two opposites; a decision that will affect several people; second sight; love versus practicality; possible new love; passion.

Look to the angels of Venus for questions of the heart, such as courtship, dating, affection, alliances, and harmony. They adore cooperation and romantic love, as well as marriage and partnerships of all kinds. Mercury angels (Tiriel, Raphael, Hasdiel, Michael, Barkiel, Zadkiel, and the Bene Seraphim) will assist in matters of communication between loved ones. If you need to make a decision, ask your guardian angel what your best move should be. Angels of the Moon bring messages, reconciliation, and love. Angels of Juno will help you if you are experiencing marital troubles. They are interested in harmony and happiness in relationships.

The Chariot: Balance through movement; bringing two opposing points under control; self-control; vehicular movement; buying or selling a car.

Angels of the Moon watch over trips and travel, as do the Cherubim (the guardians of light and stars). The Virtues are the spirits of movement, working and guiding the elemental energies that affect our planet. Sagittarius angels govern long-distance travel.

Justice: Legalities, contracts, agreements; what you sow so shall ye reap; think before you act; the Goddess will balance the situation.

The prime concern of Juno angels is the balance of power and our individual freedom. The terminator angels (Michael, Gabriel, and Uriel) are excellent in obtaining justice for those who deserve it. The Powers are warrior angels who can help you in your time of need. You can call on the Principalities in times of discrimination, destruction of animals or people, inadequate rulership, or to bring the strength to make necessary reforms. Angels of the Dark Moon deal with addictions, change, divorce, enemies, justice, obstacles, quarrels, removal, separation, criminals and their acts, and death by unjust means. Angels of the Waning Moon also deal with divorce. Angels of the Disseminating Moon assist in removing stress and negative emotions in general, and can help in a divorce case. Angels of the Full Moon will assist with general legal matters. Saturn angels take care of debts and deal with lawyers, money matters, real estate, relations with older people, and anything involving family and finance (such as wills or estates). The angels of Libra are drawn to legal incidents, the counsel of others, or when cooperation and interaction are needed between individuals. They will shine the light upon your enemies. The angels of Saturn are Orifiel, Kafziel, Michael, Maion, Mael, Zaphiel, Schebtaiel, and Zapkiel. Scorpio angels are excellent when working on criminal cases that involve homicide or an unresolved death; Virgo angels will look for minute clues. Finally, don't forget the Powers, who are warrior angels.

The Hermit: Introspection and spiritual enlightenment; planning and evaluating the next move; seeking a higher intelligence; meeting a physical teacher.

The angels of Neptune best represent the Hermit. They are the caretakers of the oppressed and the misfits of society. They like people who are visionaries or are involved with mysticism, psychic awareness, and compassion. Angels of Neptune will give you the gifts of clairvoyance, inspiration, genius, devotion, mystical experiences, and reverence. The angels of Libra are concerned with counseling.

The Wheel: Rotation of any situation or life event; tidal movement; steady and even turn of events; upward mobility.

Jupiter angels (Zachariel, Zadkiel, Sachiel, Adabiel, Barchiel, and Zadykiel) are most interested in prosperity, including self-improvement and the well-being of others. Angels of Jupiter govern the accumulation of material assets, power, and status and bolster your optimism, bringing joyful events toward you and helping you develop your aspirations. The quiet and stable angels of Taurus oversee income and assets. These angels are Tual, Asmodel, Bagdal, and Araziel.

Strength: Victory over difficulty; successful end to a tiresome event; spiritual strength; sharp and incisive mental action.

Michael, the angel of strength and victory, applies to this card. The Powers are warrior angels who will assist you when you are in trouble or when you feel you need additional strength to deal with a problem. If you are looking for emotional strength, call on Gabriel (see the invocation on page 27). Uranus angels provide the gift of strength and resourcefulness. Mars angels (Uriel, Sammael, Gabriel, and Chamael) provide independence, strength, courage, energy, determination, self-reliance, boldness where needed, and devotion. Mars angels are victory angels.

The Hanged Man: Thoughts, ideas, or projects in suspension; stuck between a rock and a hard place; getting ready to move in a definitive direction.

The angels of Chiron best represent the Hanged Man. These angels hold the key to the universe and are thought to be the male aspect of the wounded priest or wounded healer. Angels of Chiron can unlock any door, move any block, pull you from suspension, and allow you to reach below the tree of life and grasp the knowledge you need at the roots.

Death: Radical, unplanned change; old ripped away to prepare for the new; illusions swept instantly away; a new life path.

Azrael, the angel of death, brings change into the querent's life. Saturn angels also institute change and are concerned with authority, karmic lessons, boundaries, and endurance. The angels of Uranus are concerned with mass media and communication with the dead. The angels of Scorpio are extraordinarily mystical, and deal with death, rebirth, and karma.

Temperance: Ability to adapt to new circumstances; action as a result of higher self or guide information; mature love; control through wisdom; the art of mixing and matching.

This is the guardian angel card. If this card is inverted, the querent should be reminded to talk to his or her guardian angel; a message is waiting. Angels of Neptune provide patience, endurance, humility, sincerity, and seriousness. Angels of Mercury also fit here, bringing adaptability, mental activity, brilliance, eloquence, dexterity, and awareness. The angels of Mercury are Tiriel, Raphael, Hasdiel, Michael, Barkiel, Zadkiel, and the Bene Seraphim. Angels of Aquarius deal with friends, hopes, wishes, and the brilliance of our mission. The angels of Pisces are most interested in healing and energies of unseen strength and power. Temperance can be seen as the healer's card. I believe that those who gravitate toward the healing arts and the auspisces of the Pisces angels have this card turn up frequently. The Virtues can also be associated with Temperance, as they are known as "the miracle angels." Raphael, the healer, also fits comfortably here.

The Devil: Binding by thought, word, or deed; unbridled lust or deep passion; a charismatic but untrustworthy person; human frailties; drug or alcohol addiction; violence; obsession.

Angels of Ceres, the nurturing angels, will assist in counseling friends and in divination for the sole purpose of helping others. These angels find and heal lost pets and children. The angels of Neptune will assist with issues of confinement, abandonment, addiction, or physical intolerance to drugs or other substances.

The Tower: Swift breakdown of a situation; seeing things for what they really are; unexpected setbacks or repercussions; danger; fate.

Revolutionary change can be attributed to the angels of Uranus. They will help you understand unpredicted change that may look dark and dreary on the surface, but is actually for the best. To me, the Tower represents situations that hit us from the outside and difficulties that we did not cause, but are dealing with anyway. Ask the angels of Uranus for help in dealing with this sort of unexpected change of events.

The Star: Faith, confidence, and hope; positive influences; the ability to cut through illusion; new life with wider choices; fated good fortune.

This card is best linked to the Cherubim, who function as the guardians of light and stars. They also create and channel positive energy from divinity to humans. They are known as "those who intercede." The Cherubim watch over galaxies, guard any religious temple, and function as personal sword-wielding guards to help you reach your destiny.

The Moon: Dreams, intuition, vision questing, imagination, psychic prowess, emotionally charged circumstances; betting pulled in two different directions; magickal work; the possibility of deception.

Gabriel and the angels of the Moon best represent the energies of this card. Moon angels concentrate on our emotions or the emotions of others. Angels of Cancer govern intuition and sensitivity and also ward off negative energy, protecting family secrets and ensuring security. The angels of the Moon include Cael, Manuel, Muriel, Rahdar, and Phakiel.

The Sun: Joy and happiness, earned rewards; family celebrations; new and creative environment; good news on its way.

Of course, angels of the Sun are related to this card. Michael and Metatron, who represent shining personalities and success, are also important here. The angels of Leo (Verchiel, Sagham, and Seratiel) are flamboyant, optimistic, enthusiastic, and loyal. The Virtues are especially fond of those who try to go beyond their capabilities to acheive more than everyone else says they can. Angels of the Sun deal with the power of will, authority, and recognition. Issues of concern to them are advancement, health, fun, pleasures, loyalty, and generosity.

Judgement: A project or situation nearing completion; final decision has yet to be made; awakening at the end of a long process; ending may not be what is expected; the past comes back to haunt you; you are too critical of yourself.

After much consideration, I have paired the Judgement card with the Archangels (Michael, Raphael, Uriel, and Gabriel). When this card pops up, for good or ill, it is time to make a decision—although this may not be as soon as you would like. This card, for me, is the "angel red-tape" card. Not everything is finished yet. The Thrones also stand for Judgement. The Thrones create, collect, and channel incoming and outgoing positive energies that deal with justice and judgement. They are the

249

"many-eyed ones" who will send healing energy to any victim. Thrones take great interest in what humans are doing, though they may channel their energies through your guardian angel.

The World: End of a cycle in a situation, reaping your just rewards and traveling onward and upward; scenario has played itself completely out; no loose ends left; satisfactory conclusion; possibility to explore new avenues.

To me, Shekinah best represents the World card. Shekinah is known as the glory emanating from the divine and She stands for liberation, therefore this is Her card. She is the the Holy Ghost, bringing two halves (or many lines of thought or work) together. Her message is that of maturation.

Meaning of Matching Numbers

The more matching numbers you have (e.g., four kings, three aces, etc.) the faster the outcome of the situation. These combinations also have interpretations of their own.

Aces
4 Fast moving forces at work; don't be blindsided.
3 Success is ensured at a fast pace.
2 Change is afoot, such as a job or home.

Twos
4 Quick reorganization and possible shake-up.
3 Conversations (including gossip) bring quick conclusions.
2 Look for a hidden agenda in the partnership.

Threes
4 Strong finish and excellent rewards.
3 A lie is close by (look for the Moon; a giveaway).
2 Two goals moving in opposite directions or you may be hit from two different directions at the same time.

Fours
4 A strong foundation has been built at a fast pace. Are there any cracks?
3 Possible jealousy in estate matters.
2 Reorganization of assets.

Fives
4 A confrontation will hit fast and leave you spinning or running for cover.
3 Look for a love triangle.
2 Look for deceit.

Sixes
4 An attitude adjustment will hit home.
3 Look for a new, hidden opportunity in an old issue.

Sevens

   4   Grief comes quickly; hang on and flow with it.

   3   Lock your doors and windows — major theft is afoot.

Eights

   4   Quick communication on major issues.

   3   Pack your bags; you are bound for a trip.

Nines

   4   The end is fast approaching; I hope you are ready.

   3   Another person may help you bring about a speedy conclusion to the issue.

Tens

   4   Something will be bought or sold quickly; remember to read the fine print.

   3   Definite legacy with this issue.

Pages

   4   New ideas will hit soon; hang on for the creative burst.

Knights

   4   Swift action in the matter. Be careful what you wish for. Can indicate a move of house and change of job and change of relationships.

Meaning of Numbers on Cards

Not only can the number on the card indicate a time period (such as two days, two weeks, or two months for a card with the number two), it can also tell you something about the progress of the situation.

One: The beginning.

Two: The direction or first meeting point.

Three: This is where details grow and the idea solidifies.

Four: This is where roots are put down in order to build.

Five: First challenge or glitch in the situation.

Six: This is where the issue changes and grows in order to continue.

Seven: Variety is now added to expand the idea or project.

Eight: This is the evaluation period.

Nine: Moving forward to near completion.

Ten: Completion of the cycle, project, or issue.

Page: Rites of passage.

Knight: Movement and direction.

Angelic Card Spreads

Readers are always looking for new ways to gain information through their Tarot cards. Here are a few angelic spreads you may like to try.

General Rules

Sit quietly, take a few deep breaths; ground and center. Relax.

Call your guardian angel and ask him/her to assist you with the reading.

Invite the angels of prophecy into your life and ask for their assistance.

Shuffle the deck and consider your question.

When you are ready, lay the cards down in the pattern you have chosen. You can lay them face up, or choose to lay them face down, turning them over as you read.

Archangel Spread

The simplest layout is that of the Archangels. This is primarily a message spread, though it can be used for divination, if desired. Basically, each card in the pattern stands for a message from the particular angel it represents.

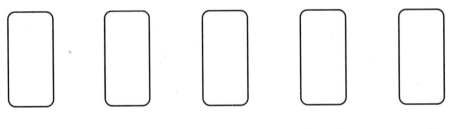

| Michael | Raphael | Gabriel | Uriel | Guardian |

Michael: Issues of intelligence, movement, and protection. Matters of the mind.

Raphael: Issues of inspiration, passion, healing, and creativity. Matters of the spirit.

Gabriel: Issues of transformation, other planes, and love. Matters of the heart.

Uriel: Issues of stability, ancestral heritage, and prophecy. Matters of the physical.

Guardian: A message from your guardian angel.

Angelic Energy Spread

Like the Archangel spread, this one is for information to help raise your consciousness.

| 1 | 2 | 3 | 4 | 5 | 6 | 7 | 8 | 9 | 10 |

1. **Guardian message:** Information from your guardian angel. This is often the issue that is most important to you at the moment.
2. **Relationship angels:** Information from angels who connect you to other people.
3. **Work environment angels:** Information from angels who oversee your work environment.
4. **Home environment angels:** Information from angels who oversee your home environment.
5. **Financial angels:** Information from angels who oversee your finances.
6. **Health angels:** Information from angels who oversee your health.
7. **Transformation angels:** Information on changes needed in your life or changes you have implemented recently.
8. **Pattern angels:** Information from angels on patterns you either need to enhance or break in your life.
9. **Attunement angels:** Information on areas in your life that may be out of joint and need a nudge toward harmony.
10. **Angels of hidden secrets:** Information that may be hidden from you either about yourself or circumstances around you.

Angelic Moon Spread

This spread moves with the phases of the Moon. You will need to check your almanac to see what phase the Moon is currently in before you begin. This phase will be your first set of two cards. In each set of cards, the card on the left indicates the circumstances during that phase; the card on the right indicates where work is needed. The third card under each phase indicates the outcome at this time. The last card (in the middle) shows the overall outlook of the month ahead. (See layout on the following page.)

Remember that when dealing with the future, divination tools show you only that which is most likely to happen, should you stay on your present course. This is

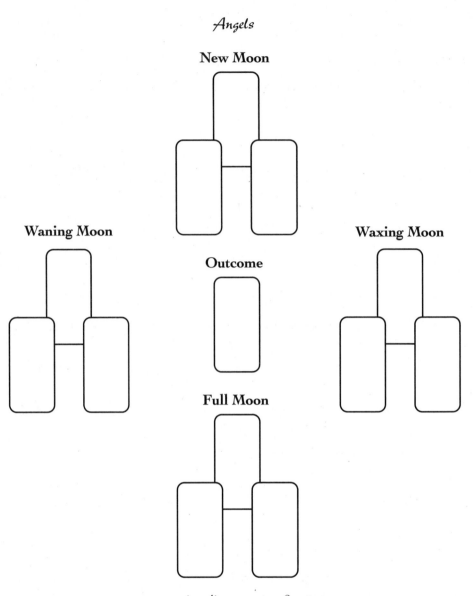

New Moon

Waning Moon

Outcome

Waxing Moon

Full Moon

Angelic moon spread

a reminder for those of us who are veteran diviners, as well as those who are just beginning to learn a tool, or individuals who seek the assistance of a diviner.

I had this point brought home to me the other evening. Once you are an old hand at handling a divinatory tool, you tend to become complacent about the experience. Sometimes we are so used to reading the future that we forget we can change it. I'll raise my hand here as being one of those who forgets this.

"Throw the cards for me," said Ina.

Fine; no problem. I obliged her. I went through the entire reading. She nodded her head, yes, this is happening; yes, that was said—blah, blah, blah. I ended with a flourish, saying, "This is the best you can hope for."

"So what do I do to change it?" said Ina.

I looked at her, dumfounded. I, the person who teaches thousands of people they have the right and the ability to change their lives, and shows them how to do it, sat looking at a client like I had lost all my senses. Ina and I then launched into a serious discussion about what she could do to change the negative outcome of the cards.

Later I took inventory of my life leading up to this particular reading. Why did I assume that Ina would not want to change the outcome of that card reading? Was it because I have many Tarot clients who do not desire to change their lives, relying solely on the outcome of the cards instead? I begin every reading by telling the client that the outcome of the cards can be changed, if desired. Why had I stopped listening to my own words?

Because I got stuck in the material plane, that's why. I looked around me. It had been a hard winter. During those months my husband and I scraped every penny together to meet the needs of our family. The material plane closed in, replacing spiritual necessities with physical ones. My life was out of whack, and I knew it.

Send in the angels. I did a mental call for help first, asking that my guardian angel assist me in raising my spiritual sights. I asked for relief from the worries of the physical plane and help to see the big picture. Finally, I thought seriously about what I felt was most important to me at the moment and why. From there I moved into action, changing various patterns in my life to relieve the physical stress.

These reality checks come to all of us at various points in our lives. No one is above them. Usually they signal a point of impending growth. Rather than allowing ourselves to sink into a grouchy existence, or worse, total despair, all we need do is ask for the angels to give us a helping hand.

If you call them, they will come.

Seventeen

Combating Chaos Using the Angels

*W*e've covered a great deal of material so far. If you have followed through with the exercises, meditations, and simple magicks, you've gotten a fairly good taste of angel magick. Now is the time to pull it all together and sink your magickal teeth into some of life's bigger issues.

Before you go any further in this chapter, review your angel journal or notes you may have kept in your adventures with the angels. Has your life changed at all since you first picked up this book and actively sought the angels in your life? Do you feel better about yourself? Are you working toward resolving some of the larger issues in your life that you may not have wanted to deal with previously? If you answer no to the majority of these questions, I suggest going back through the chapters on meeting your guardian angel, angels and ritual, and the angelic altar. Did you skip anything because you were in a hurry? If you did, you may want to rework those sections before you attempt this one.

Before starting this section, I asked a friend who works on a psychic hotline what types of questions people call and ask about most often. I figure that if someone is willing to cough up anywhere from $3.99 to $4.99 a minute, the questions must be fairly important to them. The most popular questions are on the following topics:

Love relationships: This involves everything from being lonely and seeking a relationship to the deterioration and dissolution of a relationship, and all the issues that surround this painful type of human experience. This also includes those relationships that are definitely defunct, but one individual is still holding on to the hopes and dreams that the lost partner will come to his or her senses and return.

Health issues: From minor surgeries to major, life-threatening events.

Money issues: From poverty to job-seeking, and into difficulties on the job, change of career, and hopes for the future.

Family issues: Relationships with children, step-children, parents, siblings, and extended family that affect the individual.

Most calls center on issues of self; every now and then concerns for a friend or family member. These are the issues we are going to center on first, then move to some bigger ones, such as work for the town where you live, your state or province, or your country. From there you can target global issues you see through the media.

I decided that I should give you, the reader, a project to work on here, to bring happiness to you whenever you felt the need for it. It had to be a tangible something, an item you could put your paws on when you wanted to, and something to represent your faith in the angels as well as the power you hold within yourself.

Hmmm. What to do.

Facing a blank computer screen wasn't doing me (or you) any good, so I decided to wander off to do some errands and catch some lunch. It was either that or a sink full of dishes. I opted for the fresh air, thank you very much.

In the bank I stood quietly, shifting from foot to foot. In front of me was a police officer in uniform. There were BIG angels around the police officer. I squeezed my eyes shut and peeped one open. The BIG angels were still there. At the next window was a tall man in his fifties with a little girl. She's four. She said so, you know. My guardian angel told me they are going on a trip. I saw rolling hills and a pleasant atmosphere. The man said to the teller, "We are on our way to West Virginia for the weekend."

"How nice," she said.

I thought this was all very weird.

In front of me was a man in his seventies. He had lost a son or daughter at some time in his life. My guardian angel told me the child is always nearby. At this point, I did not have the guts to open my mouth to say anything to him. As I left the bank I passed a lady in her sixties. "Heart trouble," said my guardian angel. I walked on.

There was a lady on the park bench dressed in a blue suit. The sky was azure and the sun danced off her white spring hat. The lady smiled. Beams of sunlight waltzed across something she had in her hand. I looked closer to discover it was a rosary. I turned away a moment to catch the flight of a bird, then turned back. No lady.

But I knew what to do.

The Angelic Rosary

The complete rosary stands for the five angelic mysteries. Since I developed the angelic rosary, many people have used them with great success. They are a statement of purpose, a meditative tool, an anchor when things are rough, a delight when all goes well, an aid when working spell casting, a vehicle for grounding and centering — I could go on and on.

Supplies:
> Rawhide string or leather
> 54 small beads
> 5 large beads
> 1 token of the Goddess
> 1 pentacle or miraculous medal (or both)

Tie a knot between each bead, but make sure there is enough room so each bead can turn. You could use smaller beads between each bead if you don't want to use knots. (Use the diagram on the next page as a guide.)

Don't worry if you don't want to be artsy-craftsy. I've designed this based on the standard rosary, so you can purchase a regular rosary at any inspirational store and adjust it for your needs by removing the cross and replacing it with the pentacle (or miraculous medal). However, if you are Christian and the cross is a divine symbol to you, by all means keep it where it is.

My Wiccan friends use black beads because black repels negativity. However, you may use any color beads that feels right for you. If you do not like the idea of a rosary, you may simply wish to scatter beads or gems in a decorative bowl and touch the beads in the bowl while using the prayers provided earlier. Again, it is your choice.

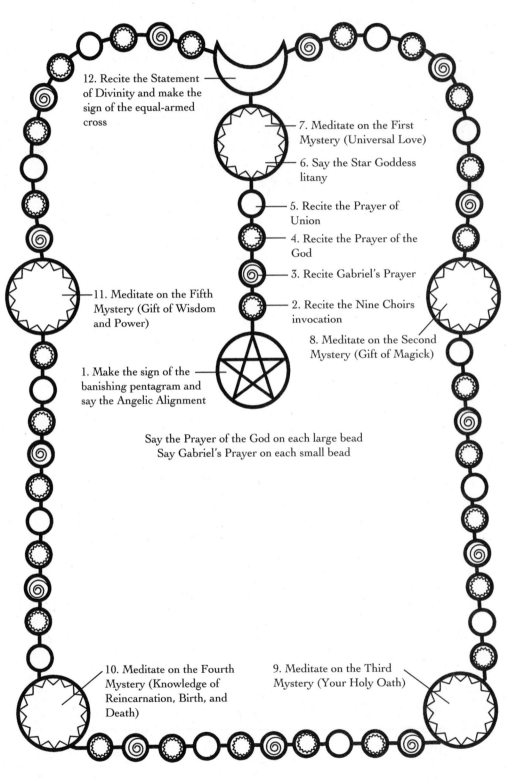

12. Recite the Statement of Divinity and make the sign of the equal-armed cross

7. Meditate on the First Mystery (Universal Love)

6. Say the Star Goddess litany

5. Recite the Prayer of Union

4. Recite the Prayer of the God

3. Recite Gabriel's Prayer

2. Recite the Nine Choirs invocation

8. Meditate on the Second Mystery (Gift of Magick)

11. Meditate on the Fifth Mystery (Gift of Wisdom and Power)

1. Make the sign of the banishing pentagram and say the Angelic Alignment

Say the Prayer of the God on each large bead
Say Gabriel's Prayer on each small bead

10. Meditate on the Fourth Mystery (Knowledge of Reincarnation, Birth, and Death)

9. Meditate on the Third Mystery (Your Holy Oath)

The angelic rosary

Does the angelic rosary take a while to memorize? Yes, it does. You will memorize it quickly if you work with it every day. You can always change the prayers to fit your religious choice. For example, I added a plain, small stone right before the pentacle because I like to recite poems by Doreen Valente. You can do this too, if you like.

Teenagers and children love the angelic rosary, especially if you go to an inspirational shop and buy ready-made ones with shiny or glittering beads. They like the idea that the rosary tells a story of mystery and magick.

Angels of prayer, should you like to call on them when you are working with your rosary, are Akatriel, Metatron, Shekinah, Raphael, Sandalphon, Gabriel, and Michael.

The angelic rosary is your first line of defense against unwanted chaos. Why do I use the word "unwanted"? Sometimes a little chaos in our lives is good. It shakes us up; it gets us thinking and (hopefully) moving.

To Say the Rosary

Begin by making a banishing pentagram on the pentacle (or medal) and saying the **Angelic Alignment:**

> *I align myself with universal harmony.*
> *I align myself with the Goddess.*
> *I am in alignment with the God.*
> *I am in alignment with my guardian angel.*
> *So mote it be.*

On the first bead, recite the **Invocation of the Nine Choirs:**

> *Brilliant Seraphim I call to thee*
> *Circle 'round, bring love to me.*
> *Mighty Cherubim guard my gate*
> *Remove from me sorrow and hate.*
> *Thrones stand firm, stable be*
> *Keep me steady on land or sea.*
> *I call Dominions, leadership true*
> *May I be fair in all I do.*
> *Circles of protection, Powers form*
> *Help me weather any storm*
> *Miraculous Virtues hover near*
> *Element energies I summon here.*
> *Principalities bring global reform*
> *Bless the world and each babe born.*
> *Glorious Archangels show me the way*
> *To bring peace and harmony every day.*

Guardian angel, Goddess delight
Gift me with your guiding light.

Say the **Prayer of Gabriel** on the second bead:

Hail, Lady, full of grace — the God is with you. Blessed are you among women and blessed is the fruit of your womb, the Consort and Son. Holy Goddess, Mother of Earth, work your mysteries for your children, now and in the hour of our need. So mote it be.

Say the **Prayer of the God** on the third bead:

Glory be to the Consort, to the Son, to the Sage, and to the Goddess. As it was in the beginning, is now, and ever shall be, spirit without end, magick with love. So mote it be.

Say the **Prayer of Union** on the fourth bead:

As the rod is to the God
So the chalice is to the Goddess
And together they are one.

Say the **Star Goddess Litany** on the next bead:

Hear the words of the Star Goddess; she in the dust of whose feet are the hosts of heaven and whose body encircles the universe. I who am the beauty of the green earth, and the white Moon among the stars, and the mystery of the waters, and the desire of the heart of man, call unto thy soul. Arise and come unto me. For I am the soul of nature, who gives life to the universe. From me all things proceed, and unto me all things must return; and before my face, beloved of Gods and of men, let thine innermost divine self be enfolded in the rapture of the infinite. Let my worship be within the heart that rejoiceth; for behold, all acts of love and pleasure are my rituals. And therefore, let there be beauty and strength, power and compassion, honor and humility, mirth and reverence within you. And thou who thinkest to seek for me, know thy seeking and yearning shall avail thee not unless thou knowest the mystery; that if that which thou seekest thou findest not within thee, thou wilt never find it without thee. For behold, I have been with thee from the beginning; and I am that which is attained at the end of desire.

The First Mystery

You are now at the point of the first mystery of the angels — universal love. Meditate on becoming one with the universal energies, opening your heart to divine love. Touch the Goddess medal to your forehead, then turn the next ten beads, reciting Gabriel's Prayer as you turn each bead. Don't forget to meditate on the mystery. See the beads glow as you become one with this sacred concept.

The Second Mystery

This is the gift of magick in our lives and the ability to change our circumstances through free will — the mystery of freedom. Begin with the Prayer of the God on the large bead, then continue with Gabriel's Prayer, turning each bead as you say each prayer. Don't forget to meditate on the mystery. See the beads glow as you become one with this sacred concept.

The Third Mystery

The third mystery is the mystery of your oath. This is the knowledge of and ability to work within the cycles of the universe in service to both the planet and our brothers and sisters. Begin with the Prayer of the God on the large bead, then continue with Gabriel's Prayer, turning the successive beads as you say each prayer. Don't forget to meditate on the mystery. See the beads glow as you become one with this sacred concept.

The Fourth Mystery

The knowledge of reincarnation and karma, birth and death, joy and sorrow teaches us that every action we perform has an equal reaction and how to live with the cycles of the seasons. Begin with the Prayer of the God on the large bead, then continue with Gabriel's Prayer, turning each bead as you say each prayer. Don't forget to meditate on the mystery. See the beads glow as you become one with this sacred concept.

The Fifth Mystery

This is the gift of wisdom and power to the hidden children of the Goddess. This mystery teaches us to be humble in our will and use our gifts for the good of all, harming none. Begin with the Prayer of the God on the bead that is by itself, then continue with Gabriel's Prayer, turning the beads as you say each prayer. Don't forget to meditate on the mystery. See the beads glow as you become one with this sacred concept.

We are now back at the Goddess medal and at the conclusion of our meditation sequence. End with the **Statement of Divinity:**

> *A great sign appears in the heavens.*
> *It is the Goddess clothed with the sun, the moon under her feet,*
> *And on her head a crown of twelve stars.*
> *The God stands behind her in his glory*
> *With his hands resting upon her shoulders*
> *And together they are one.*
> *So mote it be.*

Finish by making the sign of the equal-armed cross.

Bringing Love into Your Life with the Angels

There is nothing worse than feeling lonely and unloved. Every time these feelings come close to you, don't forget that you are never alone—your guardian angel is always with you and you are loved by all the angels and divinity combined. To bring love toward you, try this simple seven-day magick.

Day: Friday (the Venus day)

Angelic hour: Uriel

Moon phase: New (do not perform when the Moon is void of course)

Supplies: Two pink taper candles, a picture of yourself, a red heart cut out of construction paper

Angels to call: Hahaiah, who inspires positive and loving thoughts; Anael, who is in charge of love, passion, and romance; Hael, who inspires art, kindness, mercy, and beauty; Mihr, who will find you a loyal friend (or heal a broken friendship); or you may prefer a chant of angelic names: Raphael, Rahmiel, Theliel, Donquel, Anael, Liwet, Mihr

Begin by working at your angelic altar. Cleanse, consecrate, and empower the pink candles. On the back of the heart, write your desire. Do not call a specific person. That is against free will and the angels will not help you. Instead, call loving thoughts toward you (friendship, companionship, etc.). Please be specific.

Ground and center. In a ritual you design, call your guardian angel and invoke both divinity and the angel you have chosen to help you. Be honest and forthright. Be clear and operate only in harmony with the universe.

Set the two pink candles about one foot apart with your picture in the middle, between the two candles. Place the heart on top of your picture. Light the candles and let them burn for five minutes. Move the two candles a little closer together, then put them out.

Thank divinity and the angels for helping you.

The next evening at the same time, repeat this procedure, and every night thereafter until the seventh day. On the seventh day, make sure both candle holders are touching the picture and the heart. Let the candles burn until there is nothing left. Take the heart and your picture (keep them together) and put them in a safe, undisturbed place. When what you have called comes to you, be sure to go back to your altar and thank both divinity and the angels for your good fortune. You may keep the heart and picture together as long as you like.

Let the Angels Help You in the Dissolution of a Partnership

Things aren't going well and you have made up your mind that the relationship you are in is either dysfunctional, or you are just plain unhappy. You want out, but you'd like to do it amicably.

Let the angels help you. First, talk to your guardian angel about the matter and ask for guidance in all the decisions you make regarding the separation. Be prepared to spend energy and time to tie up all the loose ends. In other words, it took you time to assemble the relationship in the first place, so it will probably take you time to disassemble it.

Day: Saturday

Angelic hour: Cassiel

Moon phase: Dark of the Moon (Do not perform when the Moon is void of course)

Supplies: Two black candles (to repel negativity); a picture of yourself and the individual you wish to be separated from; a box with mirrors pasted on the sides, top, and bottom, facing outward

Angels to call: Mupiel, who fosters a tolerant "live and let live" philosophy; Nemamiah, who fights for good causes; Rhamiel, who will bring empathy, kindness, mercy, love, protection, and compassion (some believe St. Francis and this angel were intrinsically linked); Shekinah, the Jewish female angel/spirit who believes in freedom and inspires humans to be just and fair

Some preparatory magick is called for when you are dealing with separation/banishment magicks. First, remove all your jewelry, boil it, set it on ice, then either give it away or put it away. Do not wear clothing that belongs to the other person. Wash all your clothing that the other person has worn in regular detergent mixed with a sprinkle of empowered basil.

This separation/banishment working is the opposite of the previous exercise where you brought love into your life. Where you set the candles together, you will now move the black candles and the pictures apart, day by day, for seven days. On the seventh day, leave your picture in the center of the altar and remove the picture of the other person. Ask your guardian angel to surround you with love, peace, and harmony. Place your picture in the mirrored box, asking the angels to protect you through the separation process. Close the box and seal it with an equal-armed cross. Let the candles burn down to nothing. Leave your picture in the box throughout the separation process and beyond, should you feel the need.

265

When the amicable dissolution has occurred, be sure to thank the angels for their kind and loving assistance in the matter. Remember, it is your responsibility to try to keep the separation process on good terms, but what if that doesn't happen?

I've found that in severely dysfunctional relationships so much negativity has grown that sometimes the angels pack extra power to sever the abusive partner from the victimized one. You will also need to follow the mundane advice of your attorney and others who are helping you to ease your situation.

If you think that your partner is the stalking kind, or you feel that you will be harassed, threatened, or otherwise negatively affected, you may find that you need to take further measures.

File a restraining order, and research and use the stalking laws in your state.

Have as little contact with the abusive individual as possible. This means no phone calls, no visits, no chance meetings, no talking to his/her friends, etc. Be an ice cube and chill. Don't be fooled by sweet talk, flowers, candy, or gifts of any kind.

Change all the locks on your doors and learn to protect your home (it won't hurt, anyway). Get a dog, purchase an alarm system, etc.

Write down every detail when he or she tries to contact you. Use camcorders, tape recorders, private investigators, and other witnesses. These things will help you get a conviction in court, should this step be necessary.

Do not show fear around the abusive individual. That's what this type of person feeds on—your pain and your fear. Starve them.

Consider self-defense lessons. They are inexpensive and you never know when you might need the knowledge, anyway.

The Lunch Table Fracas

My teenaged daughter came home one afternoon with a long face. "What's the matter?" I asked, breaking away from my beloved computer.

"There are some boys at school that took our lunch table. Now we have to rush to the cafeteria just to get a seat. I don't like them because they throw things at us and are a real pain," said my daughter. "Who can I call to make them stop?"

"Call your guardian angel," I said.

"I thought they only hung around," she said thoughtfully. "You mean they can actually do things for you?"

I looked at her in amazement. "What have I been teaching people day and night for the last two years?"

She eyed me carefully. "Angels."

"What have I been talking about for the last three months to the point you are ready to stuff a sock in my mouth?" I asked.

She shifted from one foot to the other. "Angels."

"So, who are you going to call?"

"You are going to make this another one of your experiments, aren't you?" she asked with a slight smile on her face. She didn't wait for me to answer; she knew what it would be. "And it is going to be another one of our family stories that winds up in your book, huh?" She paused, mentally answering her own question because all she said was, "Okay, then, so who do I call?"

"Start with your guardian angel and then ask them to call the Powers for you, or you can call them yourself; your choice."

"What are the Powers?"

"Big dudes that don't like little people being pushed around."

"That will be perfect! I'll try that tomorrow!"

The problem with teenagers and magick (and some big people, too) is that they forget to work the magick. Things get so emotionally charged or so busy that the idea they can control their environment becomes a forgotten concept. You have to remind them gently, now and then, that they most certainly have the power to bring harmony in their lives. With this thought in mind, I waited patiently to see if my daughter remembered to do what I told her to do. To my surprise, the next day she told me that the boys had lost interest in her table; however, she and her friend continued to make the extra effort to get there first, just in case.

Sending Loving Angel Thoughts to a Screaming Person

Of course, you can be like my other daughter who did indeed remember to do the magick. A teacher, whom she didn't particularly care for at the time, decided the best way to handle her class was to scream at them repeatedly. I told my daughter to send loving angel thoughts to that teacher.

"They seem to fall short. Like there is a barrier around," she said sadly. "What can I do?"

"Point something at the teacher and fire the thoughts," I said. "Envision angelic healing light shooting toward the teacher."

My daughter smiled and promised to do just that. The next day, she came home with a shocked expression on her face.

"I did what you told me, Mother. I kept flicking my pencil, like I was playing, you know? And every time the end of the pencil lined up with the teacher I shot loving angel thoughts toward her."

"So what happened?" I asked, sensing something wasn't quite right.

"I really got into the flicking thing. And the pencil flew out of my hand and hit the teacher."

"Oh, no!"

She nodded. "But it's okay. Everybody laughed, and I said I was real sorry. The teacher laughed, too."

After the pencil-bombing session, my daughter and that particular teacher got along fine for the rest of the year. I guess the angels wanted to make sure the loving thoughts hit their mark, though I don't ever suggest or condone hitting anyone on purpose for any reason. Let the angels dispense the magick in the way they see fit.

Angels Will Help You Catch Criminals

If you have had something stolen or been served an injustice, the angels will help you catch the perpetrator. If you are involved in law enforcement, you should work this magick for every tough case (and those that aren't so tough if you see the need).

Days: Sunday, Tuesday, or Saturday (depending on the type of assistance needed)

Angelic hour: Michael, Camel, Uriel, or Cassiel

Moon phase: Dark of the Moon, New Moon, or Full Moon

Supplies: A piece of paper, newsclipping, etc., indicating the crime and the name of the criminal (if you know it; if you are not sure, DO NOT put anyone's name on the paper); a small cage (can be an old bird cage, a rodent cage, cricket cage, etc., as long as it has bars); two black candles; a black ribbon

Angels to call: Michael, Uriel, Cassiel—all will help with justice matters; Ambriel for communication and protection while you are working the magick (and thereafter should you feel you need her assistance); Armait grants truth, goodness, and wisdom (ask her for the "truth of the matter to be revealed to the proper authorities")

On the paper draw the symbol of the three major religions in your life. For example, my father is Christian and so Christianity plays a role in my life; I am Wiccan, of course that is important in my life; I also study Jewish mysticism (when I have the time), so that is part of my life. For me, I would draw the pentacle, the cross (it is okay to use it in this case), and the Star of David on the paper. In essence, I am asking for the religions to unite and assist me in bringing the criminal to justice.

In ritual (inside a cast circle) place the cage firmly on the altar along with the piece of paper indicating the nature of the crime, and the two black candles. Put the cage (with the door open) between the two black candles.

Ground and center. Perform the altar devotion and the angelic rosary, keeping your thoughts on the matter at hand.

Light the black candles, stating their purpose of moving negativity away from you (and the victim, if it is someone other than yourself). Slowly walk the piece of paper (you know, like you are playing with a kid's toy—the make-believe stuff) into the cage. Visualize the Powers and the Cherubim helping the perpetrator into the cage. (Don't laugh—it works; I'll tell you about it in a minute.)

Slam the cage door shut and tie it with a black ribbon.

Finish the ritual, being sure to ground and center, thank divinity and angels, and take up the circle. Allow the black candles to burn to nothing.

Wait until the criminal is caught, tried, and sentenced, then go back to your altar, thank the angels, open the cage, and burn the paper. Cleanse, consecrate, and bless the cage and put it away until the next time you need it.

Here are three cases where I have used this magick with success:

Non-payment of child support: I took his newspaper clipping and put it in the cage. In five days they found him and took him to jail. He finally coughed up the money.

Abusive partner: The client gave me the man's underwear. (No kidding.) I put that in the cage. In two days he committed himself to the psychiatric ward of a hospital and never returned to her home. I burned those sexy underwear later on.

Abduction: A teenaged girl was abducted and taken to another state. In four days she was back home, safe and sound.

I don't work magick for all my clients, though for all my clients I do ask the help of the angels in their situation. People have to learn to work magick for themselves, to understand that they can take control of their own lives and succeed. Sure, I'd probably have a lot more clients if I worked the magick for them, but then they would become dependent on me, which is not how I want to play the game of life.

Let Angels Help You Come to Terms with Unrequited Love

It's true. We've all been through it. That special someone doesn't love you anymore. What an ego-blaster. We experience a range of emotions—you hate the person, your self-esteem plummets, you hate the other woman (or man) involved, you hurt deep inside—that awful aching thing. You don't want to eat (or you are eating non-stop). Life is the pits. If someone tells you to forget it and go on, you get angry. And, if you had mutual friends, chances are you've lost their attention, too.

Bring in the angels. If you've been ditched, here's what you should do.

Talk to your guardian angel. Let it all out. Your fears, your hatred, your hurt and pain.

Let the other person go. Yes, let go. If the other person really cares about you, he or she might, maybe, possibly, come back (but don't count on it). Clean out the place. Get rid of memorabilia that makes you sad. Pack it away or give it away.

Do a bunch of nice things for yourself. Go out and eat dinner with a friend, visit an amusement park, go swimming—get out of the house! Take up a new hobby or sport where you will meet other people. You don't have to be romance shopping, just bring new life into your people network.

Work on your self-esteem. When someone leaves you, your pride is the first thing to tumble into a pile of gunk. Buy some new clothes, change your hairstyle, work on a goal that pleases you and makes you feel worthwhile, or donate some time to charity (that always helps). Do anything that makes your self-esteem rise (as long as it doesn't hurt anyone else).

Looking your best, go have your picture taken. You think I jest? Nada. You can get nice pictures for under $20.00. Set this picture on a tray on your altar.

Go to the kitchen and make some angel sugar: two cups of white sugar and one teaspoon of vanilla. Mix it together, then spread it out on tin foil or wax paper to dry for four hours (or more, depending on the climate). Smash out the lumps with a spoon. Empower all the sugar. Put some in an airtight container and take some to your altar. Spread the sugar on the tray around your picture during a ritual.

Ask the angels to heal your pain and empower you to continue your mission in life. Be specific and concentrate on what you feel you really need. Is it a change of scenery, a new job, new friends? Be fair and honest in your assessment.

Leave your picture with the sugar on your altar until you start feeling better and can see that the pain is moving away and healing has begun. Use the sugar in the container on your cereal, in your coffee, or on a dessert. Every time you take it into your body, remember that the angels are with you and you are being healed.

The angel sugar also works well in other occasions. For example, if someone at work, in the family, a friend, etc., is giving you a rough time, you can sprinkle a little angel sugar on their desk, in their food, or whatever and ask the angels to take a special look at the problem to help you resolve your differences. Call the angel Balthial to help you overcome feelings of jealousy and bitterness.

You can also take a bowl of angel sugar, put the disagreeable person's name on a piece of paper, bury it in the bowl, then stick a brown candle in the bowl and burn it, asking the angels to promote harmony. This worked so well for one of my clients that her on-the-rocks-relationship did a complete turnaround and she married the guy. They are happy and comfortable in their new life.

The Angel Egg Charm

Day: Sunday or Friday

Angelic hour: Michael or Uriel

Moon Phase: New Moon or Full Moon

Supplies: One jumbo egg, blue dye or food coloring, a marker, a needle, a cork, small items that mean harmony to you (gems, symbols, the miraculous medal, herbs, a lock of your hair, etc.), a blue candle

Angels to call: Baglis, who inspires moderation and balance; Barbelo, who brings abundance, goodness, and integrity; Camael, who brings joy, happiness, and contentment (Essene prayer: "Camael, angel of joy, descend upon the earth and give beauty to all things"); Gabriel; Hahaiah, who gives us loving thoughts; Rhamiel, who provides kindness and compassion; Samandiriel, who provides creativity and vivid imagination

Using a marker, draw a circle that is the same size as the small end of the cork on the large end of the egg. Poke a little hole in the small end of the egg with the needle. Turn the egg over and make a bigger hole on top, close to the edges of your marker line. Be careful; if you apply too much pressure, you'll break the egg. Take your time and drain the egg. Shake the egg occasionally to help it along. Let the egg dry completely.

Color the egg with the egg coloring or dye. Be careful not to break the shell. If you don't have egg dye, use markers. Paint or draw whatever symbols you like on the shell that indicate harmony to you. Take the shell and put it in direct sunlight. This is to help it dry; even if you use markers that dry immediately, you still need to put the shell in the sun for a few minutes, asking divinity to bless the shell.

On your angelic altar in ritual, fill the egg with the things that indicate harmony to you. As you place each item in the egg, you may wish to recite any of the prayers or invocations already given in this book. Then hold the filled shell in both hands out in front of you. State your purpose and call whichever divinity and angels you wish to empower the item. Ask them to bring you the harmony you seek. Light the blue candle, asking the angels to speed this work on its way. Carefully (very, very carefully) put the cork in the egg.

You may leave the egg on your altar for as long as you wish. When you are ready to part with it, bury it in the ground near your home. You may bury it right away if you like, but many people like to leave the egg on their altar for at least seven days. It is your choice.

Close down your ritual, remembering to thank divinity and the angels you have called for assistance. Let the blue candle burn until it is completely gone.

Let Angels Take the Wind out of a Conniving Person's Sails

"He's driving me insane," said my friend. "I divorced him years ago and now he's back again. I want him to go away—permanently. He's always plotting and scheming, twisting people's minds. I want him to stop! What can we do?"

Ask the angels to help you right this injustice by using an old Scottish angel charm. The caster of the charm went to where three streams met first thing in the morning and washed his or her face there, then said the following invocation. We've tried this charm here with running water from the tap, and it worked.

Goddess, I am bathing my face in the nine rays of the Sun
Sweetness be in my face,
Riches be in my pocket
Gold honey be on my tongue
My breath as the incense.
Black is yonder house,
Blacker men therein;
I am the white swan,
Queen over them.
I will go in the names of the God and Goddess
In likeness of deer, in likeness of horse
In likeness of serpent, in likeness of queen
With help from the angels, more victorious am I than all persons.

Whenever you see the person who has committed the injustice or the gossip filters down to you, say the following under your breath:

Angels sain the house
From site to summit;
My word above every person,
The word of every person below my foot.

Talking to the Deceased with the Angels

Angels will bring you messages from deceased friends and loved ones. All you need to do is ask, and be serious about it. Do the altar devotion and light a candle to represent

272

the person you wish to receive word from. You may not get a message right away. Sometimes you will hear things in your head. Don't be afraid. If the communication doesn't seem to be positive, banish it. Other times you will receive other types of signs—a favorite song you shared together plays on the radio when you are thinking about the person, or an event occurs associated with the memory of the deceased.

Let the Angels Help You Study

Are you having difficulties with your homework, or any type of study material? Ask the angels to help. Take a white candle and set it on the table where you are working. Talk to your guardian angels, indicating that you need help, what you are studying, and what your ultimate goal is. Light the white candle and keep it burning while you are working. You may also wish to ask any of the following angels for assistance: Akriel, who inspires intellectual achievement and helps improve your memory; Ecanus, who inspires writers (others are Ezra, Vretil, Enoch, and Dabriel); Iahhel, who watches over philosophers; Liwet, who presides over original ideas and thoughts; Mupiel, who helps you increase and keep your memory; Samandiriel, who helps with your imagination; or Satarel, who is the angel of knowledge. When you have finished, put the candle out and thank the angels for their assistance.

Angels of Town and Country

Every town, hamlet, burg, city, province, and country has a guardian angel. They can all use your help and are thrilled if you want to assist them by working magick. You can put a small statue on your altar or in your yard to represent this angel. In your daily devotions, don't forget to ask that energy be funneled to this angel so that he or she may keep the town (or whatever) safe from negative vibrations. If you have a particular concern about your town, bring it before its guardian. Ask angels of the Nine Choirs to help if you feel there is too much crime on your street. If you feel a development project will environmentally hurt your town, entreat the help of the angel Zuphlas, who protects and guards forests and trees; or Hayyel, who protects wild animals, along with Thuriel, Mtniel, and Jehiel.

Each week, pick at least one day to set aside a few minutes to sit at your altar sending positive energy to the guardians of your town, state or province, and country.

The Angelic Cauldron

Take a potpourri pot and fill it with your favorite herbs and spices (and of course, the necessary water). Put it in the center of your altar to burn during the day. As the scent permeates the room, ask the angels to bless your home and take care of your family. Keep a little jar of loose glitter on your altar. When you need something badly, pull the pot close to you, visualizing what you need coming your way. Sprinkle a bit of glitter in the pot, visualizing your need taking form. As the glitter and herbs "cook," your wish will manifest. Soon what you need will be in your life.

The Guardian Angel Basket

I receive lots of requests for help from people all over the country. So many pleas for assistance came in that I finally decided to create a guardian angel basket.

I purchased a "special" basket and decorated it with ribbons and bells. When someone asks for assistance, I write his or her name on a piece of paper, then stand before my angelic altar. Holding the paper close, I ground and center, then say the following:

> *Helpful angels circle 'round.*
> *Guardian angel, be near to me.*
> *I hold in my hand the name of a person who needs the help of the angels.*
> [Say the person's name.]
> *His/her problem is:*
> [I spell it all out, exactly as he or she related the situation to me.]
> *Please call forth whatever angelic forces are needed to help this person.*
> *In the name of the Goddess and the God, so mote it be.*

Sometimes I light a candle or say my angel rosary (for the really tough cases) or choose another minor magick to perform, or simply meditate, sending positive energy to the person who needs help. Then I take the paper and put it in the basket, ringing the bells to seal the request. At the end of each week I burn all the papers and scatter the ashes to the winds. The angels always help in no time at all.

Blessing of the Hearth Fire

The "lifting of the fire" by newly Christianized Celtic women was of great importance in their daily duties. The Celts successfully mixed their Pagan belief system with Christian doctrine, more so than many other tribal cultures. The hearth fire had always been blessed, and they found no need to stop the process simply because

Christianity appeared on the moors. The Celts looked upon fire as a miracle of divine power. The renewal of it reminded them that they must renew their personal spiritual and practical resources.

A Celtic blessing for the "lifting of the fire" said every morning under the woman's breath is as follows:

I will kindle my fire this morning
In the presence of the holy angels of heaven,
In presence of Ariel of the loveliest form,
In presence of Uriel of the myriad charms
Without malice, without jealousy, without envy
Without fear, without terror of any one under the Sun
But the Goddess to shield me.
Without malice, without jealousy, without envy
Without fear, without terror of any one under the Sun
But the Holy Queen of the Angels to shield me.

Goddess, kindle thou in my heart within
A flame of love to my neighbor,
To my foe, to my friend, to my kindred all,
To the brave, to the knave, to the thrall,
From the children of my loveliest Queen
From the lowliest thing that liveth,
To the Goddess that is highest of all.[1]

This encouraged the strength of the fire, the residents of the home, and brought divine blessings and the power of the angels to form.

---

1. *Carmina Gadelica Hymns and Incantations* by Alexander Carmichael, page 93.

Eighteen

Living with the Angels

*M*any of us in this part of the world search for the "right" spiritual blend. We may have grown up in one religion, then moved on to another as adults. Every day we must consciously seek to better ourselves, our family, and the planet. No aspect of divinity will ever turn away from such a person. Each of us must discover our own truths and bring divinity into our lives on our own. You can't shove concepts down someone's throat and expect them to follow blindly behind you or your truths.

I am Wiccan and angels are a part of my personal belief system. They have aided me on countless occasions, in a number of ways. I won't deny credit where credit is due. They have expanded my personal creativity, provided me with imaginative ideas, and have drawn items to me when I needed them most. I don't care if they are archetypes or a species unto themselves. It simply doesn't matter to me.

As we approach the next millennium, we humans will be called upon in greater numbers to work with the angels to bring balance to our world. This is our overall mission. Those who practice magick with the angels are doubly blessed, as they have one foot in both worlds and still maintain their dignity and personal balance. It is up to all of us, from all religions, to learn to work together to bring about harmony. If we do not, we will all fail miserably.

Working with the angels will change your life. It changed mine. Their influence and positive energies will pull you forward in your spiritual pursuits, as well as teach you how to handle the little difficulties (and sometimes big ones) of daily life. There is a plan of action you can use to help yourself work with the angels.

Discover a meaningful purpose to your life. Too often we move so fast that we fail to consider what it is we are doing here and what we wish to accomplish in the time we have. Our main mission in life does leave clues lying around. We just have to be astute enough to find them. Usually your main mission involves something you dearly love to do and a talent you possess. You need to learn to put the pieces together to determine what will be fulfilling to you. If you've made choices that have drawn you away from your mission, it may take you some time to pull yourself back in line. We all get caught up in wild goose chases from time to time; it's part of the human condition.

How does one go about discovering a meaningful life purpose? By opening your mind and heart to the wisdom of the universe. You may employ meditation, a series of relaxing walks, a weekend camping trip, or a change of daily scenery. Discovering our purpose means taking the time to think about it, and admitting that the world is full of people who need help. We have to be willing to connect with the big picture, to find our place in it.

Ask the angels to assist you in finding your life purpose. Be aware of what happens around you, conversations with others, information that comes through the media, etc. Perhaps your life purpose is a series of steps to an ultimate goal. You may need to work in one place for a few years, then move on to something different, using what you have learned in each stage of your life. You may begin a wonderful project and two years later, it falls apart. However, during the vibrant months of the experience, you may have invaluably added to someone else's life or a group of individuals' circumstances. You may never be aware of what you have done. Such is how the plan may manifest for you. Coincidence does not exist.

Learn to take effective steps to bring you toward your life mission. Don't dream about something and wait with your fingers in your nose for events to happen. Get out there and make things happen. Put action into your dreams, visions, and hopes. Take an active part in bringing the things toward you that you want. Ideas like "I can't," "I don't think I could," and "I'm not able to" are forbidden. Think positively and set yourself up for the experiences you want to draw toward yourself. Your Great American Novel won't be written if you never set pencil to paper, or fingers to keyboard. You won't get the house you always wanted if you don't actively save and seek out ways to procure it. You won't be able to move out west (or north, or east, or south) if you don't map out a plan of action. You won't be able to have the greatest invention in the world if you don't design it.

Create a support network for yourself. I know from experience that our families and friends are not always the most supportive of our dreams and visions. They will try to hold you back for a variety of reasons that usually begin with the entanglement of fear. They may think you will go away from them or spend less time with them, or that they won't be the center of your attention anymore. They may not be happy that they have to help you by relieving you of household chores or other responsibilities. They may think your dreams are foolish because they don't have the guts to get out there and fulfill their own mission, therefore they judge you by their own actions and their own failures.

Don't let negative people get you down. To combat this negativity, set up a support group of people who share a common interest in your goals. Sometimes this can include a friend or family member (it does happen). More often, though, your support network builds as you actively pull your dreams and goals toward you. You will meet these individuals along the way. Don't expect an army of them, but one or two invaluable "pillars" are really all you need.

Ask your guardian angel to help bring these people to you. Don't forget to treat these people well, respecting their mission and their dreams or goals. You must be just as supportive of them (and others) as they are of you. Learn to choose your network wisely. You don't need vapid people with rotten advice or controlling attitudes.

Learn to take responsibility for your own actions. We've turned into a society of victims, a pattern I find absolutely disgusting. You can't blame everybody in the world for your problems and expect to come out a winner. Learn to take responsibility for everything you say and do, and don't try to retreat under the myth that "somebody made you that way." Garbage! You are the sum of everything you've already done and said. If you don't like what you see, change it.

Believe in yourself. If you don't, nobody else will. Learn to be your own cheerleading squad. Do special things to raise your self-esteem. Talk positively to yourself twenty-four hours a day. If you think you aren't prepared to accomplish something, consider why. Perhaps you feel you need more knowledge. Then go about finding it. Learn to clear out the junk in your life that brings you down. Don't knowingly walk into negative circumstances; try to avoid disaster. Be positive in your approach to all things. This does take guts, but I can assure you, it is worth it.

Use your magickal skills and your newfound power with the angels to help you along the way. Don't be shy. Get out there and make life as wonderful and as full of love and laughter as you can stand. You won't regret it.

May the love of divinity and the power of the angels be with you always.

Needs and Their Associated Elements and Angels

I've given you lots of associations and correspondences through this book. Here is a quick reference list to assist you in working magick with the angels. These are not all the correspondences that could be made with the material in this book; read the sections on specific angels and check out the books in the Bibliography for more ideas.

NEED	ELEMENT(S)	ANGEL(S)
Abortion	Water	Kasdaye
Akashic records (access of)	Spirit	Metatron, angels of Chiron and the Akashic records, the Seraphim
Alcoholism (to break the addiction)	Earth	Uriel, Raphael, Dark Moon angels, angels of the Waning and Disseminating Moon, angels of Chiron and Neptune
Animals (to protect)	Earth	Behemiel, Hariel, Thegri, Mtniel, Jehiel, Thrones, angels of the Crescent Moon
Animals (to heal)	Earth and water	Manakel (water), angels of the Crescent Moon, angels of animals
Apartment (to obtain)	Earth	Uriel, angels of Jupiter and Libra, angels of apartments
Artistic endeavors	Fire	Akriel, Hael, angels of Venus (beauty), Vesta (inspiration), Pallas (intuition), Sagittarius, Mercury, Aquarius (inventing, exploring), and creativity

NEED	ELEMENT(S)	ANGEL(S)
Beauty (to obtain)	Earth	Uriel, angels of Venus, Earth, Taurus (material possessions), and beauty
Beauty (to improve)	Water	Hael, angels of Venus and the New Moon
Bills (to pay)	Earth	Uriel, Ariel, angels of the Sun, Jupiter, Taurus, the Waning and Disseminating Moon, and personal finances
Birds (to protect)	Earth or air	Ariel, Anpiel, angels of birds
Business (success)	Earth or fire	Anauel, Dominions, Principalities, angels of the Sun, Jupiter, Leo, the New and Crescent Moon, Taurus, Gemini, and business
Car (to obtain)	Earth	Uriel, Angels of the Sun, Libra (for a fair deal), Taurus (finding a good car), Pallas (truth), and vehicles
Childbirth	Water	Ardousious, Gabriel, Queen of Angels, Virtues, angels of Chiron (healing), Virgo, Ceres (protection), Vesta, and childbirth
Children (to protect)	Water or earth	Gabriel, Dina, Queen of Angels, Uriel, Ariel, angels of Ceres, Vesta, and children
Cocaine addiction (to break)	Water	Raphael, Gabriel, angels of Neptune, the Dark Moon, and Chiron
Courage	Fire	Michael, Raphael, Metatron, Powers (defense), Virtues (miracles), angels of the Sun, Leo, the Crescent and Waxing Moon, Ceres, and courage
Divination	All	Adad, Teiaiel, Isiaiel, Bath Kol, angels of the Full Moon and divination
Divorce	All	Archangels, Powers (defense), angels of the Waning and Dark Moon, Libra (fair treatment), Scorpio, Saturn, Chiron (healing after the divorce), Pallas (truth, protection), Gemini (communication), Mars (if you are forced to fight), Taurus (to get your share of the property), and Ceres
Domestic violence (to stop)	All	Michael, Uriel, archangels, Thrones (ferret out injustice), Virtues (miracles), Cherubim (those who intercede), angels of Saturn, the Dark and Disseminating Moon, Scorpio, Aries, Mars, Ceres (protection), Juno (freedom), Uranus (freedom, independence), Vesta (guardians of magickal women), and protection
Domestic violence (to heal)	Water	Gabriel, angels of Chiron, the Waning and Disseminating Moon, and healing
Dreams	Air and water	Gabriel, any Moon angel, angels of Cancer, Pallas (intuition), Scorpio, and dreams

NEED	ELEMENT(S)	ANGEL(S)
Drowsiness (to prevent)	Fire	Raphael
Employment	Earth	Uriel, Anauel, Principalities (protection against discrimination), angels of earth, the Sun, the Full and New Moon, Virgo, and employment
Fertility	Earth	Samandriel, Yushamin, Anahita, Gabriel, Queen of Angels, angels of Virgo, the Sun, and fertility
Friendship	Water and earth	Mihr, Cambiel, Ausiel, angels of the Sun, the New and Waxing Moon, Venus, Juno (harmony), Leo (loyalty), Virgo (eloquence), Sagittarius (laughter and parties), Aquarius, Mercury, Gemini, and friendship
Gardens	Earth	Uriel, Ariel, angels of the New Moon, Leo, Virgo (harvest), Aries, and agriculture
Hatred (to release)	Water	Gabriel, angels of the Dark, Waning, and Disseminating Moon
Healing	All	Michael, Gabriel, Uriel, Raphael, Cherubim (those who intercede), Virtues (miracles), angels of the Sun, the Full Moon, Chiron, Virgo, Sagittarius, and healing
House (to obtain)	Earth	Uriel, angels of the Full and New Moon, Jupiter, Libra (for a fair deal), Cancer (to hold on to your house), Saturn (financing), and houses
Interviews	Fire	Ambriel, Anauel, guardians of the business, angels of the Full and New Moon, Jupiter, Libra (for fair treatment), Virgo, Gemini (communication), and Mercury
Jealousy (to release)	Water or earth	Gabriel, Uriel, Ariel, angels of the Dark and Disseminating Moon, Neptune, Chiron (healing), Juno (freedom), and Gemini (communication)
Karmic issues	Spirit	Metatron, angels of the Waning Moon and Karma
Love	Water to begin, Earth to maintain	Gabriel, Anael, Shekinah, Seraphim (divine and universal love), angels of Venus, the Full and New Moon, the Sun (success), Cancer, Juno (relationships), Mercury (communication), Virgo (structure), and love
Magickal energy	All	Uriel, Ariel, Seraphim, Virtues (miracles), Cherubim (those who intercede), angels of the Full Moon, Vesta (pure power), Scorpio, and magick

NEED	ELEMENT(S)	ANGEL(S)
Marriage (harmony)	Water, earth	Gabriel, Thrones (smooth out problems), angels of Venus (love), the Moon, Vesta (protection), Juno (relationships), Virgo (structure), Capricorn (stability), Libra (balance), Sagittarius (laughter), Gemini (communication), and marriages
Money	Earth	Uriel, Anauel, Ariel, angels of the Sun (success), Jupiter (to make), Taurus (to get debtors to pay up), Vesta (protection), Capricorn (stability), and prosperity
Overeating (to stop)	Air	Raphael, angels of the Dark and Waning Moon, Neptune, and Chiron
Peace	Water	Gabriel, Gavreel, Spheres, Shekinah, Seraphim, Virtues (miracles), Thrones (smooth out difficulties), Cherubim (those who intercede), Principalities, angels of the Sun, the Moon, Pluto (global change), Juno (harmony), and peace
Patience	Water	Gabriel, angels of the Gibbous Moon, Juno (harmony), Capricorn, and patience
Peer pressure (to stop)	Water	Gabriel, Cherubim, angels of the Dark Moon, Saturn, Juno (freedom), and protection
Protection	All	Archangels, Dina, Ambriel, Cherubim (personal protectors), Virtues (miracles), angels of the Full Moon, Ceres, Cancer, Mars, and protection
Psychic awareness	All	Archangels, Dominions (divine wisdom), angels of the Full Moon, Uranus, Pallas, Scorpio (mysticism), Neptune (psychic healing), Uranus (astrology), and psychism
Purification	All	Archangels, angels of the Full Moon, Vesta (temple guardians), Juno (harmony), and purification
Sleep (to bring about)	Water	Moon angels, Gabriel, Raphael, angels of Venus and sleep
Smoking (to break the addiction)	Water	Raphael, Gabriel, angels of the Dark Moon, Neptune, and Chiron
Stress (to ease)	Air or water	Raphael, angels of the Moon, Chiron, and harmony
Studying	Air or fire or earth	Uriel, Michael, Raphael, angels of Chiron (for religious study), Vesta (guardians of knowledge), Pallas (new ideas and theories), Scorpio (mystical study), Sagittarius, Gemini (to understand concepts), and learning

Bibliography

Andrews, Ted. *How to Meet and Work with Spirit Guides.* St Paul, MN: Llewellyn Publications, 1992.

Buckland, Raymond. *Bockland's Complete Book of Witchcraft.* St Paul, MN: Llewellyn Publications, 1987.

Buckland, Raymond. *Practical Color Magick.* St Paul, MN: Llewellyn Publications, 1987.

Burnham, Sophy. *A Book of Angels.* New York, NY: Walker & Company, 1990.

Carmichael, Alexander. *Carmina Gadelica Hymns and Incantations.* Floris Books, 1992.

Connell, Janice. *Angel Power.* New York, NY: Ballantine Books, 1995.

Connolly, David. *In Search of Angels.* New York, NY: Perigee, 1993.

Cunningham, Scott. *Living Wicca.* St Paul, MN: Llewellyn Publications, 1993.

Cunningham, Scott. *Magical Aromatherapy.* St Paul, MN: Llewellyn Publications, 1989.

Daniel, Alma et al. *Ask Your Angels.* New York, NY: Ballantine Books, 1992.

Davidson, Gustav. *A Dictionary of Angels.* New York, NY: Free Press, 1971.

Delaney, John J. *A Woman Clothed with the Sun.* New York, NY: Image/Doubleday, 1990.

Frater, U. D. *Practical Sigil Magic.* St Paul, MN: Llewellyn Publications, 1990.

Freeman, Eileen Elias. *Touched by Angels.* New York, NY: Warner Books, 1993.

Freeman, Eileen Elias. *Angelic Healing.* New York, NY: Warner Books, 1994.

Georgian, Linda. *Your Guardian Angels.* St. Louis, MO: Fireside Books, 1994.

Godwin, Malcolm. *Angels: An Endangered Species.* New York, NY: Simon and Schuster, 1990.

Hauck, Rex. *Angels: The Mysterious Messengers.* New York, NY: Ballantine Books, 1994.

Howard, Jane M. *Commune with the Angels.* Virginia Beach, VA: A.R.E. Press, 1992.

Kraig, Donald Michael. *Modern Magick.* St Paul, MN: Llewellyn Publications, 1988.

Moolenburgh, H.C. *A Handbook of Angels.* The C. W. Daniel Company Limited, 1984.

Pearsal, Paul, Ph.D. "The Power of Your Own Thinking to Strengthen Your Immune System," *Going Bonkers Magazine,* March 1995.

Price, John Randolph. *The Angels Within Us.* New York, NY: Fawcett Columbine, 1993.

Pruitt, James. *Angels Beside You.* New York, NY: Avon, 1994.

Pruitt, James. *The Complete Angel.* New York, NY: Avon, 1995.

RavenWolf, Silver. *HexCraft.* St Paul, MN: Llewellyn Publications, 1995.

RavenWolf, Silver. *To Ride a Silver Broomstick.* St Paul, MN: Llewellyn Publications, 1993.

RavenWolf, Silver. *To Stir a Magick Cauldron.* St Paul, MN: Llewellyn Publications, 1996.

Ronner, John. *Know Your Angels.* Oxford, AL: Mamre Press, 1993.

Ronner, John. *Do You Have a Guardian Angel?* Oxford, AL: Mamre Press, 1985.

Skalka, Julia Lupton. *The Instant Horoscope Reader.* St Paul, MN: Llewellyn Publications, 1994.

Taylor, Terry Lynn. *Creating with the Angels.* H. J. Kramer, Inc., 1993.

Taylor, Terry Lynn. *Guardians of Hope.* H. J. Kramer, Inc., 1992.

Taylor, Terry Lynn. *Messengers of Light.* H. J. Kramer, Inc, 1990.

Tyl, Noel. *Astrology's Special Measurements.* St Paul, MN: Llewellyn Publications, 1993.

Tyson, Donald. *New Millennium Magic.* St Paul, MN: Llewellyn Publications, 1996.

Index

Stay in Touch. . .

Llewellyn publishes hundreds of books on your favorite subjects!

Order by Phone

Call toll-free within the U.S. and Canada, **1-800-THE MOON.** In Minnesota call **(612) 291–1970.** We accept Visa, MasterCard, and American Express.

Order by Mail

Send the full price of your order (MN residents add 7% sales tax) in U.S. funds to:
> Llewellyn Worldwide
> P.O. Box 64383, Dept. K724-2
> St. Paul, MN 55164–0383, U.S.A.

Postage and Handling

- ◆ $4.00 for orders $15.00 and under
- ◆ $5.00 for orders over $15.00
- ◆ No charge for orders over $100.00

We ship UPS in the continental United States. We cannot ship to P.O. boxes. Orders shipped to Alaska, Hawaii, Canada, Mexico, and Puerto Rico will be sent first-class mail.

International orders: Airmail—add freight equal to price of each book to the total price of order, plus $5.00 for each non-book item (audiotapes, etc.). Surface mail— Add $1.00 per item.

Allow 4–6 weeks delivery on all orders. Postage and handling rates subject to change.

Group Discounts

We offer a 20% quantity discount to group leaders or agents. You must order a minimum of 5 copies of the same book to get our special quantity price.

Free Catalog

Get a free copy of our color catalog, *New Worlds of Mind and Spirit.* Subscribe for just $10.00 in the United States and Canada ($20.00 overseas, first class mail). Many bookstores carry New Worlds—ask for it!